T0354946

HE WAS ALWAYS THERE

BETTY HOOPER PITTMAN

authorHOUSE®

AuthorHouse™
1663 Liberty Drive
Bloomington, IN 47403
www.authorhouse.com
Phone: 1 (800) 839-8640

Published by AuthorHouse 06/11/2020

ISBN: 978-1-7283-6486-5 (sc)
ISBN: 978-1-7283-6485-8 (e)

Library of Congress Control Number: 2020911110

Print information available on the last page.

Scripture quotations marked KJV are from the Holy Bible, King James
Version (Authorized Version). First published in 1611. Quoted from the KJV
Classic Reference Bible, Copyright © 1983 by The Zondervan Corporation.

This book is printed on acid-free paper.

INTRODUCTION

I owe a debt of gratitude to my daughter, Theresa, for getting me started on the research of our family. **<u>And</u>** to my late cousins Harry Gordon Pettey and Vivian Pettey who were the first ones to write the stories about our Family and peaked my interest for doing the same.

I have quoted many Bible Verses telling My Story, but there are still many more I would like to quote that may help you understand My Story even better. They may even help someone who reads my story to make better decisions than I did. You can't Pray God's Word back to Him if you don't know His Word. He only answers prayers that are prayed using His Word and His Promises.

Study His Word every day. When you quote Scripture, look on them and at them with your eyes, and Pray them.

Proverbs 4:20 My Son (or Daughter), attend to My Words; incline thine ear unto My Sayings. :21 Let them not depart from thine eyes; keep then in the midst of thine heart. :22 For they are life unto those that find them, and health to all their flesh. :23 Keep thy heart with all diligence; for out of it are the issues of life.

Psalm 118:23 This was the LORD'S doing, and it is marvelous in our eyes.

Matthew 19:26 With men this is impossible, but with God all things are possible.

I John 5:14 And this is the confidence that we have in Him, that, if we ask any thing according to **His Will**, He hears us; :15 And if we know that He hears us, whatsoever we ask, we know that we have the petitions that we desired of Him.

III John 2, Beloved, I wish (pray) above all things that you may prosper and be in (good) health, even as thy soul prospers.

The Verses that I prayed many times while waiting for God to bring Gene and I back together and He did, are found in-

Psalm 37:3 Trust in the LORD, and do good; so shalt thou dwell in the land, and verily thou shalt be fed. :4 Delight thyself also in the LORD; and He shall give thee the desires of thine heart. :5 Commit thy way unto the LORD; trust also in Him; and He shall bring it to pass.

All Scripture is from the King James Version of the Bible.

CHAPTER 1
MY BIRTH AND YOUNGER YEARS

It may have been morning. It may have been night. It could have been cold or sunny. No one ever told me, because I never thought to ask. I waited until it was too late to ask. Everyone that knew about my birth, or was present at my birth, has gone on to Heaven to await my arrival there. I know I'm going to Heaven, because I gave my life to the LORD when I was nine years old at the church my Dad built and again on October 20, 1995 at my Step Brother Tommy's church when I was 67 years old.

Most of us think we had some kind of control over our birth, but we do not. In Jeremiah 1:5 God speaks to Jeremiah saying, "Before I formed thee in the belly, I knew thee; and before thou camest forth out of the womb I sanctified thee, and I ordained thee a prophet unto the nations." KJV God chooses us. We do not choose God. He has plans for us before we are born. My question is, "Father, why did you choose me? I'm nothing special. I'm certainly not the smartest kid on the block. I have done some good things, but I also have done some bad things."

It was October 18, 1932 when I entered into this world with the help of my dear, sweet Grandmother, Mamaw Ida, my Dad's mother. She was the midwife when I was born in her home somewhere near Center, in Shelby County, Texas.

No doctor was present at my birth. I don't know why we were there at Mamaw's house. It could have been because my Mother had a hard time when my older brother, Sammie, was born, and Mamaw thought she could be a better midwife than the doctors were in delivering me into this world. It was not unusual to have a midwife present at a birth in those days.

I could have been born early, or premature, because of what my Uncle Paul, Dad's Brother, always said to me whenever I saw him. After greeting and hugging me, he would always put his hand out and say, "I remember when I could hold you in the palm of my hand, because you were so little."

In those days, it was not unusual for a baby to weigh 10 or 12 pounds at birth. The women did not go to a doctor when they were pregnant, but waited until it was time for the baby to be born and did not always eat properly. Unlike today, most of the time the doctor came to the home when the baby was ready to be born.

Later, I'll tell you about the time the doctor came to our house to deliver another baby.

Mamaw took me to see the house I was born in when I was about 5 or 6 years old.

The house was small, like a log cabin, but it was a frame house. The lady who lived there was very nice and allowed us to come in and look around.

In October the weather can be either hot or chilly. Since the fireplace was the only heat available in the house in those days, that's why I was born next to the fire-place in the front room. During the middle of October, after a cool spell, the weather can turn very hot for a few days or a week. Then it will turn cold or cool again. The warm spell is called Indian Summer. I was born during Indian Summer.

In 1930, according to the United States Federal Census, my parents and brother Sammie were living on the corner of Mobberly Avenue and Electra Street, but does not indicate what type of structure they were living in, and if the house was on Mobberly Avenue or Electra Street.

My first memory of our house that my Dad built on Culver Street, was when I may have been three or four years old. Sammie was four years older than me. We were playing in the driveway next to the house. We were having a wonderful time making "mud cakes." To make a "mud cake" you need a large jar lid which you fill with mud. Then you gather some leaves and flowers to decorate the cake.

When it is finished and decorated nice and pretty – you eat it!! Well, at least that was what I had in mind, until our Mother opened the door and caught us. She forbid us from eating our "cakes." That's all I remember about "mud cakes."

Since we were outside the house, my Dad may have completed building our house. It's hard for me to remember about that.

The next thing I tell you, you may not approve of now, but remember, those were different times, the Depression was still going on in the middle of the "30s. Dad was either trying to complete the girl's bedroom or add on to it. I never was sure.

The bedroom was not finished because there was no East wall on our room. My brother, Sammie and I were playing on the floor – what game I don't know. Dad started scolding Sammie for something he had or had not done. There was a "space heater" in the room that was connected to the gas outlet with a rubber hose. That was the way houses were heated in those days.

Dad went over to the heater and pulled the rubber hose lose. Then he grabbed Sammie. That's when our Mother stepped up to him and said, "No, you don't. You're not going to whip him with that hose." I only remember the part where my Dad backed off. I don't know what happened after that.

As the years passed, I noticed that all of us children seemed to have a "very bad temper." I knew it came from Dad, but don't know how far back it went in our family. Dad was still a young man, thirty years old when I was born, and learned to control his temper as time passed. And so did I.

Dad had bought a corner lot on Culver Street with lots of trees. The house was the largest and most beautiful in the neighborhood. It had three bedrooms and one bathroom. Most of the houses in our neighborhood had only four rooms. They did not have indoor bathrooms in them.

In the master bedroom, he built a nice closet with a clothes rack on one side and built in shelves on the other. He put doors on part of the shelves.

There was a door that went outside onto the front porch from the master bedroom. It was customary to have more than one outside door for a house. Those doors were usually in the bedrooms, leading outside the house. That was a safety factor in case of fire. Remember, there were no telephones to call the fire department.

The bathroom was between the master bedroom and the girl's bedroom, with a short hallway extending to the living room. The bathroom had a built in bathtub, no shower. Bathrooms did not have showers in those days. There was a closed in shelf area with doors for linens and large items that were kept in the bathroom, and a built in dirty clothes hamper. There may have been other houses in town that had bathrooms as nice as ours, but not in our neighborhood.

Most of the neighbors had what we might called "outside facilities." In other words, it was an outhouse. Their bathing was done in a number 3 wash tub that was put in the kitchen where it would be warm and had a little privacy.

On bath day, the tub would be brought in and filled with hot water that had been heated on the kitchen stove. The youngest person always took a bath first, and then the older people were next according to age. I'm sure the water may have been changed several times before the "bathing" was finished. This usually happened on Saturday so everyone would be nice and clean for church Sunday.

The girl's bedroom was next after the bathroom. As you open the door, there were two small closets on each side. The closets each had doors on them, and that determined the size of the closet, as well as the width of the door. Today, that would not be sufficient for a one year old because he or she would have more clothes and they would not all fit in those small closets.

I shared my bedroom with my two sisters. We barely did have enough clothes to fill up those closets, and that included our winter coats. There wasn't any shoes in the closets because they were on our feet. If there was any shoes in the closets, they were probably the Sunday or Dress shoes. Everyone didn't have dress shoes.

There was also a built in cabinet/shelf area with doors on it on the opposite wall for linens and whatever we needed it to be. My two sisters had a "Double Bed" that was large enough for the two of them. My bed was actually a three quarter bed. It was slightly larger than a twin bed. I was the only person in the family with my own bed. Everyone else had to share a bed.

We had a dresser, with a mirror on it, and a stool. We also had a chest-of-drawers, four drawers, for our fold-up clothes. When I was older there was a "treadle" sewing machine that had been my Step Mom's mother's machine that was given to us. It was in our bedroom because there wasn't any other place to put it.

A "treadle" sewing machine had a large "pedal" thing that you pumped with your feet to make it run. It had no electrical wire to plug it into an outlet. It was all manual, but I learned to sew on it when I was in Junior High School. That's when I learned to love sewing and I've been sewing ever since. Of course, I now have a nice sewing machine that will sew anything and make any type of stitch you may desire.

There was a door on the east wall of our bedroom that led to the outside in case of fire. Since most, or nearly all of the, people did not have telephones in their house, it would be hard to notify the Fire Department when there was a fire. We were very fortunate in our neighborhood that no one ever had a house fire.

There was a door from the girl's bedroom into the boy's bedroom. Their bedroom was on the back of the house. It was for my brothers, Sammie, Charlie, Jackie, and my Stepbrother Tommy. In their bedroom was a chest-of-drawers and a nice size closet with a rack for their clothes and built-in shelves on one side and a ladder built onto the other wall to access the attic.

One day, being the climber that I was, I decided to climb up into the attic – why, I don't know, that's just the things we did, Climb. There never was anything in the attic. Half way up, I slipped and fell back down. I was skinned up a little and had hit my head, but that didn't stop my climbing. After all, we all were climbers and you will read about it later.

From the boy's bedroom, there also was a door that opened onto the back porch. On the back porch is where the laundry, or washing, was done every Monday.

We did own an electric washing machine that had a wringer arm attached to it.

For those who don't know, the washing machine had a paddle in it that swished around to clean, or wash, the clothes. When the clothes were washed, you put them, one at a time thru the wringer arm to squeeze all the water out of the clothes. They were then dropped into a wash tub with clear water to rinse the clothes.

This process was continued through three rinse cycles into three number three wash tubs filled with clear clean water. To the last rinse tub was added some "bluing" to help the white clothes look cleaner and whiter. Yes, the bluing was actually blue. That's why it was named "bluing." It was sold at the Piggly Wiggly Grocery Store where my Dad and Mom bought our groceries.

This may seem like a tedious job, but it was much nicer and easier than what came before it which was the large cast iron pot in the back yard. This was before we had a washing machine. Also remember this was in the 1930's and very few, if any, of the people in our neighborhood had electricity.

To wash in the cast iron pot, one had to get up early, gather firewood for the pot, light the fire and heat the water in the wash pot. Both of these procedures took all day long to complete. I was the oldest girl and it was my duty, chore, to help in the house. The breakfast dishes would be on the table with dried eggs on them when I can home from school to help. When I finished that, I would check if any of the clothes that were hung out on the clothes line were dry. If they were dry, I gathered them and took them into the house to be folded and put away.

The wet clothes were attached to the clothes line with clothes pins. I'm sure most people think clothes pins are only for making crafts. Long before people had time for crafts, they were used to attach the wet clothes to the clothes lines which were strung across the back yard. Most of the lines were quite long, so we had to put a pole in the middle of the line to hold up the clothes line so the clothes would not drag the ground. If it was a windy day, the clothes would have gotten dirty again from being blown by the wind and drug on the ground.

I don't remember what we had for Supper, we never had "Dinner" on wash day. We probably had some kind of soup or stew that had cooked all day and would be hot and ready for Supper. Whatever it was, it was always delicious, and served with a hot pan of cornbread.

To enter the house you came across the front porch, through the front door and into the living room. Dad had made a beautiful entrance with a large door and small "French" type windows on each side. The door was also a "French" style with small windows in it so that we could see anyone coming up to our front door.

Dad built an "artificial" fire place on the west wall that had a gas stove in it which looked like logs burning. On the east wall he built a book shelf from the ceiling to the floor.

There wasn't much of anything in the book shelf until I was in Junior High School. I had a history class and had to do research. That meant going to the Library next to the Junior High School.

I don't know when, where, or how, Dad bought a set of Encyclopedias that were put into the book shelf. Now I did not need to go to the Library any more, I could study at home. I didn't realize what was happening until years later. Dad was also reading the Encyclopedias. In fact, my Step Mom told me he had read each one of them. He loved to read and study.

He had gone to school and some college, and he still liked to read and study. After he died, it was my duty to go through his things. To my amazement, he had several different kinds of Encyclopedia sets. I'm sure he read every word in each of them.

There was a large couch on the north wall with a beautiful Dutch type painting with flower carts and canals. I loved that picture. Dad had hung a chandelier over a glass top coffee table that sat in front of the couch.

All of the rooms in the house had "real hardwood flooring." None of the rooms had any type of carpet or rug. None of the people I knew had any carpet on their floors. The bathroom and kitchen had some type of tile flooring.

When I was in my teens, it was my job to wax and polish the living room and dining room floors. That meant, the paste wax was applied while crawling on your hands and knees. The wax was in a metal can with a soft cloth. Then came the buffing. Dad had gotten some type of buffer that looked similar to a huge upside down hammer with a long handle. The buffer was operated manually. It was a very heavy rectangular metal thing with some brushes on it that you had to swing back and forth to polish the floor. Thank God, we only waxed the living room.

From the living room, you go into the dining room. The west wall had three large windows. There was a Buffet on the east wall that had drawers and doors on it to hold the silverware and table cloths. The only time we used the tablecloth was at Christmas, Thanksgiving, and our Birthday Dinner. The dining room table was large enough to seat ten people. By the time our family finished growing, we were ten total.

The west wall in the kitchen is where the kitchen sink and cabinets were. Cabinets were built into each corner. One set of cabinets held the dishes and the other side held the spices and things for cooking. The water for the sink was piped in from the water well outside the kitchen window.

The City had not put water pipes to the houses in our area at that time. That would come later, but Dad had anticipated it would be done and had allowed for it. He must have also piped the water from the well to the bathroom, because we had water in the bathroom also.

The counter top was "L" shaped. Under the end of the counter top on the north wall Dad had built a bin for storing flour and shelves for pots and pas. The stove had gas burners and an oven and was on the south wall.

On the East wall, Dad had made a breakfast nook which was a small room with two benches and a built-in table. The nook was very practical when our family was fairly small, but as it grew, the breakfast nook was too small and useless.

Dad then turned it into a storage room with lots of large, long shelves to hold all the groceries and the things that our Step Mom had canned. She canned black-eyed peas, corn, and other vegetables from her Mother's farm. She and her Mother also canned meat to be used in stews, or for whatever it was need.

Once we went out to the farm and picked black-eyed peas in a cotton picking sack. That sack was about four feet long. We shelled so many peas that day that I made myself a bed out of the hulls to lay on when we finished. We also went to her cousin's orchard and picked peaches, which she later canned.

I saw and did things that most people never saw. I watched when some of the food was canned in a tin can. The food, whatever it was, was put into the tin car, then a lid was placed on it and put under a thing that looked like a "can opener." In fact, the "sealing of a can" is just the opposite from opening it, only done in reverse. To me it looked exactly like a can opener, but when it was turned it would seal the can instead of opening it. Then the can was placed in a pressure cooker filled with hot water and cooked for a given amount of time which sealed it.

Some of the food was canned in glass jars and were processed almost the same.

The jar was filled with the hot food, then a metal lid was screwed onto the jar. The jar was then placed into a pressure cooker or a "water bath cooker" with water in it for a given amount of time to seal the jars properly.

That may seem like a lot of work, and it was. But those "home canned foods" sure did taste good on a cold winter night.

When I was a teenager, Dad decided to enlarge the kitchen and enclose the back porch. Atop the kitchen counter he made an eating bar where we could have breakfast or snacks. The porch area was used mostly like a den area. Later Dad also built a garage with a covered walkway to the house.

After the garage was finished, Dad purchased an electric washing machine and an electric dryer that was kept in a room at the rear end of the garage out of the weather and out of the house. Laundry was not done in the house in those days. I'm sure my Step Mom was very happy to have the new conveniences. No one else in the neighborhood had the nice things she had.

I Believe God helped Dad design our house because it had so many nice features in it that most houses did not have. That may be why God called my Dad to build His Church. If he could build a house with so many beautiful built-ins and other features, I believe God knew he could build His Church. He did, and it was a very beautiful Church.

CHAPTER 2

PNEUMONIA AND WHOOPING COUGH STRIKES

My Grandmother Della Ellis, my Mother's Mother, lived in Houston and came to visit us in Longview when I was four or five years old. She took me home with her on the bus to Houston. It was a long ride that continued into the night. I became very cold during the ride, so Grandmother took her coat off and spread it over me. After that, I slept most of the way. I don't know when we arrive at Houston or how we got to Grandmother's home.

When we arrived at her home, Granddad was already in bed because it was very late at night. He saw that I was very cold and told me to get in bed with him and sleep in the middle between him and Grandmother so I could get warm.

It seems I had double pneumonia and the whooping cough and was very ill for some time. My grandparents didn't think I would live through it. I believe that was the first time God took over my life, and He never let me go after that. I could have died because whooping cough was a very serious illness and the pneumonia made it much worse. The medicines we have now weren't available then.

Most people died from one or the other, but God had work for me to do in my golden years, and He would not let me go. Whooping Cough has almost been eradicated today. But people still die from pneumonia even today.

My aunt and her husband, my Mother's brother Thurman, lived next door to my Grandparents. Aunt Lucy had just given birth to her first baby, a girl named Mary Jane, and my aunt took the whooping cough from me. It seems that it's not very pleasant to have the whooping cough just after a woman has given birth.

Aunt Lucy was sort of upset with me. I know that she didn't really hold it against me for giving her the whooping cough. She just liked to remind me of it quite often, especially when I hadn't seen her for some time. That was in the '30's and the medicines we have now were not available then.

I can't remember exactly how long I stayed with my Grandparents, or when or how I went back home. It was late September, but I was not old enough to go to school, so I may have stayed for quite some time.

Whenever my parents and I visited my Grandparents, I would play with Mary Jane in our Grandparents back yard.

I didn't know until years later that my Mother's new husband, the one she left us to be with, had forbidden my grandparents from having any contact with my Dad and us children. He threatened to take my Mother far away so that they would never see her again if her parents or family told where they were.

I never knew this and couldn't understand why my Mother's family never tried to contact us, write to us, send birthday cards or Christmas cards or presents to us. It made me very bitter towards them. That was because I didn't know the truth.

Sammie and his family and I decided in about 1953 that we would all go to Houston to see Mother's family. The insurance company that I worked for had transferred me to their office in Oklahoma City at that time. I rode the "milk train" that stopped at every crossroad from Oklahoma City to Houston, but Sammie and his family drove to Houston.

Uncle Thurman, his new wife, and young son seemed very pleased to see us. Uncle Thurman cooked some Bar-B-Que and we all relaxed in the back yard. Uncle Thurman was a policeman or detective on the Houston Police Force.

I mentioned I would like to see my grandparents to Uncle Thurman and he send his son next door to tell my grandparents we were there and to come over and visit with us. My grandparents house was about 20 feet away. When the boy came back he told us, "They said they were getting ready for church and would come over to see us later when they returned home."

Needless to say, I was very disappointed. I had not seen or had any contact with my grandparents in about fifteen years. I know they could see us by looking out their window, but would not walk across the yard to make any contact with us.

I have grandchildren of my own now and I cannot imagine a grandparent that would not be filled with joy any time they were able to see their grandchildren.

It was probably thirty years later that my Mother called to tell me that my granddad had died. I tried to be as kind as possible in telling her that I would not be coming to the funeral. A few years after that, she called to tell me my grandmother had died. Again, I tried to be kind because I knew she was grieving over the death of her parents. But it was very hard form me to erase the way my grandparents had treated us. And it still is. I pray that God will help me to forgive them.

When I was in my 80's, I visited my half sister, Patricia and her husband at their home in Lonoke, Arkansas. She was the daughter of my Mother and her new husband. She was showing me some old pictures of my Grandparents, the Ellises, and my Mother's sister and brother and their children.

She said that Grandmother, Della Ellis, was very, very strict and hard to get along with, but Granddad, Dean Ellis, was very pleasant and easy to please. That helped me to understand more about them, and especially after I learned the truth about what had happened, and how my Mother's new husband had threatened my Grandparents if they told where my Mother and her husband were.

God's Word says that the Truth will make you free. It sure helped me to under-stand what had changed my life so drastically when I was only eight years old.

CHAPTER 3
A BLESSED HERITAGE

God Blessed me by letting me be born into a Christian family. I always believed my Dad wanted to be a Preacher, and don't know why he wasn't. It was probably because he had eight children. That would have been a lot of family to feed on a Preacher's pay in those days. But, I know now, it didn't matter how many were in the family, God would have provided.

My Mamaw liked to preach to me when she came to visit. One of her daughters, Kate, and one of her sons, Paul, were both Pentecostal preachers. Two of her brothers, my Great Uncles Oliver Newton and William, were also Pentecostal preachers.

I believe all of those relatives lived to be in their late nineties, except for one Great Uncle who lived to be 103. I always heard a lot of preaching whenever my relatives came around. That gave me a good start in life.

I know my uncle Paul, Dad's brother, was 98 when he died and had preached, I believe, until he was eighty. My Mamaw was also 98 when she died, but she was only one year and three months away from her 100th birthday. I wanted so much for her to live to be 100 years old. All of Mamaw's family lived long and Blessed lives. God did promise us 120 years.

Mamaw and her family had lived hard lives and were raised on a farm. Times were hard for them, but God saw them through all of their trials. I'm now 87 years old and plan to be around for a long time according to God's Word and His promises.

Please Note This! I may be wrong, but I don't know of any of my Father's relatives who died of a heart attack or any disease. They usually just went to sleep one night and woke up in heaven with Jesus.

Dad didn't know very much about his family because his Father died when he was about three years old. He told me the only thing he remembered was standing on the front porch of their house wearing a long white dress. Young boys and babies didn't wear pants in those days. Most of their clothes were hand-made.

Mamaw told me that her husband, my Dad's Father, went out in the Spring to plow the field to get ready for the Spring Crops, and it started to rain on him. I don't know if he knew that he had the measles or not. He was soaked with the rain and then sick with the measles. That made the measles go in on him and gave him pneumonia.

Mamaw said she held him while he coughed, and seemed to cough his lungs up. I'm sure that was a very hard time for her. Mamaw was pregnant with a girl baby who never saw her Father. She is my Aunt Kate that became a preacher.

I know that Mamaw had a very hard life living on the farm without a husband and pregnant. This was in 1904 and a woman could not go out and get a job as we do today.

God's Word never changes. What He promised, He will do, and He will do the same for you if you only Believe. I only wear glasses to read small print. With large print, I can read well without them. I take three prescribed medications and a hand full of vitamins each day. I consider myself to be pretty healthy, compared to other people.

I look forward to a long and healthy life according to God's promise. He promised us 120 years, and I believe He will give that to me.

CHAPTER 4

MY DAD AND THE CHURCH HE BUILT

My Dad would tell us true stories about things that happen when he was growing up and after he became a young man. He said he was walking home from town through the woods when he was about thirty-two years old, and heard a sound. It seemed as though he heard a voice speaking to him.

He thought it was some of "those old boys from town, following him, and 'funnin' with him." Since he didn't see anyone, he kept on walking. Again he heard what seemed like a voice saying, "Sam build my church." He looked around again, but no one was there so he walked on through the woods towards home.

The third time he heard the voice very clearly saying, "Sam, build my church." He said, "LORD, I don't know anything about building a church." The voice answered and said, "I'll teach you." And God Did.

My Dad built that Church in town, on the corner of Fourth and Marshal Avenue, with God telling him how to do some of the construction work which had never been done before, to his knowledge.

I remember playing under the church while it was being built. It was a pier and beam building on a slight incline because the ground was not level. The front of the church seemed higher off the ground than the rear of the church which was touching the ground. The smell of "fresh cement" was very strong under the church. That smell still lingers in my memories to this very day. Sometimes I get a whiff of that cement small even today.

There wasn't much parking space between the Church and the highway. In the late 1930's everyone didn't have a car, so there was no need for a large parking lot.

Some times we would walk to Church which took us from the south of town to the north of town. Our house, the one Dad built for us, was on the south edge of town, one block inside the city limits. The Church was on the north side of town on Highway 80. That was a nice long walk, especially for a little girl.

My Dad was very tall and had very long legs. For me to keep up with him while we were walking, I had to take two steps to his one step.

For years I have heard something about, read some about, and inquired some about the Revival on Azusa Street in Los Angeles, California when the Holy Spirit came down on that church like **FIRE!**

Our nation was still considered a small nation. The Wright Brothers had flown an airplane in 1903 and our president was Theodore Roosevelt. A black Christian man had come to Los Angeles on February 22, William Seymour, and became Pastor of the Azusa Street Church. He had already been filled with the Holy Spirit and was speaking in tongues. A small majority of white people had joined the church which was held in a small two story building.

Churches across the United States were divided for different reasons. But, in April 1906, during the service, Reverend Seymour began to read from the Book of Acts Chapter 2 in the Bible and things began to change because The Holy Spirit came down like **FIRE** and filled that little church.

They had been having Prayer and Worship Service three times a day, seven days a week. The Baptism of the Holy Spirit with the evidence of Speaking in tongues gave them boldness such as they had never had before. If you want to know more about The Azusa Street Revival, check it out on the Internet. Either before you do or after you do, read Matthew 5:6 where Jesus said, "Blessed are they which do hunger and thirst after righteousness for they shall be filled." The filling of the Holy Spirit is a promise from God Himself.

God's Holy Spirit was moving across the United States and the world. Some may disagree with me, but I think God was getting ready for a mighty move of the Holy Spirit and wanted His People to be ready in our town. That's why He had my Dad build His Church when and where He did. This is my opinion and some may agree or disagree with me.

There was no TV and very few radios in those days and news traveled very slowly. Usually by word of mouth, which took a long time to go from California to Texas.

A couple of years after the Church was finished, some of the Church Members came to our house to talk to Dad. It seems they thought he may have taken some of the building fund money. No formal charges were ever filed against my Dad, but nevertheless, it broke my Dad's heart.

My Dad would never take a penny that didn't belong to him. He was always helping others. He had poured everything, his strength and knowledge and time, into building the Church that God told him to build, and built it according to God's Plan. That was God's Church.

Years later some of the Members came again to see Dad. They came to apologize to him. They had now discovered that the Pastor at the time of the construction, had taken some of the money. That Pastor had moved on and they had a new Pastor now. Dad and my family went back to the Church, but it was never quite the same. Dad was no longer "on fire for the LORD" as he was before that happened.

I grew up in that Church. My Cousin Bill, Uncle Paul's step son, and I would sing for the Sunday morning service. But one night we didn't sing, we ran. I don't know what caused us to run during the Sunday Night Service. I guess Bill and I decided to have a race back and forth across the front of the church and the altars.

I cannot believe that we would have done that if the preacher had been preaching or the singers singing. But we did. We would have been pretty dumb to race back and forth during any of the service procedures. I do remember Uncle Paul grabbing Bill and took him out the side door. That was about the same time Dad grabbed me and took me out that same door. That was the last race we ever had inside the church.

It was during this time that my Aunt Kate, Dad's sister, was involved in her own ministry. She would take my older brother, Sammie, and I to the radio station on Sunday morning and have us sing during her Sunday Morning broadcast. I know I was small, because they had me stand up on a piano bench to sing because I couldn't reach the microphone.

I believe my Aunt Kate, my Uncle Paul, and my Great Uncle Will, and possibly my Mamaw, were members of the Church my Dad built. There could have been many others, too. One of Mamaw's Brothers, Uncle Will, with his wife Alice, was pastor of the Church at one time. They have all gone on to be with Jesus and their Dads and Mothers and sisters and brothers, and all the other relatives are now in heaven.

No matter where I am, from time to time, maybe God is letting me smell that cement smell again to remind me what my Dad did and how he obeyed God. Those were fun days for me, I played under the church while he built it. Dad had obeyed God and built a beautiful Church for God.

My Dad's name was Samuel. There is a beautiful store in the Bible about a woman named Hannah who was barren (childless). She prayed to God for a son and promised God she would turn her son over to the Priest when he was weaned.

God gave her a son and she named him Samuel. You can read about her and her son in I Samuel, and how God gave her a child.

Hannah promised to dedicate Samuel to God. Therefore, when Samuel was old enough and weaned, she took him to the Priest Eli and gave her son to Eli to be dedicated to God. Chapter 3 tells about how God spoke to Samuel three times one night. It's a beautiful story, you should read it. It reminds me of my Dad.

During a Sunday night service when I was about nine years old, and the pastor or an evangelist was preaching "Hell Fire and Brimstone," I went to the altar and gave my life to God. I can still remember that day very well.

The next day, I was a little confused and asked God if I was really saved. I said if I was, would He please take the big rock off the tub that held it down over the pump on our well so that I would know I was really saved. When I went out the next day, God had answered my prayer because the rock was off the tub. Glory!! He sometimes answers children's prayers according to the way a child thinks no matter how silly it may seem to others.

Little kids don't always know the proper way to pray, but God hears them anyhow. Who do you think taught your Father to be a father. It was God. We are God's children and He treats us like children until we are grown. Until then we are taught different things, like how to ride a bike and climbing a tree.

My Cousin Bill and I were about the same age, maybe eight or nine, when our parents decided they wanted us to sing during the Sunday Morning Worship Service. I don't know if we sang well or not, but the members asked us to sing several other times, so we must have been "fair singers."

I came home to visit many, many years later after a long time of being away. I was with my oldest brother, Sammie, and we were traveling east on Highway 80 where the church was built. I could not believe my eyes. The Church was gone and a large Doctor's Building was in its place.

I yelled at my brother, "Where's the Church?" He said they sold the lot and tore the Church down. A much larger church was built on north on Fourth Street with a huge parking lot, and was made with bricks. The Church Dad built was built with lumber. I sat back in my seat stunned and in tears because "our church," my Dad's Church was gone.

There is now a Doctor's Building on the corner where the Church once stood. My Doctor's office is in the Doctor's

Building. I told him about the church Dad built on the corner where his office is. In fact, if we measured it, his office may be sitting where the altars and the platform were. That would be a nice place to have a doctor's office who is trying to help people get well.

But, the actual healer's name is Jesus. He loves to heal people. He always said, "Only Believe." For with those who Believe, all things are possible. But, if you don't Believe, don't expect anything from God, not healing, and not prosperity.

CHAPTER 5

THE BREAKUP THAT CHANGED OUR LIVES

I'm sure my Dad may have had men working for him and with him while building the Church God told him to build. There was a family we became friends with and I believe were also members of the Church. I mention this because things were about to happen that would change my life forever and all of my family.

My youngest brother, Jackie was born on March 7, 1941. That made us a family of five children, and my Dad and my Mother made us seven. I was eight years old and school was out for the summer. I went to stay with Mamaw and Granddad for a few weeks in northeast Texas about 50 miles from my home. I loved to stay with Mamaw and Granddad because I was the only child staying with them and I got all of the attention.

They lived in Jefferson in an apartment on the second floor which had a balcony. I could stand out there and look down toward the sawmill where Granddad worked. The smell of fresh cut wood was always in the air. I was having such a good time.

One day my Aunt Kate came to see us. I didn't know why, but when she and Mamaw finished talking, she told me to get my things because I was going home. I was having such a wonderful time and did not want to go. That's when she told me exactly why she had come. She said that my Mother had left and my Dad wanted me to come back home. I didn't really understand what all of that meant.

She got a bed sheet from somewhere and laid it on the floor and piled my few things on it and tied it up. We went out to her car and she put the sheet with my things in it on the back seat.

I got in and sat on the sheet to make me sit taller and so I could look out the window because I was small and couldn't see out otherwise. I knew that if I watched for my Mother and saw her walking down the road, then I would tell my Aunt to stop and we could take her back home. I was only eight years old and was thinking as a child would. We did not see my Mother walking on the road and did not get to take her home.

After arriving home, I learned part of what had happened. My Dad had taken my two brothers to get hair cuts. Another Aunt, my Dad's youngest sister Alpha, had taken my younger sister, Della, with her to the Beauty Shop. That left my Mother alone at home with my baby brother Jackie, who was just three months old.

I guess my Mother and her friend had planned to leave us when they got the chance, and this was that day. I know they could never have imagined what their leaving would do to the two families and the children they left behind. I don't hate my Mother, in fact, I love her. I think it would be very hard for a person to hate their Mother.

She came back to get a divorce about the last of September after being away only four months. My Dad begged her to come back and take care of the children. He promised her that he would take care of her and the children, and he would live somewhere else. But, she said no. I guess she knew she had gone too far.

My Dad agreed to the divorce, but only if she would give him all of the children.

That meant, she would have to give up my baby brother, who was now eight months old and still nursing. She reluctantly agreed and the divorce was final on October 31, 1941. That was really a terrible Birthday Present for My Dad, my oldest Brother Sammie, and Me whose birthdays we had just celebrated in October.

I remember that day so well. It was a chilly, cloudy day. There was a fireplace in our house that my Dad had built and it had a gas heater in it that looked like logs. My Dad's youngest sister, my Aunt Alpha, the nurse, was there. I sat in her lap while she rocked me and waited for my Dad to come back home. It was a terrible, gloomy day.

I don't remember anything else about that day, and it's probably best that I don't. It was a very painful day for all of us. Aunt Alpha had agreed to stay with us during the day while Dad worked. As a nurse, she was working the night shift and would be there in the daytime, sleeping, if we needed her.

When I was about twelve years old and even older, I would spend several weeks in the summer with my Mother and her new husband. They eventually had eight more children and were divorced after twenty plus years of marriage.

Yes, add it up. My Mother had five children with my Dad. Then she had eight children with the man she left with. She was the mother of thirteen children. And if it was true what they told me later about her having a miscarriage between my older brother and myself, she actually was pregnant fourteen times.

Nevertheless, you cannot build a happy life and family by tearing up two other families to do so. Someone told me when I was growing up, that you cannot build happiness over another person's ashes. It never works. There is always too much heartbreak involved.

My Mother had married my Dad when she was only thirteen or fourteen years old. As adults, we know now that she never had a "childhood." People married quite young in those days, but she went from childhood into motherhood at a very young age. She had been married to my Dad only twelve or thirteen years, and was only about 26 years old when she left us. The man she married was about fifteen years older than she. It's hard for me to imagine what she felt or thought.

She and her new husband lived in Galveston for a number of years, then moved to Arkansas. Her oldest daughter, Patricia, by her new husband, told me years later that all of her siblings were born in Galveston. I had not known that.

Once, when I was grown and married, I visited them in Arkansas. One afternoon my Mother called me into her bedroom because she wanted to talk to me. She didn't say much, but the most important thing I remember is that she told me the worst mistake she ever made was when she left my Dad.

She knew she had made a mistake and that mistake could never be undone. I think that's why I never could hate her. She regretted what she had done.

My family never talked about the time when our Mother left. I know it was hard for me, and probably just as hard for them – my sister and two younger brothers. My older brother, Sammie, and I would visit her occasionally, and knew she regretted leaving us. That's why we were more able to cope with the situation. That doesn't mean I did not cry many night in my bed, even when I was in my forties. We can never go back and change the past.

Our Mother came to see us at our home a couple of times when we were growing up. She didn't stay very long and she didn't ask us any questions. I now own the one picture that was taken of us children when she visited. Aunt

Kate was holding my baby brother, Jackie, in the picture, He's the one she had to give up.

The picture was taken after My Dad had married our Step Mom. In the picture was Sammie, me, Charlie, Della, Jackie and our new Step brother, Tommy. He was too young, and did not know exactly what was going on. He just wanted to be in the picture. She gave each of us a shiny half dollar. I don't know if she gave one to Tommy or not.

One summer, while they lived in Galveston, I went to visit my Mother for a few weeks. She took me shopping at one of the department stores downtown and told me to pick out a dress that I wanted. I was only about twelve years old. I picked a pretty pink formal. She didn't saw anything about my choice, she just paid for it.

I did not need or had any use for a formal. I guess she just wanted to please me. I would take it out of my closet sometimes and look at it, and put it on, then put it back into the closet. I never went anywhere that I could wear the formal. The only time I wore any kind of formal was at the Junior Prom and then at the Senior Prom. By that time, the dress was too small, old and ragged, and of no value.

Mother did come to visit me after I was married and lived in Euless. She was divorced from the man she left with and married to D. C. Underwood. They were living in Little Rock, Arkansas and had come to the Dallas area to see the football game between Arkansas University and Texas

University. That was one of the big games during the year. They were there for the ball game, not to see me.

She and I were talking and she asked if I would call my brother Jackie. He was the baby she had to give up so that Dad would give her the divorce. Jackie didn't live very far from my house, so I called him. He and his wife came over.

My husband and I, and Mother and D.C. were sitting in the Den visiting. Jackie and his wife came in through the kitchen door. I think I must have said something like, Jackie, "This is Mother." I really don't remember.

As soon as I finished speaking, Jackie and his wife sat down on the couch at the opposite side of the room. I have no memory of the conversation, if there was one, or when they all left. Jackie was always very quiet and didn't talk much. I don't remember Jackie saying anything to Mother. He never mentioned the incident to me.

I was living in Mineral Wells in West Texas and decided to have a Family Reunion so that we could all get together and have some "Fun Time." Jackie and our Step Mom had died and we had enjoyed some family weddings and needed some "Fun Time" just to relax and enjoy each other.

I invited our Mother to the Reunion. One of her sons, Philip and his family, brought her in their camper trailer. Two huge pecan trees grew in my yard for everyone to sit under and relax. I was visiting with Mother and she asked me, "Do you think your Dad would come out of the house and talk with me." I asked Dad and he said, "NO!!" I didn't purse the matter any further. However; after a few minutes, I noticed he got up from the table and went outside and sat down next to Mother.

For our family, this was a Historical Moment. As to my knowledge, the last time they had seen or spoken to each other was the day of their divorce some forty years earlier. I know from the conversations I had with my Mother that she wanted to apologize to my Dad. We don't know what was said. It was a personal thing between them.

Me and my siblings that were watching this historical event from afar, considered the matter closed and perhaps the "brokenness mended" so they could be "civil" to each other. None of us knew for sure. I believe this happened in the Summer of about 1981.

Her husband D.C. brought her to another Reunion on July 4, 1984. They stayed for only a couple of hours, which was strange since they had traveled so far. She told me something about going across an open field from their apartment to the Drug Store to get a prescription filled and someone attacked her. Her story didn't make much sense. D.C. told me she had been hit on the head and had not fully recovered from the injury.

She and D.C. were living at an "Assisted Living" Nursing Home in Jacksonville, Arkansas after they returned home. My half sister, Patricia, called me and said Mother wasn't doing well. She had Alzheimer's Disease and the Doctor's did not expect her to live for very long. She died in January 1985.

Sammie and his wife Marie were living with me and helping me do some re-modeling on my home in Mineral Wells when we got the news. The three of us were the only children from her marriage to my Dad that went to her funeral. That was the end of a long story and the end of an era in our lives.

Afterwards everyone went to Patricia's house to visit and look at pictures. She had pictures of family members she didn't even know. Sammie and I helped them and told them who the family members were.

We did have an enjoyable time looking through pictures and visiting with some of my half brothers and half sister. They all knew me because I had visited with my mother and them when they were young and growing up.

CHAPTER 6

MY AUNT ALPHA, THE NURSE TO THE RESCUE

I had one older brother, two younger brothers, and a sister. My older brother, Sammie, was four years older than me. The younger brother, Jackie, was eight years younger than me. He's the one my Mother took with her when she left us. The other brother, Charlie, was two years younger than me. We called him the "Clown" because he was always doing crazy stunts. My sister, Della, was five years younger than me.

Charlie and I were playing around the driveway which had been covered with road oil to make it harden. That's what was used on some of the roads and streets because we lived in the middle of the Oil Field Boom in east Texas, and the oil "boom" was on. Oil was very plentiful and probably cheap.

My Dad had planted Poplar trees along the front edge of the property. Poplar trees were not designed for climbing. The branches grew straight up and were very thin. However, my "Crazy" brother, Charlie, decided he wanted to climb up the tree next to the driveway.

There were a number of other trees on our property that we liked to climb, but he wanted to climb that one. He only got up about nine feet when the limb broke and he fell flat of his back on the oil paved driveway.

I was about eight years old at the time. I looked at him as he laid there lifeless. Then I ran into the house to get Aunt Alpha, yelling, "He's dead!! He's dead!!" I think I really scared my Aunt awake. She was sleeping because she had worked the night shift at the hospital. She worked for and with Dr. Khoury, who was also our Family Doctor.

Thank God, she knew exactly what to do. She grabbed him up in her arms, he wasn't very big, and took him in to the bathroom. She ran cold water into the tub and doused him in it. He only had the wind knocked out of him. No bones were broken and he didn't have any bruises or scrapes that we could see. This would be only the first of many serious tragedies for my brother Charlie.

I was maybe four years old when I was hurt. We had a wagon that my brother Sammie and I played with. Usually, he would let me ride and he would pull the wagon. I guess, this particular day I wanted to be a "big girl" and pull him in the wagon. Our driveway was a little steep and had large planks across the ditch at the bottom of the driveway. Going down the driveway was always easy. It was the coming up that was the hardest.

I was pulling and Sammie was riding. We were going at a pretty fast pace down the driveway, then I slipped just as we got to the planks. I went sprawling out on my stomach with my arms and hands stretched out in front of me. I caught my fourth finger nail on my right hand on one of the plants and almost tore it off.

I still remember that pain! Sammie helped me into the house where our Aunt Alpha was. She made me lay down on my bed and proceeded to jerk my fingernail off. It was loose enough to just fall off, but I wouldn't let anyone touch it because it hurt so much. She bandaged it and I believe I fell asleep because I don't remember anything after than and I had been through a very traumatic experience.

My Aunt Alpha's sister was our Aunt Kate. She had one of her fingernails torn off many years earlier and it was an ugly, hard, thick, yellowish nail now. I did not want my nail to grow out to look like hers and I cried about it. She was the sweetest person you would ever want to meet. She just had an ugly fingernail.

CHAPTER 7
THE NOSE BLEED

You must know how kids pick at things, break things, change things, lose things – it never seems to end. Well, I have always had problems with my nose. I may have been about nine years old and in the bathroom one night and picking at my nose because it was dry. It started to bleed. I grabbed the tissue paper and tried to stop it to no avail.

I came out of the bathroom and told my Dad and Step Mom, that my nose was bleeding – as if they couldn't see it for themselves. By this time it was running pretty fast. She and Dad tried holding my head back. They also put a penny under my tongue and an ice pack on my nose. None of these worked. It only got worse.

The next thing I remember was that I was lying on the front porch with my head hanging off the edge. I know my Dad had sent for my Uncle Paul, his brother, and his wife, Aunt Connie, to come help who lived on the street behind our house.

They were both Christians and I know they were praying for me very diligently. My Dad and Step Mom were on the porch, and my Uncle and Aunt were standing on the ground in the flower bed next to the porch by the shrubbery.

There was a bright, full moon shining that night. I think it was the brightest and most beautiful moon I had ever seen. I don't know how long it took to stop the bleeding, probably all night. I either fell asleep or passed out.

The next memory I have is waking up in my bed. I got up, feeling fair, and headed for the kitchen to get some breakfast. Dad had enlarged our kitchen by extending it out and incorporating the back porch into the kitchen-breakfast-dining-den area.

Over in one corner of the dining area, next to the back door, was a Number 3 wash tub and it was completely full of bloody rags and blood. While I'm standing there looking at it, Uncle Paul came in the door. He looked at me and said, "We thought we lost you last night."

That's the last memory I have of the incident, but I'm sure those who were there remembered it for a long time. By my telling you, you know I have remembered it all of my life. I know when I was looking up at that bright moon, God was looking down at me and healing me and protecting me. I know God was always there when I was facing any difficulty.

I had problems with nose bleeds all of my life. Once when I was, grown and on a date, my date was driving and talking about something. He flung his hand toward me and hit me in the nose. Yes, you're right. My nose started gushing. He was so embarrassed. I finally got it to stop while my date was still apologizing to me.

When I was married and pregnant with my son, Michael, I seemed to have lots of nose bleeds. I told my doctor and he gave me some nose drops to help make the membranes stronger, and the drops did help. When I was being taken into the Delivery Room, I was getting pretty foggy, but I told them, "I need to take my nose drops with me." At that time I never went anywhere without my nose drops.

They didn't give them to me, but after all the problems I had all my life with nose bleeds, I didn't want to take a chance. I do believe God healed me, because after that, I never had a serious nose bleed again.

CHAPTER 8

MAIDS CAME AND WENT, BUT ONE STAYED

Finally, my Dad began to hire maids to stay with us in the daytime and cook and clean house. It had become too hard for Aunt Alpha to work all night, then try to watch over us and sleep in the daytime. The maids would cook and clean the house and do the laundry. But someone needed to watch over the "wild children" we had become.

I don't know exactly what we did, but none of them ever stayed very long. It may have been that we were just too rowdy and almost uncivilized for anyone to stay around us very long. Maybe after not having any actual supervision in the day-time for a long period, we went back to our "wild nature."

Some days Dad would come home exhausted. I remember one of those days when he came home and laid down on my bed. I was the only one in the family that had a twin bed all to myself. The others shared beds. I think he had walked all day selling insurance, and I know we had a car most of the time. Only several families in our neighborhood had cars. I don't know why he was walking.

He started to cry, while we were rubbing his legs because they hurt and ached. He told us he would probably have to take us to The Buckner Orphans Home near Dallas, because that was the only one he knew about. We all started to cry, and said, "No, No, please don't take us there. We want to stay here at home with you." We stayed in our home and he continued to hire maids to take care of us.

We may not have had any supervision in the daytime, but we were not alone. God was watching over us every minute of every day. HE was always there.

One day Dad asked me if I would like to take a ride with him. Naturally, I wanted to go. I always loved to go anywhere my Dad would take me. We went out to a small suburban town, Greggton, on Highway 80. He stopped at a small shop on the south side of the highway and took me in with him. It was a Beauty Shop and he had gone there to talk to a lady.

I don't know what they talked about. I guess I was more interested in looking at all the "gadgets" they used in the Beauty Shop. A few days later he brought the lady home and told us she was to be our new maid. She had a son that she brought with her who was about 4 years old. We were all pleased with the situation, and we also had another playmate.

It wasn't until years later that I actually realized the situation. My Dad had five children without a Mother and she had a son without a Dad. She lived with her Mother and Step-Dad on a farm where she grew up which was about 8 miles out East Cotton Street. That distance of eight miles was counting from the city limits to their home in the country, not from our house.

Each morning she had to walk that eight miles to the city limits to catch the town bus and ride into downtown. There she would transfer from that bus onto another bus that went out Highway 80 to the Beauty Shop were she worked as a Beautician all day – might I add – standing on her feet. She was only about 23 years old.

When her workday was over, she rode the bus back to town and transferred to the bus that took her out to the edge of the city limits. Then she would walk that same eight miles home. Most of the time she would leave for work in the dark and go home in the dark.

Those were some very hard times for many people in 1940. She did that five or six days a week. She had been married to a man that was much older than her and did not treat her well. They had one son but were now Divorced. Her son would stay with her Mother on the farm during the day while she worked.

I have lived through times like that and the children very seldom saw their Mother because the Mother left before daylight to go to work, and came home after dark in the winter time. Only in the summer time would the Mother return home while it was still daylight.

Now she lived with us and did not need to take that long journey to work and back each day. Her Mother had been taking care of her son Tommy, but now she could have her son with her all day long.

This was, as they say "A no lose situation." She was a very nice lady. We all benefited from the arrangement. It must have been instigated by God.

Time passed and one day her son, Tommy, ran into the house and asked her to make him a "Sugar Sandwich." We were all right behind him yelling, "Mama, make me a "Sugar Sandwich."

Because you probably don't know what a "Sugar Sandwich" is, I'll tell you. You take a piece of bread and spread some butter on it. Then you sprinkle sugar on it and fold it over. For hungry little kids there wasn't much to make a sandwich with in those days. However, "a sugar sandwich" was delicious. We also made onion sandwiches.

You may wonder why we made "weird" sandwiches. Because Lunch Meat and some of those delicacies had not yet been invented. We ate what was available.

One day my Dad was there and heard us calling her "Mother" or "Mama." Later he sat us all down on the couch in the living room and asked, "Would you like to have her for your Mother?" We all said, "Yes."

He had asked us that same question about other ladies he knew. When he asked that question the other times, the answer had always been, "No." I know he never would have married anyone we did not like or approve of.

They were married July 30, 1942 by Dad's Uncle Will, one of Mamaw's brothers. Uncle Will was the pastor of the church my Dad built. She was 24 years old with one child, and Dad was 38 with five children. It wasn't until many years later, and all of these dear people had already gone to be with the LORD, that I asked my Uncle Paul, my Dad's brother, about what had happened.

Uncle Paul had also been a member of the church Dad built. My Great Uncle Will performed the wedding ceremony in his home, not in the church. Uncle Paul said that it was against the Church's Rules and Regulations for Uncle Will to perform the Ceremony for my Dad and this Lady because both of them had been divorced.

Uncle Paul said that Uncle Will could have had his pastor's license revoked if anyone had found out about the marriage. No one ever found out and my Great Uncle Will lived to be 103 years old and was a pastor, probably until he was well into his late eighties or early nineties.

Growing up, I felt a special love for both my Great Uncle Will and my Uncle Paul, who also lived to be ninety-eight years old. He was also a pastor of different churches until he was in his eighties. He was the pastor of a church in Mobile, Alabama for many years.

Many years later, and after he had retired, whenever I would go to visit him, he would always say, "I remember when I could hold you in my one hand because you were so small." His house and our house had been back to back for most of my childhood there in Longview.

In his later years, he and his wife lived in Tyler, Texas. He attended church services until he wasn't physically able to get around. He said that during the Pastor's Sermon, when the Pastor would quote a verse or reference from the Bible or other information, he would always look at my Uncle and ask, "Isn't that right, Brother Paul?" Uncle Paul said he would always answer his question.

Anyone could ask him about any verse in the Bible and he could quote it and tell you the meaning. I believe he and I always had a special "bond." Once he showed me a letter he got from the mayor of Tyler congratulating him and his wife for being married seventy years. THAT'S A LONG TIME.

He said that a couple of years earlier they had gone to a Church Conference being held at another church. Aunt Connie was walking up the steps to the Church and lost her balance and fell back down the steps and hit her head. She was never the same after that.

She was then living in a Nursing Home because the hit to her head had caused her to lose her memory and was not able to function properly. I never was able to see her again until her funeral. She was a very sweet lady and very special to me.

Tyler was about forty miles from my home. That's why I didn't get to see them very often. Aunt Connie was never able to go home and finally died in the Nursing Home.

Uncle Paul was very proud of her. She had been the president of the Women's Ministry in that area for a long time. He gave me the magazine that had a story about her and her devotion to the Women's Ministry, which I have kept and treasured for many years.

They were both devoted to the LORD. Before He died, He gave me one of his Bibles, which was a study Bible for Pastors. I have that Bible on my desk with my other Bibles and Reference Books to use during my studies. I treasure His Bible very dearly.

Mamaw once told me about Uncle Paul, her son, and his wife, Aunt Connie. She said that my Aunt Connie had a baby "out of wedlock." That's the way everyone explained it in those days. She did not agree to their getting married. Mamaw went on to say that out of her two Daughter-in-laws, Connie was the kindest and the sweetest. She said that Aunt Connie always tried to help Mamaw any way she could and was the most devoted Christian she had ever known.

I don't know how, when, or where she became pregnant. That doesn't matter. She was devoted to the LORD and delighted in doing His Work.

Mamaw also told me about Uncle Paul and when he became a Christian. This was before he met and married my Aunt Connie. He was very excited one day and told his mother, my Mamaw, he needed to talk to her brother Ollie. By this time, Ollie had already become a Christian Preacher.

Uncle Paul had accepted Jesus as his Savior and needed to ask his Uncle Ollie about it. Mama had two brothers who followed and preached about Our LORD all of their lives, Will and Ollie. Now one of her sons was going to follow in their footsteps. Then later her daughter Kate would also.

Her daughter Kate is the one who never saw her father because he died of the measles and pneumonia before she was born, was also a preacher all of her adult life. I am blessed to have lived and known these people who were devoted to our God and our LORD Jesus Christ, our Savior. They served Him all of their adult lives right up to their deaths.

These were my aunts and uncles. I was blessed to be born into such a renowned and distinguished family.

CHAPTER 9

BIKE RIDING AND NEIGHBORS VISITING

Those were the days when children could ride their bikes anywhere without fear of being harmed. Our town, at that time, was only about 14,000 residents.

I don't remember how old I was when I decided I wanted to learn how to ride a bike. Everyone else was riding bikes except for me. I asked Sammie if he would teach me and he did.

Of course, he had a boy's bike, so that's what I learned to ride. There was a small hill at the east end of our street which made a perfect place to start riding. He went with me to the top of the hill. I got on and he pushed me off. I went sailing down the hill and it was a wonderful feeling of freedom. I looked back and much to my amazement, he was still standing at the top of the hill. I had ridden down the hill without any help. That settled it. I was now a bike rider. The only thing I needed now was a girl's bike.

One Summer day, my girlfriend, Madeline, and I decided we would take some sandwiches and ride our bikes to the Sabine River. That's how FREE we were in those days. We could go anywhere we desired without fear of anything or anyone. It was about ten miles from my home to the River and took us most of the morning to get there. We were tired when we got there, so we rested, ate our sandwiches and started back on the long ride home. It took us most of the afternoon to get home.

Those were wonderful days when my girlfriend and I had no fear of anyone molesting us or harming us. It was wonderful freedom. No one locked their car or their front door. We could walk or ride our bikes wherever we pleased.

None of the houses were air conditioned, but Dad had installed an attic fan in our house which helped during the heat of the day and night. In fact, only several stores and restaurants were air conditioned.

My Dad had gotten a huge box type fan and put it in front of the Front Door to draw the cool air in at night. It was in a wooden box frame with chicken wire on the front and back to keep "curious little children" from sticking their fingers in it. It was big and very loud, and the blades were very sharp. It sounded like an airplane taking off, but it sure did put out the cool air.

Early one morning, when everyone was still asleep, our neighbor friend, Lopez, came to ask my Dad for help. He stepped around the fan and came into the house calling for my Dad. Remember, no one locked their doors and if your neighbor needed help, you helped him.

We played with his children, and they spent many hours at our house. For some reason, I was sleeping on the cough in the living room. I didn't get up because I knew it did not concern me and that my Dad would take care of him and help him.

I was also told that sometimes, when no one was at home, and a neighbor needed something, the neighbor would go in and help himself. Later, they would tell their neighbor what they had done and repay them for what they had taken or return it.

We never considered it to be stealing. We helped each other. We trusted our neighbors and our neighbors trusted us.

We were the only family in the neighborhood that had a telephone. The neighbors would come to our house when they needed to make a phone call.

Not many people had cars. When they needed to go somewhere, they would go to the neighbor that had a car and ask that neighbor to take them wherever they needed to go. They didn't do that very often, only when they really needed help.

Everyone was friendly. Everyone knew all the children in the neighborhood and who their parents were. One day they may play in our front yard, and the next day they may all be next door playing. We didn't fuss or fight, we just had fun.

On Saturday afternoon, my Step Mom would take us to the movies. Before she could get out of the driveway the car would be filled with us and all of the neighbor kids. We always went to the "Double Feature Cowboy Movie."

The boys would sit on the front row and pretend they were cowboys, too.

It was my job to watch over all of them because I was the oldest. After watching the movies, I would call home for My Step Mom to come and get us. I called and we waited in front of the theater for her to come and get us. I was holding onto Jackie's hand because he was still little. She came up on the opposite side of the street and when Jackie saw her, he pulled his hand away and ran out into the street.

There was a car coming and he ran in front of the car. Everyone was watching in horror. The front bumper of the car knocked him down and ran over him. When the car was stopped, his right leg was pinned down with the edge of the right rear tire. It did not run over his leg, just pinned it down.

Yes, the car ran "over him" and left some black tire marks on his leg, but did not run over his leg. The man got out of his car and "plopped down" on the "running board." He was about to pass out. I grabbed Jackie up and to everyone's amazement, he was not hurt. Someone who saw the accident had called the police and the police came with an ambulance.

They were talking to our Step Mom and she told them that Jackie was not hurt and he was okay. But, they better check the driver of the car because he looked like he was going to have a heart attack. Everyone decided that Jackie was not hurt and we went home. Shortly after we arrived home, the driver of the car called to ask if Jackie was okay. Dad assured him that Jackie was okay and thanked him for calling.

I hope I don't need to tell you that God was at work during that situation. The Devil had tried to kill Jackie, but God would not let him and Jackie came through it without any injuries. Praise God!!

One night on November 15, 1949, when I was a senior in High School, my friend Margaret came running in the house and into the kitchen where I was washing dishes and cried, "Daddy was killed." Her father had been crossing the highway and was hit and killed by a car. That's all we were told. I don't know why it happened. He had ridden the bus out onto Highway 80 to a bar where he was planning to be with some friends and drink.

He walked in front of the bus and stepped out into the oncoming traffic and was killed instantly.

She had said at times that she hated her Dad. I know it was because he was very strict with the children. There were six children in the family, plus him and his wife. That was a large family to take care of. I know he wanted his children to grow up respectful and able to care for themselves. He and his wife raised some very fine children. We grew up like "brothers and sisters" and they are all still very dear to me. I believe they all accepted Jesus as their LORD and Savior before they died.

There are only three of the boys alive today and we are all still very close. At this writing, both the girls and one boy have gone on to be with their LORD and Savior. I was given the privilege and honor of speaking at each of their funerals.

Now, my Stepbrother and I are the only two left in our family. Our relationship with our neighbors started at "the sand box" and has lasted to the grave. We have always treated each other like brothers and sisters. I have always called them my "other brothers and sisters."

CHAPTER 10
GRADE SCHOOL DAYS

I was born in the month of October, and could not start to school in the fall as the other children did. At that time, children could start First Grade in January after their sixth birthday. Our Elementary School was South Ward and about 8 or 9 blocks from our house.

During the Spring in my second year of school, I was now in the first half of Second Grade. I developed the measles and did not get to finish the beginning of Second Grade.

When I went back to school in the Fall, the Principal put me in the Third Grade thinking he was doing me a favor. That put me in a class that had already learned about adding and subtracting and division.

I had missed all of that teaching and had no clue as to what the teacher was talking about. They were studying the Multiplication Tables. Because I did not know the basics, multiplication was very hard for me and I was failing.

My Dad went to talk to the Principal about putting me back to finish the second half of the Second Grade. He did, and I did fairly well then. I was not the smartest kid in the class, but I did make fair grades. I had to study hard because it did not come easy for me. Some of my brothers did very well in school, when they stayed in school. That was the hard part, keeping them in school.

Since we did not have a Mother to watch over us and help us – especially with our clothes and dressing, I was doing a very bad job of dressing myself. Sometimes I would wear my brother Sammie's brogan shoes. If you don't know, they were actually boots to be worn outside while working, and came up past the ankle.

My shoes were wearing out. They had holes in them and the sole was coming loose. I would put new newspaper in them every day and put a rubber band around the toes to keep the sole from flopping. I'm sure I was a "raving beauty" then.

In Third Grade we had a teacher that taught Art. I loved that class because she told us how and what to draw. Our pictures were usually of buildings and streets and black and white. Many years later I put that teaching to use and started painting.

These Grade School days were during World War II. On Friday our Spelling Teacher would have a test to find out who could spell the most words without making a mistake. If you could do that, you were given a Hershey Bar.

Any form of Candy was scarce. The teacher's husband was in the Army and could buy the Hershey Bars at the Commissary on the base. Since there wasn't actually a base in Longview, I now presume that her husband was stationed at Herman General Hospital and Prisoner of War Camp in the south part of Longview.

Since I loved Hershey Bars, I would study extra hard before the test. I believe I may have won the Hershey Bar almost every Friday. That may have been when I fell in love with Hershey Bars, and still do. I call myself a chock-a-holic.

The class was asked to bring a piece of yarn to school, for what reason I don't remember. It was a very cold day and I had gloves on. I held the yarn very tight in my hand, but when I arrived at school and opened my hand, the yarn was gone. I cried because I wouldn't get to participate in the project that day.

The girls were never allowed to wear any type of pants to school. In fact, I didn't have any pants or jeans to wear. I don't think they had yet started making jeans for anyone to wear, and they certainly did not make pants for girls.

If you think that was bad, when my oldest daughter, Theresa, was in First Grade and the days were very cold, they were not allowed to wear pants. Finally, the School Board bent the rules and let the girls wear pants to school under their dresses. They were told to take the pants off in the Cloak Room, while in school and only had a dress on during class.

I started to school in 1939 and Theresa started to school in 1963. Wasn't that Good Progress. Hooray!! She could wear pants to walk through the cold and snow going to school, but not in the classroom.

In my school, each class had its own Cloak Room where we would hang our coats up in the morning and take off our galoshes, rubber shoes we worn on rainy days. But, I never had any galoshes. Dad couldn't afford them.

If you misbehaved, you would be told to stand in the corner in the rear of the room. I was blessed, because I never did stand in the corner. The first day in Second Grade, the Teacher would assign us our seats (desks). I believe her name was Mrs. Peterson. She told me to sit up front next to her desk because she wanted me near her because I was always quiet. She made the "rowdy boys" sit on the back row because they were so loud.

In the Sixth Grade our music teacher was Mrs Murphy. Her daughter, Pat Murphy, was also in that grade. I thought it was "neat" for Pat to have her mother as her teacher. Many years later, at our High School reunion, I talked with Pat about her mother and how much I admired her mother. She told me that her mother had died several years earlier.

There wasn't a cafeteria or any place to buy lunch in Grade School. Everyone brought their lunch and ate at their desk. If I remember right, after lunch we would go out for Physical Education, recess, and usually played baseball.

Once I was waiting for my turn at bat, when the batter hit the ball, then slung the bat behind her. Do I even need to tell you what happened. That bat hit me across my chest, knocked me down, and started the bells to ringing in my head. I don't know if I finished the day at school or went home.

I never did like P.E. after that. I asked my Dad if he would ask his sister, my Aunt Alpha, to get a note from our family doctor, Dr. Khoury whom she worked with that would excuse me from playing baseball. She did, and I never did play baseball in Grade School again. Or in High School!! Or in College!! Thank God for that. My Dad always acquired me an excuse.

I have some good memories of Grade School, but I also have some bad memories. I think I was in third grade when my Mother left us and also of the time I was hit with a bat. But, I also had some very kind and nice teachers.

CHAPTER 11
THE TREE CLIMBERS

We had lots of trees in our yard and in the fenced-in area for the cow and chickens. That's where the pond was that my older brother, Sammie, and I went "swimming" in. I should say, the one I almost drowned in. Dad always had a cow and some chickens and a pond.

With eight kids and two grown-ups, he had to do something to stretch that "old dollar bill." Dad had built our home on one acre of land with lots of trees. The trees were mostly plain old willow trees, except for one Sweetgum tree, and one Weeping Willow tree. The only trees he planted on the property were the Poplar trees that lined the front of the property. I liked those stately tall trees.

Dad got a pig once and put it in the fenced in area, but also built another fence around it to keep it separate from the cow and chickens. He was going to raise it and then butcher it for us some meat. Since our New Step Mom was raised on a farm the same as my Dad, they both knew about canning vegetables and meat.

I don't know how long he had had the pig, but it was getting pretty big. Then a person, an authority person, came to see the pig. Dad showed it to the man and the man told Dad he could not have a pig inside the city limits.

Even though our house was at the edge of town, it was inside the city limits by one block. The man told Dad he had to get rid of the pig. I don't know what happened to it, but we never did get any bacon for our breakfast from it. We could have cows and chickens, but NO PIGS.

Sammie and Charlie had built a tree house, or should I say a platform, in one of the trees outside the fenced area. They nailed pieces of boards to the trunk for us to hold on to and step on to so we could climb up the tree to the platform which was about fifteen feet from the ground.

We all liked to climb trees. That gave us a perch high above the ground. One afternoon there wasn't anyone around when I decided to climb up to the platform. I had gotten almost to the top, when I grabbed the board to pull myself up to the platform and the board broke in two pieces and I went air born down to the ground.

I fell flat on my back and heard all kinds of whistles and some of the brightest and most beautiful stars I have ever seen. I don't know how long I lay there, but when I was alert again, I walked to the house and entered through the back door. My Step Mom was in the kitchen cooking Supper (we ate Supper, not Dinner).

I told her what had happened and she told me I probably needed to sit down. I don't think I told anyone else right away what had happened. No one took me to the doctor or the hospital to see if I was hurt or okay.

After I felt better, I went back outside to play. That's the way things were handled back then. You didn't run to the doctor just because you fell out of a tree or got cut on something.

There was a family that lived a couple of houses from us, the Lopez family that I have mentioned. They had children the same ages as us kids. They had only one large Cottonwood tree in their front yard. Their Dad told them to never climb up in that tree!

You know you should never tell kids not to do something they like to do, or something that all the other kids are doing. Because that is exactly what they will do. The oldest boy, Eddie, climbed up in that tree and fell out. He broke his arm. He only wanted to be like the other kids.

My brothers and I always fell out of the trees. The difference was, we never got hurt. The secret to that may have been because we were always relaxed when we fell because we were never told to stay out of the trees. We were not afraid of being caught climbing the trees, or of falling out of the trees. We were not disobeying our parents.

Their Dad told them not to climb in that tree because they might get hurt. Since they were disobeying him, they may have been tensed up and afraid they would be in trouble for climbing the tree. That may be why he broke his arm when he fell.

In the fenced in area where the cow and chickens were, we put a rope in one of the trees so we could swing out over the pond. You know, like Tarzan. We also took some jar lids and caps and can lids and found a "Y" where two large branches met in one of the trees. We took our lids and nailed them onto the tree. This was our airplane. We could sit up there for hours and fly our planes all over the world. Of course, this was done mostly in the summer time. During the winter it was too cold to be up in the trees.

Nevertheless, we always found plenty of things to do to keep us amused, no matter if it were summer or winter. With our eight and all the neighbor kids, there was always someone to play with.

My Step Mom's mother still lived eight miles out in the country. Everyone called her Big Mama. She had lots of relatives that lived up the road and down the road from her. Almost every Sunday we would go to her house for Sunday Dinner. She cooked on a wood burning stove. I had never seen a wood burning cook stove before. She had to keep the fire going in the stove all of the time. That's what heated the burners and the oven.

One Sunday I had on my blue taffeta dress from church. It may have been Easter time and the weather was still a little chilly. I thought I would walk between the cook stove and the wall where it was warmer.

Do you know what happens to taffeta when it gets near or touches heat? It seems to draw the material toward the heat. Before I knew what was happening, my dress skirt touched the hot stove and curled up my dress on one side. My beautiful new dress was ruined.

Another time we were there for Sunday dinner, and after dinner, I went out to play. One of their Mulberry trees had fallen down, so naturally I wanted to walk on the trunk and on the limbs. I caught my dress on one of the limbs and tore a "V" shape in it. There went another one of my pretty Sunday dresses.

In those days, people had special clothes to wear on Sunday that they never wore any other day. I had now ruined two of mine, and I'm sure those were the only "nice" dresses I had to wear on Sunday. I didn't have a closet full of clothes as kids do now. I had three dresses for school that my parents had ordered from the Spiegel Catalog. I don't know where they bought my Sunday Dresses.

I had one pair of shoes to wear to school. When school was out, those shoes were pretty well worn out and ready to be tossed. I did not like to go barefooted, so I must have found some way to wear my worn out shoes during the summer.

We were all happy and never complained about what we didn't have. We really didn't know what we DIDN'T have. At least, I didn't. No one else in our neighborhood had any more than we did. I grew up during the last part of the Depression Era.

We never thought of ourselves as being poor, because we were in the same financial condition as everyone else. If you didn't have a car or a bicycle, you walked to wherever you wanted to go. If you did not own an electric washing machine, you built a fire under the "old wash pot" in the back yard to wash your clothes and hung them out on the clothes line to dry.

Everyone was the same and was treated the same. Thank God for His mercy and grace.

CHAPTER 12
PERILOUS SWIMMING DAYS

When I was about 4 or 5 my older brother, Sammie, and I decided we would go swimming in the pond on our property. The pond provided the water for the cow and chickens and was inside a large fenced area. We did not know that Dad had it dredged, dug out, to make it deeper and help the water to stay fresher.

We both stepped in at one end and when I hit the water, I just kept going down. I couldn't swim a stroke. That was my first experience with drowning. There would be two other times. I was blessed that Sammie was four years older than me and taller than me and he could swim. He pulled me out before I drowned, I guess you surmised that. We were out there alone that day and things could have ended very badly for us. But, never fear, God was always watching over us and kids who do stupid things.

My family loved to go swimming in the river south of town. One afternoon, I may have been about 9 years old. Uncle Paul was swimming with us and he saw that I could not swim. So he decided he was going to teach me. He held out his arms and had me lay across them. He told me to kick, and I did. Then he pulled his hands back and let me go. I went down, down, down like a rock.

Trees were growing in the water and some of the roots were showing. I tried to grab a root or something and swim, but didn't go anywhere. Uncle Paul finally found me and pulled me out from the tree roots and said, "I thought I had lost you," I thought so, too.

I had tried to swim in the pond and now in the river and neither one turned out very well. I never gave up though. Someone always wanted to teach me how to swim. I had a college professor who taught swimming try to teach me once and couldn't. There would still be a third time. I never gave up and neither did anyone else. No one told me it would be impossible to teach me to swim. Never fear, God was always there protecting children who could not swim, and simple minded people who thought they could teach children who would never learn to swim.

Thinking about swimming and drowning, reminds me of a time when my Dad, our new Step Mom, her son, Tommy, and the five of us went to the Sabine River to swim and have a cookout. We had taken wienies and buns and all the "fixins'" and watermelons. This was not the same location on the River where my Uncle Paul tried to teach me how to swim. That was on the South side of town, we were now on the North side of town.

We all had been to this area several times and were quite familiar with it. The water was only up to our waist where we kids were walking and wading. My Dad and Step Mom were a very short distance from us up stream.

I was watching our brother, Tommy, walk downstream when I blinked my eyes and he suddenly disappeared. I yelled to my Dad, "He's drowning!!" My Dad's reply was, "Well, pull him out." Being the obedient daughter that I was, I stepped forward to pull him out. I guess I thought that since he was shorter than me, that the water would still be shallow enough for me to reach him. WRONG!!!

I started going down, down, and still further down. I was trying with all my might to swim, but couldn't. My mind was still clear enough to know that we had stepped off into a hole. I thought that if I could get to the edge of the hole, I could climb back up. I may not have been too smart, but I certainly was not stupid.

My Dad was six foot and two inches tall. I guess he thought he could stand up in the water even if we couldn't. He also was WRONG!! But I still felt that long, strong arm and hand grab me and "put my feet on higher ground." Then I saw him pull our brother Tommy out of the water as he was gasping for air. I guess he took the two of us back to the shore. I really don't remember.

The next thing we noticed was Sammie with our younger sister, Della. None of us had noticed that Della had stepped into the river to follow us. BUT, Sammie, did. He pulled her out and put her on the bank of the river. If he hadn't seen her, she would have drowned that day, but God was still at work.

We didn't know she was following us into the water. She was only about three or four years old. And if my Dad had not been the good swimmer he was and was able to get to us quickly, my brother, Tommy, and I would have drowned. I remember that I was going down for the third time which was not good.

My Dad realized later that it had rained very much a few days before we went to the River to swim. The heavy rain had caused the bed of the River to shift and deep, deep holes had appeared that were not there the times before when we went swimming there.

This was a serious lesson I learned that day, and I believe the others did, too. To this day, I have not learned to swim. I guess I was suppose to be a fish and swim under the water. You would think that I would be very afraid to go into deep water, but I wasn't.

I told you how Charlie didn't seem to be afraid of anything. Well, I guess I have a little bit of that "bravery" in me, too. I have been on deep sea cruises, shallow water cruises, and any other kind that there is. I am not afraid of the water, and I do have a very deep respect for water. It may have been after this incident that Dad got inner-tubes for each of us. I remember we had them a few years later when we went to Merrill Lake in the White Oak Area.

I know God was watching over my family that day to keep it from being a horrible tragedy for us. He knew what we had already been through, some horrible and heartbreaking trials and had mercy on us. God loves little children and His eyes were always on us, watching and protecting us and continued to do so throughout our lives.

CHAPTER 13
MY OLDEST BROTHER SAMMIE

Sammie was four years older than I, but even with the age difference, we had always been very close. Maybe it was because there weren't many children in the neighborhood at that time for us to play with. That would change as the years passed, because each family was adding children to their family all the time.

One Sunday, after the morning service, we were leaving the Church when my Dad pulled into the little grocery store driveway next to the Church. He told Sammie to go in and get a loaf of bread for our Sunday dinner.

When Sammie opened the door and stepped out, he was hit by a young man on a motorcycle. I only remember that we took him to Gregg Memorial Hospital, now known as Good Shepherd Hospital, which was across the street from the Church. He must not have had any serious injuries, because they did not keep him at the hospital. God was always at work taking care of us.

Once he told me about his bicycle being stolen when he was a boy. One Sunday morning during church, he told our Dad that God had told him where his bicycle was and wanted to go and get it. Dad did not want to leave church during the service, but he did and took Sammie where he said his bicycle was. They had taken a police officer with them.

When they saw the bicycle, Dad said it was not Sammie's bicycle because it was a different color. Someone scraped on it and they could see that it had been re-painted a different color, but the old paint and color was visible when the new paint was scraped away. Sammie got his bicycle back because God told him where it was located.

As Sammie grew older, about 10 or twelve years old, he ventured out into selling ice cream. Probably Dad helped him build and attach an insulated box to the rear fender of his bike. Each morning, in the Summertime, he would ride his bike to the ice cream factory and buy enough pop cycles and various forms of ice cream to fill up his insulated box. Then he was off to sell them.

I don't know where he went through town, but he usually sold all of his "ice cream goodies." Some days, he would have a couple left and we were allowed to eat them. They sure were good on a hot summer day, and was the only time we ate ice cream. We never had many "goodies" to snack on as people do today.

When I walking home from Junior High School, I would spend my nickle bus fare for a fudge cycle. I didn't mind the long walk as long as I had my fudge cycle.

When Sammie was older, he had a paper route. That meant getting up really early in the morning to go to the newspaper plant and pick up papers to sell. The papers had to be folded or rolled for tossing into the subscriber's yards. He probably switched to the papers because it may have been difficult to sell ice cream in the winter time, but people read the newspaper year round.

I don't know how much money he made from selling ice cream and papers, but he always seemed to have a little spending money. He emptied his pockets at night onto the chest-of-drawers in the boy's room. I was just a kid, but it seemed to me he always had lots of change. I don't remember ever seeing any dollar bills.

As he grew, he had more responsibilities. One was to mow the grass. Dad came home from work one day and the yard had not been mowed. Evidently, he had told Sammie to mow the grass that day. He took Sammie out into the back yard and was whipping him with a branch, a limb, from one of the trees.

A neighbor must have heard the "commotion" and called the Police and said that my Dad was "killing" my brother." Dad told the Officer what had happened, and the Officer agreed with my Dad about issuing punishment. My brothers were well known for yelling as if they were being killed when being punished. They were only punished when they did not obey our Dad.

Dad knew the Bible, and in Proverbs 13:24 we read, "He that spareth his rod hateth his son; but he that loveth him chasteneth him bedtimes (early)." KJV And also in

22:15 we read, "Foolishness is bound in the heart of a child; but the rod of correction shall drive it far from him." KJV

These are God's Words and God's Teachings. When I disobeyed my Dad, I was corrected with the rod and it did not kill me, but made me a better person. We must understand that when we disobey or do terrible things, we will be punished.

Those who are not punished, grow up thinking it is okay to disobey, whether it be parent, teacher, the law, or police officers, because they were never punished for doing wrong.

Perhaps if the rod were used more today, we would not be seeing and experiencing all the violence and rebellion and killing that is going on in our schools, our towns, and in the world. People don't seem to understand that there is a price to pay for stealing, lying, and killing.

Our family went to visit our Mamaw in Galveston one summer. Sammie had made his money from selling ice cream and newspapers and took me to ride the Roller Coaster. It was at a small amusement park across from the seawall and not far from Mamaw's house. I believe it cost ten cents each and we rode for what seemed to me to be all afternoon. Riding the Roller Coaster was always one of my favorite things to do while visiting in Galveston.

That night we went back to the amusement park area to ride some of the other rides. Our Aunt Alpha, who was living with Mamaw at the time, went with us.

We three rode the Tilt-a-Whirl. When we got off, I thought Aunt Alpha was going to be sick at her stomach or pass out. She didn't, but said she had had enough "riding" for the night.

Sammie and I went back to the park the next night. Sammie had saved his money and paid for everything we did. As we were walking around looking that everything, we saw a couple of boys. One of them made a remark about "it must be his sister" or something of that nature. Sammie said to the boys very sternly, "She's my sister." I don't know what they said, but I know Sammie didn't like it. He always seemed to be protective of me. Between him and God, I was always in good hands.

Sammie quit school without finishing. I don't know what grade. He told me about stopping off at our Dad's Office at the corner of Mobberly and Young Streets. It was a rectangular shaped building, some called those buildings "Flat Iron Build-ings." Dad worked drawing Plans and Specifications for building houses for Mr. Haskins.

Sammie told me he was trying to finish drawing the plans Dad had been working on when Dad returned to the office. Dad was amazed when he came in and saw what Sammie had been doing without any professional training. In his later years, he would get the professional training he needed to be an architect like our Dad.

When he was older and married with children, he became my Dad's foreman on his building projects. But for Sammie, things would change and times would change. After all, there was a big War coming, World War II.

I believe Sammie was about 16 when he quit school and joined the Merchant Marines and the War was almost over. Dad must have signed for him, or gave his permission, to join the Merchant Marines because he was under age. He was stationed at Galveston, but was able to come to see us sometimes on a weekend.

Mamaw and her husband had moved to Galveston so Granddad could work in the shipyards building ships during the war. We always went to Galveston to visit her in the summer. One summer my girlfriend, Madeline, went with me. Sammie was on leave from his ship in Galveston. He arranged for us to go out for the day with him and his friend and shipmate Johnnie.

We spent the day swimming and riding two-seater bikes along the seawall. We were young and just having fun. I don't think many older brothers would have taken their younger sister with them as my brother did. We always had fun together, just as we did when we were making "mud pies" that day at home.

We discovered one day that my Mamaw was married to Madeline's Uncle Jim. It wasn't like we were blood relatives, only by marriage. My Mamaw had buried her former husbands and was now married to her fourth husband, Jim. Our religion forbids a person to remarry after a divorce. But, if the spouse had died, then it was okay to marry again.

Sammie began dated Madeline when he came home on the weekends. Then he asked her to marry him and she said yes. She was too young to get married, but her mother had given her permission. She had already quit school months earlier and had been working at the T&P Cafe, at the train depot.

I was also working that summer at the Malt Shop. Dad did not want me to work because he was afraid I would not want to go back to school as most of the others did. I promised him I would go back to school after the summer, and I did.

When Sammie came home the next weekend, much to our dismay, Madeline had gone off with one of the customers of the cafe. They had gone to Shreveport and got married. Sammie and I were both devastated. I was supposed to be her best friend, and never dreamed she would do something like that. She did all that without confiding in me at all. I was crushed and could not forgive her.

Several years later, I was walking to the bus stop at the end of our street. I looked up and there she was walking towards me. I walked as close to the edge of the street as I could to get away from her. We never spoke or looked at each other. It would be about forty years when we would see and speak to each other again.

After Sammie got over her "ditching" him, I introduced him to another girl friend of mine, Alene, who was now working at the same T & P Cafe. I wasn't paying too much attention, but they started going together when he came home on the weekends.

They had been going together for some time, and one Sunday afternoon when Sammie was home on leave, he asked me if I would like to take a ride with them to the town where Alene was raised. They also asked my Uncle Junior, my Step Mom's brother who was only one year older than I, if he would like to go with us. Alene was from Karnack, a small (little-tiny) town about forty miles east of Longview.

After graduation from High School, Alene had moved to Longview to live with her Aunt Josie and to get a job. Karnack was just a "spot in the road, which meant there wasn't any employment there.

When we arrived at Karnack, Sammie stopped at a house, and we all went in. That's when he told me that he and Alene were getting married and this was the preacher's house. I was completely shocked, but also happy for them. I cried during the ceremony. I told them I thought it was the custom to cry at weddings. After the ceremony, we went back home. I have always said that Alene was my friend long before she was my sister-in-law.

Our family tradition was to have a huge dinner with all the trimmings, and a three tier birthday cake with our five names on the cake, because there were five of us with birthdays within one week in October.

It just so happened that today was my 16th birthday, October 18, 1948. Dad's birthday was the 14th. Sammie's birthday was the 15th. My birthday was the 18th. Our Step Mom's birthday was the 20th and, Lynn, our new baby brother's birthday was the 21st. Since there was five of us with birthdays within one week, we had Leonard's Sweet Shop on Green Street, across from the Junior High, bake us a three tiered cake for our birthdays each year.

The top layer had Lynn's name, the second layer had mine and Sammie's name, and the bottom layer had our Step Mom and Dad's names on it. When we arrived back home, there was a huge, delicious dinner waiting and our three tier cake.

My Aunt Alpha, was now married, and her husband, my Uncle Bob, had come up from Galveston with Sammie for the weekend. I believe Uncle Bob wanted to talk to Dad about coming to work for him in his "House Building Business."

Sammie had to report for duty the next day, so my Step Mom drove Sammie and Alene and Aunt Alpha and Uncle Bob back to Galveston. I don't know how they managed to get to our house without a car.

Sammie and Alene lived in Galveston while Sammie was in the Merchant Marines. When he was discharged, in 1950, they came back to Longview to live and that's when Sammie began working for Dad as his foreman.

They bought a vacant lot across the street, and a couple of houses up the street from our house. Since Dad had a crew of men working for him, they decided to have an old fashioned "Barn Raising," except it was a "House Raising." Alene and my Step Mom cooked fried chicken with all the trimmings for the men to eat at lunch. When they finished working that Saturday afternoon, the house was up.

The house was a simple four room house, with two bedrooms, a living room, kitchen, and bath. Sammie put lots of nice finishing touches on it like built-in shelves in the closet with doors on them to put shirts and handkerchiefs on. He put nice things in his house the same as Dad did when he built our house.

It was on March 16, 1950 that their first child, a girl they named Linda Diane Hooper, was born. I was a Senior in High School and getting ready for school, when Alene came through the front door. She was in labor and her "water had broken." I begged to go with them to the hospital, but was refused. After all, this was my first niece.

I was now an Aunt. They had another daughter, Brenda Jo, born November 12, 1951. I was living in Dallas at that time. Their third child was a boy, James Terry, born June 7, 1953.

A few years later, Dad's construction business went bad and they moved to Alene's home town, Karnack so that Sammie could work at the ammunition plant there. After that, Baton Rouge, and then Monroe, Louisiana. Later they moved to Decatur, Illinois and stayed there for quite a while.

We may have been miles apart, but we always kept in touch and visited whenever we could. This is not the end to this story. There's lots more to tell.

CHAPTER 14
THE CLOWN MY BROTHER CHARLIE

Charlie was the brother just younger than I. He was born on February 5, 1935 in Longview, Texas. I don't know if he got his carefree spirit from being born third in line, or if it was because he was born in February, or if he just came by it naturally. Circumstances didn't seem to bother him and pain wasn't a big problem either.

Our home on Culver Street had a nice, large front porch on it. I didn't see him, but Dad told us that one day Charlie had fallen off the end of the porch, but it didn't hurt him. Later that day, a man came by to see Dad. While they were talking, Charlie interrupted and told him how he fell off the porch. He even proceeded to show him how it happened by falling off again. Maybe that's why we called him The Clown-Our Crazy Brother Charlie. This name didn't mean we didn't love him. It was mostly a name of description.

There wasn't anything Charlie wouldn't do if you dared him. He also liked to tell jokes and stories. He was happiest making someone laugh.

Charlie was two years younger than I, and seemed to always be looking for some-thing that would get him into trouble. The time I remember is when the Sheriff brought him home and told my Dad, "I'm going to put him in jail for a long time, or you can put him in the Army."

It seems he and a couple of his friends had broken into the street-level rear window of a restaurant in town and stole some beer. That was a pretty bad offense. I also believe this was not the first time the Sheriff had caught him. It was the first time I had heard about it. Dad knew the Sheriff, and everyone else in town, so the Sheriff was trying to do my Dad, and my brother, a favor.

Dad took him down to the Recruiting Office, lied about his age, and enlisted him in the Army. That was the only way to save him at that time. But, don't give up on Charlie. Wait and see what he grew up to be.

Our Mother left when Charlie was 4 years old. This little story happened about that time. Dad would buy frog legs and Mother would fry them. One night we were all standing in the kitchen when Charlie started jumping up and down. Dad said, "What's wrong with you boy?" Charlie said he had eaten so many frog legs it made him jump around like a frog. We all thought that was very funny. It was probably the beginning of his clown act. He also jumped off the front porch, on purpose, and stuck a sewing needle into his foot. I don't know how we thought or knew it was a needle. Maybe we decided from the looks of the puncture wound.

Dad took him to the doctor and he cut a big cross on the heel of Charlie's foot trying to find the needle, but couldn't. It was several months later that Charlie came running into the house yelling. The needle was sticking out the back of his heel. Either Dad or Mother pulled it out and he went about feeling fine. Pain doesn't seem to bother some people, especially Charlie.

One day a man came walking down our street and saw Charlie and Sammie out in the yard. He told Charlie he would give him a dime if he would climb up to our Tree House platform and jump off.

You guessed it – Charlie jumped. The Tree House we had built was about 15 feet off the ground, but that didn't slow Charlie down. He also fell out of the Poplar Tree at the edge of the driveway that he was trying to climb. Aunt Alpha, the nurse, was staying with us after our Mother left and she knew what to do.

It may have been in 1939 or 1940 when times became very hard for everyone. Jobs were scarce. My Dad heard of a place in New Mexico where they were hiring workers, I believe, to pick cotton. Dad took my oldest brother, Sammie, and my brother, Charlie with him. They rode the train to somewhere in New Mexico. Dad was raised on a farm and in the country, which lets me know he knew about pick-ing cotton and harvesting crops. He always had a beautiful vegetable garden.

I don't think they were gone very long when they came back home on the train. Charlie had been badly burned on his right leg and was taken from the train station directly to the hospital.

I was told that they were camping out at the cotton field along with other people. There was a young boy there that was about the same age as Charlie. They had played together and seemed to get along well.

One night they were all sitting around the camp fire before bedtime. Charlie was sitting on an axle with two wagon wheels attached to it. His "so called friend" walked up to him, picked up a can of kerosene, threw it on him, and pushed him out over the fire. Naturally, Charlie's pants caught on fire and burned his knee, leg, and ankle very seriously. I never knew why the boy did that, or what happened to him. I don't know if he was charged with any crime or not.

Charlie's leg looked like "raw hamburger meat." When I saw him at the hospital, his leg was held up inside a wire cage by a cord so that nothing could touch his leg. There was also an electric light hanging inside the cage for heat and to aid in the healing process.

I don't know how many days or months he remained in the hospital, but it must have been a very long time. It was my duty to stay with Charlie at the hospital to get him water or whatever he wanted to eat or whatever he needed. I'm sure it was very painful for him and I know it took a long time to heal completely. The Doctor said he would never walk right again.

When Charlie came home from the hospital, I remember that he walked with his leg crooked and on his toes. That didn't stop him. He was still running every where he wanted to go. Eventually his leg straightened out and he walked normally. He even joined and retired from the Army and no one noticed his "burned leg."

It seems Charlie and I were the only ones in the family to have curly or wavy hair. I don't know how mine turned out that way, but I do remember when our Step Mom's friend, Doreen, said to Charlie, "Come here and let me comb your hair." She must have seen something none of us could see.

That was when he was a teenager, and she combed his hair into waves. His hair seemed to stay that way, or either he combed it that way. Actually, it stayed that way and was curlier the older he grew.

I was 16 when my Step Mom decided to give me a permanent. Since she was a beautician she knew how to do all those things, like cutting hair and permanents. So I got my permanent, and my hair always seemed to stay a little wavy and curly. I didn't want my hair to be too curly. I liked it just the way it was, wavy.

One day she looked at me and said, "I think I'll style your hair like Rita Hayworth. That thrilled me, because I thought Rita Hayworth was beautiful. My Step Mom always cut my hair and styled my hair. I never had another permanent because my hair had just enough wave in it that it styled well. She was the only one to cut my hair until I was

27 years old. I was living in Dallas then and it was a little too far to go home to Longview every time I needed a haircut.

Dad bought a new car, a Frazier, at the end of the War when metal and cars were still scarce. Our Step Mom would take all of us to school in the new car. She would let the little ones out at South Ward Elementary, then Charlie at Junior High School, and then take me to the High School. She didn't wait to see if Charlie stayed at school or not.

Later, we found out he did not stay. The school had large double doors on the front of the building and also on the back. Charlie would go in the front doors and then out the back doors. He was either playing hooky with his friends, or just killing time alone out in the fields. Dad told him if he didn't want to go to school, he would put him to work on his building jobs. Dad said Charlie would work for a while, then crawl up under a tree and go to sleep. His excuse was that hard work never hurt him, because he could go right to sleep next to it.

Charlie did work enough to make the money to buy an old Plymouth pickup. His best friend, Eddie, told me that one day Charlie got mad at his truck because it wouldn't start. He picked up a 2×4 board and started hitting it on the hood of the truck. I don't know what he thought that would solve. Charlie did have sort of a temper. We all did. I do believe we got it from our Dad.

When we were all grown up and had children of our own, I had our Family Reunion at my house on the Brazos

River in Mineral Wells, Texas. Charlie kept us all entertained telling his stories and about his adventures.

Charlie and two of his buddies were cruising, riding, around one day and decided to go into Oklahoma. He said they were looking for "girls." Whatever the reason, I'm sure they were up to no good.

I don't remember exactly how the story went, but the Sheriff in a little town in Oklahoma put two of them in jail, probably for loitering. They were trying to figure out how to get out of the mess they were in, when the other buddy showed up at the back window of the jail.

His buddy proceeded to come inside, get the keys, unlock the cell door, and they ran out as fast as they could. They high-tailed it out of town before the Sheriff knew they were gone.

When he told the story, years later, he said he thought the Sheriff left one of them on the outside so they could escape because he didn't know what to do with them. They were just kids exploring life.

Nevertheless, they never did go back to Oklahoma again. They presumed there was a warrant out for their arrest. I believe the Sheriff did the right thing and best thing to get rid of them. I don't think the Sheriff wanted to keep them in his jail because he didn't want to be bothered with those kids from Texas. It probably would have caused him a lot of paper work.

I remember the time, the three "outlaws," got some potatoes out of our pantry and headed for the Sabine River. A block or so from our house lived a man who was raising pheasants. They stole one of his pheasants and took it to the river with the potatoes, cooked then, and ate them, potatoes and pheasants and all.

I also remember the Gregg County Sheriff coming to our house inquiring about the pheasants. Charlie seemed to do "crazy" things because he was not afraid of anything or anybody. I think he thought it was all funny.

He was the largest and tallest of my brothers. Trouble seemed to find him like a magnet even when he was standing still or sleeping. I understand him better now. He had a lot of energy and drive and needed to let it out some way. I also believe he had some anger and resentment, and maybe some hurt feelings about our Mother leaving us when he was such a young boy.

Charlie was a good, kind, and sweet person. It may not seem like it to those who read his story, but his story thus far does not tell all of who he was. He did not get into fights, except maybe with his friends, but never street fights. He did not have a gun or a knife. Well maybe a pocket knife to cut up the potatoes and pheasant.

He did not do drugs or get drunk. He was just a boy with a lot of energy and trying to use up that energy.

Charlie was very dear to me. I know God had his hand on him or he would have been killed or died, or something worse before he was grown. Think of all the trials he went through, his leg was burned, he fell out of trees, he was put in jail in a strange town. Satan was trying to kill him, but God would not let him.

Charlie had been working for my Dad because he would not stay in school. Dad was in the business of designing nice homes for people and then building them. He usually had several jobs going at one time. Dad told me he would drop Charlie off at one of the building sites, and then go on to check the others. If they needed supplies, or extra help, my Dad would take care of it.

After he made his rounds, he would go back to see how Charlie was doing. Dad said he would always find him asleep under a tree. At least, that was better than breaking into restaurants or cooking pheasants.

My "Clown" Brother joined the Army the day Dad took him to the Recruiting Office. He told me he wasn't sure if they would let him in the Army with a "bad leg," but they did. No one knew he had a bad leg unless he wore short pants where they could see the scars. He walked **perfectly** even though his leg had huge scars.

He was in the Army for four years, which was the length of his enlistment. During his service time he had gotten into trouble. Once was for hitting his Sergeant and trying to kill him. He didn't do so well taking orders. I believe all of his problems were caused from our Mother leaving us when we were all very young.

He tried to get jobs in different places, but nothing seemed right for him. He came to stay with me for a short time when I lived in Dallas. He was working at the Ford Motor Company in Arlington, Texas on the assembly line, when he decided to go to California to "seek his fortune."

He had bought a chartreuse green 1930 or older Dodge sedan. That was one of the colors that was popular then. It was a good car and a nice looking car. But, I guess someone else liked it as much as my brother, because it was stolen.

The Police found his car somewhere in Oklahoma. In those days, if your car was stolen and then recovered, you had to go and get it yourself. It wasn't in the best shape when he got it back, but he still liked his car. I don't know how long it was until it was stolen again. I believe he gave up on it that time.

He had made friends with a man, "Red," that worked with him, and they both left Texas to find their fame and fortune in California. No one told them that the Gold Rush was over many years ago and that jobs in California weren't any better than they were in Texas.

They eventually met two sisters around the Oakland Area and married them. For his friend, it would be his first time in the Army, but for my brother, it would be the second time. He told me years later that he and his friend and their wives were about to "starve," so they joined the Army. However, his buddy could not pass the physical because he had some serious health problems – it may have been his heart. So Charlie went into the Army alone.

This time he had settled down and was more mature. After Basic Training he was shipped to Berlin, Germany to work in the hospital. He had his choice of working in the Children's Burn Section or working as a Dental Assistant. He told me that he chose the Children's Burn Section because of how he had been burned. He could sympathize with the children and knew their pain.

While in Berlin, he and his wife, Deanna, had a baby girl, Michelle. Since she was born in Germany and not the United States, before they could returned to the States, they had to get a special Passport and Birth Certificate for their daughter.

He was in Berlin for several years, then he returned to the States. He was first sent to Fort Lewis, Washington and called me from there. When he told me where he was, I said, "You might have just stayed in Berlin. I don't know when I'll be able to come and see you." I never did get to go see him at Fort Lewis.

Later he was transferred to Fort Ord, California. At Fort Ord he was put in charge of the "artificial arms and legs and braces unit. While there at Fort Ord, they bought a house for them and their three girls, Michelle, Renae', and Colleen. Once Charlie told me he was surrounded by females – his wife, three daughters, and even the dog and cat were females.

My family and I went to see them at Fort Ord and then again after they were transferred to Fort Carson, Colorado during our vacation times in the summer. His wife and girls were the best hosts anyone could ever want. One day we went driving up the mountains to Cripple Creek and Victor where the Gold Mines had been. They were all vacant then, but interesting.

We went into one of the museums with lots of antiques from the "Gold Age." We were having a grand time. We had brought all the "fixins" for a wienie roast. It was a little chilly up in the mountains, even in July. We were on the east side of the Rocky Mountains. My sister-in-law, Deanna, had warned me to bring coats or sweaters because after the sun went down below the mountains about 4:00 o'clock in the afternoon, it would get chilly there on the base.

We went up towards Pikes' Peak in the "deserted mines" area to have our wiener roast. We built a fire, and the fire felt quite nice as I stood to warm myself. Suddenly there was a pop, and my left ankle had sharp pains going through it and started to bleed profusely.

I was lucky my brother knew how to "doctor" people. He put a compress on it and we all started back down the mountain. The cut wasn't too bad and a butterfly bandage fixed it up proper after my brother cleaned it up thoroughly with alcohol. After all, he didn't get many chances to work on a "bleeding" patient.

We could not understand what had caused the injury to my ankle. Charlie thought it may have been from a bullet left over from the Gold Rush days, or it may have been from some kind of rock that exploded. It could have been some kind of flint rock. We never did know, but it sure spoiled our excursion into the Gold Field and Mines of Colorado.

He was our "Crazy Brother" who would never stay in school in Junior High School. When he was taken to school, he would go in the front doors, and then go straight to the back doors and out into a field behind the school.

He remained in the Army at Fort Ord, California until his retirement after twenty years of service. He had a hard start, but finished with "flying colors." He was now a Doctor and opened his own clinic in Salinas, California.

Dad went to visit him at his clinic in Salinas. When Dad came to see me, he told me about his visit and how he had helped Charlie remodel his new clinic. He brought some pictures to show me of the clinic and Charlie's family. He had one of Charlie coming out of one of his offices wearing a white doctor's coat.

I said, "He's What, a Doctor?" It was hard for me to believe that my "Crazy Brother Charlie" was now a very well respected Doctor in that area of California. This was the same brother my Dad could not keep in school and had a hard time keeping him out of jail.

We also called him "Our Dumb Brother." I was talking with my Dad once about him, and my Dad asked me why we always called him "Dumb." I said it was because he never would stay in school, and didn't study, and made bad grades.

Dad was very quick to correct me. He said that as long as Charlie stayed in school, he made excellent grades and learned very quickly. It seems he was very smart and was bored with school because he would always finish his work ahead of the class. Now I understood a little more about Charlie.

Charlie opened his clinic in Salinas for making artificial arm and leg braces. He said four of the doctors in the Salinas area had told him that if he opened his clinic they would recommend patients to him, but he would be required to have a "Certified Person" working there. He could either hire a "Certified Person" or he could be "Certified" himself. He decided it would be best if he were Certified. He took all the training and studies to do so. My "Crazy" brother was now a DOCTOR, Certified and true.

He kept the Clinic for a few years, then decided to actually retire. After all, he had his Army Retirement Pay and was leasing out the Clinic.

He had wandered all over the world, and was now ready to come back home to Texas and settle down. We all traveled around the world at different times, but always came back to our home area in Texas.

Sammie, our sister Sandra, Crazy Doctor brother Charlie, and myself were told of a house on some acreage in the White Oak area in East Texas by our stepbrother

Tommy. The property wasn't but a few blocks from Tommy's church.

We decided to buy all of it and split it up. My sister wanted the house that was on the property, and that was okay with us. As for me, I had been working on my house plans for several years and wanted to build my own house.

Sammie, had worked with my Dad while he was building houses and knew how to build one. We all grew up in the "house building" business and had a fair knowledge of what to do.

I had been living in West Texas for twenty plus years, my husband had died and I was coming back home. Sammie had lived in the Houston Area and in the Illinois area for a long time and was ready to come home also.

Sandra and her husband had been in the Army and traveled all over and were now retired and ready to come back home, and the same was for our Crazy "Doctor" brother and his wife. Charlie was ready to move back to Texas. We were going to teach that California Girl what it means to be a TEXAN! We would teach her how to cook black-eyed-peas and cornbread.

CHAPTER 15
MY UNCLE JUNIOR

My Step Mom had a brother, Junior, who was one year older than me. Everyone called him "Junior" because he was named after his Father who had died many years earlier. I never met the man.

They all called their Mother "Big Mama." I never knew why, but she certainly wasn't "Big." She was a very small person and nay have weighed about one hundred pounds.

While Junior was going to High School, he was living on the farm with his Mom and Step-dad, Daddy Bill. It was the same farm where my Step Mom had lived – eight miles from town.

I called him my "uncle" because we thought that was pretty keen to have an uncle that was almost my age. When he was in his "teen" years, he would come to our house on the weekends. That was good because he had a drivers license, and Dad let him drive the company pickup truck sometimes on the weekend.

Just like his sister, our Step Mom, when he wanted to come in to town, he walked that eight miles. Dad let him work on some of his jobs in the summer time to make some money.

He played football in High School. It was a small School and they only had a seven-man football team. Only occasionally did I get to see him play because my School's football team played on Friday night and his team played on Thursday night. That would have been a late night out for me on a school night.

One summer night there was a "Donkey Baseball" Game in the city park. Two of my girlfriends and I and Junior, decided we would like to see a "Donkey Baseball Game" because we had never seen one. We took Dad's company pick-up truck, that was okay because Junior was driving and my Dad let us use it occasionally. Neither of us girls could drive.

The game was on the west side of town at the park. We were all having a good time telling silly jokes and laughing while Junior drove. One of the girls, Margaret, and I were riding in the back bed of the truck and her sister, Anita, was riding up front. Junior turned to see what we were doing – and at that instant our truck came in contact with a "new tractor-semi trailer" parked in front of a house.

I don't know why we did it, but we were so scared and probably said, "Let's get out of here," so Junior drove away. When we got home, Dad and Mom were not home yet from the movies. We were very scared. We began to get our money out and count to see how much we had to pay for the damages of Dad's truck. We did not think about the damages we caused to the tractor-trailer.

We all had summer jobs, which gave us some spending money – not any huge amount. Between the four of us, I think we gathered up $20.00. That wouldn't have paid to have even one headlight or fender repaired.

When my parents came home, we told Dad what had happened. He talked to Junior and got all the details and both of them set out to find the truck that had been hit.

They did find it parked in front of a resident a couple of blocks from the park. Dad went to the door and told the young man who was the driver of the truck what had happened.

It seems that young man had just driven this "**New** Truck" out of the terminal and had gone by his Mother's house to tell his family good-by and where he was going when he heard this loud "Bang" outside. He ran out to see what was wrong and saw that his **New** Truck had been hit and the auto that hit it was driving away.

He was frantic, because he thought he would lose his job. He was very glad to see my Dad and Junior who told him what had happened.

None of us were old enough to know about "Insurance." Dad's insurance paid for the repairs on both trucks and the driver did not get fired. We also learned" not to leave an accident." because that was against the law and we could get into serious trouble, or go to jail for leaving the scene of an accident. To this day, I have never seen a "Donkey Baseball Game."

After our little excursion, we were getting older and had all calmed down a little. We all had jobs. I had a job at the Malt Shop and Anita worked at the Cafe at the Train Station, the T & P Cafe. Margaret stayed home to help her mother. They never did go back to school.

After Junior and I graduated from High School, he joined the Army, and my Dad sent me off to college. We only got to see each other rarely after that.

One weekend I came home to visit my step brother, Tommy, and then I went to see Junior. Junior was actually Tommy's Uncle, he was Tommy's Mother's brother.

He had inherited part of the farm land from his parents and had built a house on it. When I drove up in the driveway, I saw him out by some trees and he came to see who I was. We hadn't seen each other in about twenty plus years.

He seemed a little strange and "distant" to me. He did ask me into the house and I tried to talk with him, but he still seemed "distant."

His wife was cooking supper while we sat and talked. I could not quite understand what was wrong at the time. When his wife had the supper on the table, she told him it was ready. He told me good-by and went to sit at the table. I was not asked to join them, so naturally I left. I did not understand what was going on.

It was much later, when my youngest sister, Sandra, told me he had Alzheimer's Disease. That explained his strange behavior. He may not have actually known who I was. Later on he was put in a Nursing Home where trained people could take care of him. He had four boys that went to visit him often and took him home to their house occasionally.

Sandra said she was at the oldest son's house for Thanksgiving and they brought him home to have dinner with the family. He would try to eat out of the plate of the person sitting next to him instead of his own plate. And when they were ready to take him back to the Nursing Home, he could not get his legs to lift up so he could step up into the truck. He died in the Nursing Home shortly after that.

Actually, I'm glad I never did get to see him when he was in that condition. I'll keep my memories of all the good times we had together and they were many.

Not only were they my "Cousin Bill and Uncle Junior," they were my best friends when I was growing up and in my teens. We didn't get to share our "Golden Years" together, but the ones we did share were Fantastic!!

CHAPTER 16
MY COUSIN BILL

Uncle Paul had a Stepson that was my age, my Cousin Bill. Their house was behind ours on the next street when we were growing up and Bill would come over to play with me. We would sometimes get things from the garden or from inside the house and play "Grocery Store."

One particular day, we got some peppers from the garden, HOT Tabasco Peppers. We were playing "Buy and Sell" when Bill handled the peppers and then rubbed his eyes. We did not know that the peppers were "HOT." He jumped up and ran out of the house crying. His eyes were burning terribly.

Actually, that stopped our game of "Grocery Store." We never played it again. I knew from that day, and I'm sure he did, too, that peppers can burn your eyes by rubbing your eyes after you handle HOT Peppers. They have an oil on them that is transferred to your skin as you handle them.

My Dad and Step Mom liked to go to the movies on Saturday night. It was my job to take care of the younger children while they had their night out and away from all the kids. Bill would come over to play with us while they were gone. He was quite a rowdy boy and big for his age. He and my brother Charlie made a good pair.

I was the only one who had a bed to myself, a twin bed. Actually it was a ¾ bed and just a bit larger than a twin bed. All the others had to share a bed.

Bill was, I guess, feeling quite rowdy that night, and ran into my bedroom and jumped up on my bed. Naturally, the slats broke as well as the box springs from his weight – and jumping. But, my Dad could fix anything, being the carpenter that he was.

Dad had installed a chandelier in the living room which hung over a glass-top coffee table that sat in front of the couch. Bill wanted to be Tarzan, so he ran down the hall and into the living room and took a flying leap, jumping up to catch the chandelier as he yelled the yodel that Tarzan did. He only got to make one swing, because the chandelier broke and he and the chandelier came crashing down onto the coffee table.

I was so shocked to see all of this. My bed was broken and now the chandelier was broken and lying on the floor with the coffee table. We were all rowdy kids, but we never did anything like that. Thank God, Bill was not hurt, but I believe he went home after that. He had done enough damage for one night and it was about time for my parents to come home.

I told Dad what had happened. He said he could repair my bed, but the chandelier and coffee table were a total loss. The really bad part about the whole thing was that the coffee table was my Step Mom's favorite piece of furniture in the whole house. I don't remember if Dad replaced the chandelier or not. I do know that we never had another glass top coffee table. It just wasn't practical with so many children around.

When Bill was old enough he went into the Army. By then he was staying mostly with his Grandmother who lived in Gladewater. He also would stay at our house occasionally. Since he did not have a car, he would hitchhike to our house or walk. People could do that in those days without any fear of being harmed. Sometimes my Step Mom and I would take him home to his Grandmother's house.

He came to see me one day, while on leave, to show me his new motorcycle he had bought and wanted to take me for a ride. I had never ridden on a motorcycle before. I didn't know about the "hot" exhaust.

While we were riding, I let my ankle touch the exhaust and got a terrible burn. That ended our ride for the day, and ended my ever riding on a motorcycle for the remainder of my life. It was too painful.

I would write Bill letters and put some sachet (perfumed powder) in the envelope to make it smell good. I did that with all the letters I wrote.

He came home on leave and came to see me. He asked me to please always put the sachet in his envelopes because his Buddies were going crazy trying to find out who "that girl was who kept sending him those good smelling" letters. He never did tell them it was only his cousin.

Another time when he was home on leave, he was at our house and went with us to Big Mama's, my Step Mom's Mother's house in the country. It was that same dirt road that she had walked into town to catch the bus and go to work before she and my Dad were married.

About half way to Big Mama's house, there was a flat on the car. We didn't know that Bill had just had a hernia operation. He changed the tire and I know it hurt him, but we didn't know how much. No matter how rowdy he may have been, he was always ready to help us whenever we needed him.

My Clown Brother, Charlie, came home on leave from the Army and asked about Bill. Bill was now out of the Army and we didn't know exactly where he was. Charlie said he went looking for him at several places, then he went to a local Bar. Behind the bar were mirrors and the outside light was reflecting on them so that he could not see the faces of the people sitting at the bar.

Charlie said he yelled some "obscene remark" and watched the mirrors. A very big person stood up to answer his call and Charlie could see then that it was Bill and he had come out of his seat ready to fight. They were glad to see each other and had a very good time visiting that afternoon.

I soon moved to the "Big City," Dallas, to make my fortune. No, that's not exactly true. I went to the "Big City" to get a job, because there were no jobs available in Longview at that time. I had tried but did not even get a "call-back" from any of my applications.

The next time I saw Bill, I was married and living near the Dallas-Fort Worth Airport when it was under construction. He was driving a truck, long haul, loaded down and called me at my home. I gave him directions to my house and he came to see me.

I did not see his truck, but he said it was a very large truck. He parked it at a service station and asked the manager if the parking area was strong enough to hold up the weight of his truck. The manager told him it was.

Later he told me that when he went back to his truck, it had sunk down quite a bit on the asphalt and he had to get a wrecker to pull him out. He was on his way to Washington State and wasn't having a very good start on his trip. He told me he had gotten married and had a son and that his wife had divorced him.

The next time I heard about him was from my brother Sammie. Bill had driven his truck to the terminal in Houston. The guard told him to park it on the back of the lot since he planned to stay in Houston for a few days to visit relatives. The park-ing lot was a huge lot.

The next day, one of the attendants found him unconscious hanging with half his body outside the truck and the other half inside the truck. He was taken to the hospital by ambulance. He had had a stroke when he was getting out of the truck and that's why he was hanging half way in and half way out. He had planned to visit some of his relatives in Houston. Sammie and Alene lived there at that time as well as our Aunt Alpha.

The hospital attendants found two phone numbers on him. One was his Aunt Alpha, Uncle Paul's sister. The other was Sammie, who went immediately to see him. He still could not talk and had lost the use of his right hand and right side.

His Mother, Connie, and his Step Father, Paul, were notified about him. At that time they were living in Mobile, Alabama. Bill spent a few months in the hospital in Houston, then they transferred him to Tyler where his wife and son lived. Tyler is about thirty miles from Longview.

His parents moved from Mobile to Tyler to be near him, and they lived in Tyler the remainder of their lives. I went to see him once in the hospital in Tyler when I came home to Longview to visit. He was speaking better, but he never regained the use of his right hand and part of his right leg.

Months later, he was released from the hospital. He lived in the Longview area until his death, which was several years later.

He was separated from his wife and son and lived alone. A friend went to check on him and found him. I got to meet his wife and son at his Mother's funeral, my Aunt Connie, in Tyler, Texas. We sure had some good and crazy times together. I loved him and miss him. God Bless you Bill.

CHAPTER 17
MY YOUNGER SISTER, DELLA

I was Blessed with two sisters. The oldest one, Della, was born to my Mother and Dad. The youngest, Sandra, was born to my Step Mom and my Dad. But they were both younger than I. Maybe this would be a good time to tell about the birth sequence.

I had an older brother, Sammie, then I was born, then a younger brother, Charlie, then my first sister, Della, then the baby brother, Jackie that my Mother took with her when she left us. There was five of us born to my Dad and Mother.

Then my Dad married our Step Mom and brought with her our Step Brother, Tommy. Then my Dad and Step Mom had a daughter, Sandra. She would be my baby sister and my half sister. After her, they had a son, Alfred Leonard, which would be my youngest and half brother and the youngest and last of the children. That gave us a full total of eight children in our family.

Counting Dad and our Step Mom, we were a Family of Ten. There was a movie came out about that time, "Yours, Mine, and Ours." We said, THAT'S US!!

We all got along very well. Each of us had playmates in the neighborhood that were our respective ages. I guess, if we ever fought, it was with our playmates, not our brothers or sisters. But I don't remember any of us fighting with anyone.

Of course there was one exception. I started keeping a Five Year Diary when I was thirteen years old. I kept it in a night stand next to my bed. It had always been safe there. I don't know if he saw it or if someone told him I had a Diary.

Tommy Hubbard, one of the neighbor boys, got my Diary out and read it and when I found out I was HOPPING MAD!! I found Tommy Hubbard and scratched his face till it bled and rolled down the embankment at the side of our house with him. My brother Tommy said he was yelling "Let me go, let me go."

I was a couple of years older than him and a little bit bigger. I was told that he never did bother anything that belonged to the girls in the neighborhood again.

My younger sister, Della, was six years younger than I and I remember the day she was born. The doctor came to our house with his black bag and Dad told me to go outside because the Doctor was bring us a new baby. I thought he brought it in the black bag.

I was standing outside Dad and Mother's bedroom when I heard a baby cry. I went into the house and they told me we had a new baby girl. As a child myself, I only remember parts of things that happened.

The years passed quickly and three years later we were Blessed with a baby boy. That was Jackie, the baby my

Mother took with her when she left us, but had to give him up during the divorce.

Our Step Mom was very loving and kind and took good care of us. Thank God she was a beautician and could do something with our hair.

Della, had long blond hair styled into long blond curls. I know our Step Mom took care of Della just as she did me. One day she told me to come over to her and sit down. She wanted to look at my hair.

Since I was the oldest girl, it was my duty to help take care of the younger ones, help with the housework, and wash the dishes. I Hated Washing Dishes!! I know it couldn't be helped, but instead of putting water in the dirty pans, my Step Mom would just put them in the sink which let the leftover food dry in the pans. Mashed Potatoes are very, very hard to scrape out of the pan after it sat for an hour or two.

Whenever I asked my Dad permission to go anywhere, he would always tell me, "Go see if your Mom needs help in the kitchen." I knew what that meant – I could go after I washed the dishes. There was always a lot of dishes for ten people.

Monday was wash day at our house. The beds were all stripped, towels were washed, and clothes washed. When my Step Mom came to live with us, the laundry was done in a "wash pot" over a fire. The wash pot was in the back yard, put over a "camp fire." My Dad would help by lighting the fire under the wash pot before he left for work.

In those days, houses didn't always have a hot water heater, or even hot water piped throughout the house. At first, the wash pot was all we had to wash clothes in. We lived in a beautiful modern home my Dad had built, but we lived one block inside the city limits. The city had not put in water lines, gas lines, and sewer lines to our location yet. Those were added as the city grew and was able to do so.

As each load was washed, it was taken out of the wash pot with some kind of stick or rod and put into the rinse tubs. There was usually two or three rinse tubs. The laundry was dumped into each wash tub, swished around by hand and wrung out by hand and placed into the next tub. That procedure was repeated in each rinse tub until the last one. As each tub of laundry was finished, it was hung out on the clothesline to dry.

The laundry procedure usually took all day to complete. There was at least five beds to change, plus the baby bed. Then came all the towels and wash cloths, some for bathing and some for washing dishes. When those were finished, then there was all the clothes for ten people. This was an all day task.

Needless to say, there wasn't much time left for doing other chores. Usually my Step Mom would still be doing the laundry when I came home from school. It was my job to wash the breakfast dishes which were still on the table with dried food and dried eggs in them.

I don't quite remember what we ate for our evening meal. There wasn't any "lunch meat" or "sliced bread." Those had not been invented yet. If any of you younger people think that was bad – There Was No TV either. But, we did have a radio which we all listened to at night. Some days, after school, if we didn't have chores, we listened to the radio – The Lone Ranger, Hopalong Cassidy, Superman, and others.

At night we listened to Inner-sanctum, which was supposed to be a scary program that started with what sounded like a squeaking door opening and slamming. At night when our parents were present, we listened to The Bob Hope Show, The Ed Sullivan Show, and lots of interesting stories. Times were quiet and days were slow and easy in the summertime.

As I mentioned before, we were the only ones in the neighborhood who had a car or a telephone. I don't know if anyone else had a radio. The car was for Dad to get to the houses he was building. The phone was for him to call his clients and for them to call him. Him and my Step Mom would travel to Dallas to buy special door knobs or fixtures for his clients. He built some very expensive and beautiful houses that anyone could be proud of.

Della seemed very rebellious, but you must remember what happened to her and all of us children. None of us knew how to cope or fight back against our emotions. We were all very young when our Mother left us. No one thought to take us to a Psychiatrist. That wasn't done in those days.

I think we reacted like a hurt animal when it gets it's paw or foot hurt. That animal will lash out at anything or anyone that comes near it for fear it will be hurt more.

No one ever suggested taking us to a therapist. I don't think we knew what a therapist was. Now, today, if anything happens to you, you are always taken to a therapist right away. I believe we all depended on God in those days to see us through, and He always did.

I think part of her problem may have been that after I went to Dallas to work, she inherited all of my chores. When she rebelled, I'm sure Dad punished her, and it made her even more rebellious. She and Charlie both rebelled against punishment.

I was now living in Dallas, but came home for the weekend. Dad told me that Della, had "run away" twice to Houston. The Police had informed him that she was in Houston. He went there and brought her back home each time. He suggested I take her back to Dallas with me and help her find a job. Maybe that would make her happy.

I did, but she was in such a rebellious mood that she didn't want to listen to advice from anyone. We clashed because she did not want to go to work one day, and she left my home. I did not know where she went. I only presumed she went back home.

I didn't hear anything about her for some time. She had joined the Army and was stationed somewhere in New Mexico. I also heard she was stationed in New York State for a short time.

Things had gone very badly for Dad and he lost our house. He took the family and moved to Galveston where his sister, Kate and her husband Artis, lived. Kate told him she was sure he could get a job at the wharves as a night watchman as her husband Artis had done.

I did not hear from Della or know where she was for several years. When I did, she was out of the Army and living with Dad and our Step Mom and the other children who were still at home. She was pregnant, but was not married. Dad took her in and she had a beautiful baby girl. One of the nurses at the hospital said the baby was just a precious "Joy." So that became her middle name, Theresa Joy.

Later, she got married and her and he husband, Charles, had four children, one boy and three girls. They lived in Galveston for several years with Dad. Dad told me he had shaved and reached into the cabinet to get his after shave lotion, and it was gone. He said that was the worst thing you can do to a man, take his after shave lotion.

Someone also took Sandra's baby sitting money out of the sugar jar in the kitchen cabinet. I do believe Dad ordered them out of the house, because the next I knew, they had moved out. But, he helped them get an apartment and buy groceries. Dad wasn't making much money as a night watchman, but he always tried to help his children whenever he could.

Charles was arrested for writing "Hot Checks." This was the time the stores took your picture when you gave them a check. I thought that was pretty "dumb" of him. Anybody would have known better.

One Saturday they appeared at my house in Euless, which is between Dallas and Fort Worth. They had Theresa, Pattie, and Kenneth with them. They needed a place to stay and Charles needed a job.

By this time, I was married with a child of my own. We let them stay, and on Monday I took Charles with me into Dallas when I went to work at the Insurance Company. I gave him a dollar for lunch and he walked away to find a job. That evening he was back at my car and ready to go home. He told me he had gotten a job with a roofing company.

The next day he rode with me to work, I gave him a dollar, and he left for his new job the same as before. That evening he was there waiting for me in the parking lot. This procedure was followed every day until Friday. I should have suspected something, but I didn't.

His mother, who lived in Dallas, called me at work to inquire how they were doing. I told her that Charles had a job with a roofing company and had been working all week. She asked the name of the company and I told her the name.

It was only a short time until she called me back. She had called the roofing company and they told her they had never heard of her son. Evidently, she knew her son much better than I did.

He was waiting at my car in the parking lot when I finished that Friday. I did not tell him what his mother had told me. But, when I got home, I told my husband. He was so angry his blood was boiling. He confronted Charles and I thought he was going to hit him, but he didn't.

He stood nose to nose with Charles and told him he had to find a ride, because he was not welcome in our home any longer. Charles called his sister and she came and got them and as far as I know, took them to Dallas.

Della called me one day and asked if I would come to Dallas and help her because she was in jail. She wanted me to fail her out. I did. After all, she was my sister.

They ended up back in Galveston, but I did not hear from them or see them for several years. Dad called me one night in February to tell me that Charles was in jail and the Social Services had taken the children because they needed help and didn't have much food.

At this time, they had added another girl to their family and she was still a baby. Dad was afraid the children, his grandchildren, would be adopted out and he would never see them again. He asked if I would take one of the children.

At this time, I had a daughter of my own and expecting another baby. I had known Theresa Joy since her birth, and told him that I would like to take her. He had also contacted my brother Sammie, but Sammie said he had three children already and didn't think he could take care any more.

Dad also asked his sisters, Alpha and Kate, if they would each take one of the children. It turned out that they were judged to be too old. The children remained in Foster Care for the time being.

The Court Date was set for May. Dad and my Step Mon, Aunt Kate, Aunt Alpha, my husband and I were all there in the courtroom in Galveston for the hearing. Della appeared before the judge. Charles, we presume, was still in jail because he was not there. The judge told Della that if she would get a job and a place to stay for her and the children, he would release them into her custody in thirty days.

Della left the courtroom first, and we all followed. As she was going down the steps of the Court House, she looked back and said, "You all are just trying to take my kids away from me." She was very angry.

She did not return after those thirty day or even later. We never saw her again for ten years. We did find out later that she and Charles had gotten back together and they had another little girl.

The next time I saw her was at my Dad and Step Mom's house in Galveston. I had taken our family to Galveston for Theresa's 16th Birthday because that's what she had requested for her birthday. That's a story for another time and a later date.

Nevertheless, I know with all my heart, that God was still with us. Sometimes we create the messes we are in and it takes some time and God's Grace to see us through and change the situation. It's always easier to look back and see what happened, than to look ahead and not know what is in store for us.

Jesus promised us He would never leave us nor forsake us. He's always there just waiting for us to call on Him. We fail Him, but He never fails us.

CHAPTER 18

THE ARMY HOSPITAL COMES TO TOWN

About four months after our nation entered World War II, some of our Civic leaders tried to obtain an army hospital for our city, and succeeded. It was built on the south side of town and not very far from our home. Our home was located on the last street within the city limits.

The hospital was built on 156 acres of farm land and opened on November 24, 1942. It was made up of some 157 buildings and had space for almost three thousand beds. The hospital was named after Col. Daniel Warrick Harmon who had been in the Army Medical Corps for thirty-six years – thus, Harmon General Hospital.

This was not the only hospital built during the war years. There were fifty-eight across the nation. There was one in El Paso, one in McKinney, one in San Antonio, and one in Temple, Texas, not to mention the others.

The hospital also housed 270 Women's Army Corps personnel. In addition, it held German Prisoners of war. Sometimes there were as many as 200. During its peak period, the Hospital held 4,000 to 5,000 staff, trainees, and patients served by a railroad spur and depot, bank, chapel, newspaper, Western Union office, library, and Post Exchange.

The average daily patient load in 1943 rose from 824 to 1,247 in 1944. The peak load was 2,804 on April 4, 1945. Over 73 percent of the patients in 1944 and 1945 were admitted due to disease, and less than 15 percent for battle wounds, and 12 percent for injuries. Only 38 deaths occurred.

The Hospital also provided various recreational and entertainment opportunities for the patients. There was a gymnasium which helped relieve the monotony. The more physically fit patients took bicycle tours around the countryside, refreshed their marching skills, and participated in athletic tournaments. A circular swimming pool was opened in 1945.

The Hospital also provided USO celebrity sponsored performances, had a patient band and orchestra, and a movie theater. A Shreveport Radio Station broadcast from the wards daily named "Heroes Come to Harmon."

East Texas citizens contributed their time, money, and household items to various needs at the hospital. Dozens of ladies volunteered as Red Cross Gray Ladies to provide games and reading material to the patients and to write letters for them. Other women formed the Red Cross Motor Corps and ran errands for the patients and took them on outings.

The Hospital helped Longview to continue the economic and population growth that had begun a decade earlier in the East Texas oil boom. The population grew from 14,000 in 1940 to 30,000 in 1946. The Hospital also brought in people in large numbers from outside the South.

The Federal Housing Administration designated Longview as a Defense Housing Area, an act that enabled the city to construct houses and apartments during the war. In October 1945 the process of closing the hospital began.

The last patient was released and all wards were closed on December 6th. In February 1946 Christian Industrialist R. G. LeTourneau acquired the 156 acre hospital and all equipment and auxiliary buildings from the federal government for an industrial training school for veterans.

The site today is the main campus of LeTourneau University. All of the old barrack buildings have been removed except for a few, including the hospital chapel, which has been refurbished as a memorial to the hospital personnel and patients.

The majority of the buildings and land were located east of the highway and not completely visible. It did not appear that this large hospital and grounds were even there. But, the area where my Dad worked and where the German prisoners were housed was visible from the highway. The Chapel was awarded a Texas State Historical Marker in 1999.

In another story about my Dad, you may remember that I mentioned he had worked at the Hospital with some of the German Prisoners.

CHAPTER 19

A VERY FAMOUS PERSON & THE SALE OF THE ARMY HOSPITAL

I don't remember which class it was in Senior High School, but I think it was in tenth grade. The Senior High School teachers always made us sit in alphabetical order in their classes. There was a boy who sat across the isle from me whose last name was a very well known name, probably around the world-LeTourneau.

He was a very nice and polite boy. His Father was quite wealthy and was the man who purchased Harmon General Hospital in our town from the government after World War II was over.

The Hospital housed 23,405 of our military men who were treated during the war. It also had 200 German prisoners there, too. My Dad worked at the Hospital with the German Prisoners. He said they were very polite and friendly. I don't know the reason why they were brought to Texas or how they got here and how long they stayed here.

Dad made friends with them and one day he brought home a hand made wooden "cigarette case." It was a beautiful, small, wooden house in which a person could keep cigarettes. When you pushed down on the chimney, a cigarette would roll out from under the front steps. All of us liked to play with it. My brothers liked to play with it, and they were very "hard on everything." Naturally, they destroyed it. They did the same thing with some of my toys.

My friend, Madeline, and I rode our bikes to watch the formal ceremony in February when R. G. LeTourneau took over the hospital. He owned a company that manufactured very, very large earth moving equipment. The largest ever made. He was very famous all over the world.

His company also had a huge machine that made houses out of cement. The machine was made like a four room house, without a roof. Cement was poured into the sections that were to be the walls. When the Cement was hardened, the machine was moved away and the house could be finished on the inside with kitchen and bathroom fixtures and a roof.

His machine was a marvel. The machine was demonstrated on the day of the formal ceremony. Madeline and I stayed all day to see the ceremonies.

Our service men were coming home from the war to get married and settle down.

They needed houses quickly. He also made several large domed structures to be used in manufacturing his earth moving machines. The buildings had to be very large in order to build the earth moving machines in them. Those domed buildings are still in use today. My girlfriend and I stayed all day and got a terrible blister, but it was worth it.

This man was very famous among Christians, and in my home town, because of his Tithing. His story went something like this: "I started out tithing ten percent as the Bible instructs us to to. I had plenty of money left over, so I upped my tithing to twenty percent.

There was still a huge amount of money left over, so I upped my tithing to thirty percent. This went on for years until I was tithing ninety percent and still had plenty of money left over."

My feelings about his story is this: You cannot out give God. The more you give, the more He pours out His Blessings on you. After all, the ones God loved the most in the Bible and Blessed, were the ones that always wanted to please Him and do His Will. They also Gave.

God's Will has always been for us to help those in need. It's like a well. God will keep the well full, if we keep drawing from it to help others and show them God's Love and Mercy.

God loves all of His People very much, but sometimes they need a little help. He Blesses us so that we can help others. It is said that "We don't work for a living, we work for a giving." God blesses those who help others.

CHAPTER 20

MORE SCHOOLING ~~AND~~ JUNIOR HIGH SCHOOL

When I was in about the fourth grade, the teacher asked us to bring a jar to school, for what, I do not know. All jars were glass then, there wasn't any plastic. I was outside the girl's restroom and dropped my jar. Naturally, it broke. I knew I was going to be in trouble, and I was. Not only that, I was embarrassed because I had to sit in the back of the class that day. That was not my usually seat.

One of the other Grade Schools, Campus Ward, on the north side of town caught on fire. Everyone thought some of the school boys there set it on fire. Even through High School and graduation, we were still talking about it and trying to find out who burned the Campus Ward School down.

Since they did not have a school, we had to share with them. We attended classes in the morning, up to lunch, and a School bus delivered them to our school in the afternoon. We never saw the other students, because we were never at school during the same time of day.

The Junior High School was next to down town, which was a little too far for me to walk to school each morning, so my Step Mom would drive the younger ones to South Ward, then take me to the Junior High School.

I was given a nickel to ride the city bus home each day. But, instead of riding the bus, I would stop at the Drug Store on the way home and buy a Fudgecycle, and eat it on the way home. I really did like Fudgecycles, and I still do to this day. I didn't mind the walk home since I had a Fudgecycle to eat on the way.

I had a History Teacher in Junior High that I thought was soooo! Handsome. I think the reason I really liked him was because he looked like my Uncle Paul.

My Uncle was a very handsome man. He had beautiful curly hair. Years later he told us that the Church he was pastor of in Mobile, Alabama was thinking about asking him to resign because they though he was "curling" his hair. Maybe they never saw a man with natural curly hair before in Alabama.

In Junior High School it was different. We had basketball and volleyball to play for P.E.. I still hadn't learned to like the idea of a ball flying through the air toward or around me since my encounter in Grade School. Again I asked my Dad if he would ask our family doctor to write me an excuse so that I didn't have to play any sports. He did, and that excused me from ever playing sports.

There was a couple of other girls that did not play sports either. Why, I do not know. But we were to play some sort of game while sitting on a mat. That suited me fine. I did not like playing any ball games, and was not required to.

In Junior High School I had a class that I really liked. We were taught how to sew. I loved to sew, and still do. I have used that skill all my life. I have made shorts, blouses, shirts, pajamas, dresses, formals, wedding dresses, coats, curtains, quilts, fur coats, etc. I made things for other people and for my family and my children.

Elementary School had taken me through sixth grade, and in Junior High School I was finishing ninth grade. We had a special day in Junior High named 9B Day. We had a picnic held at Tyler State Park which was 30 miles away. I guess that was to make us feel "grown up" because we had a picnic away from home.

We had a formal graduation. The girls were required to wear a white dress. It just happened that my Dad and Step Mom were going to Dallas to buy some special door knobs, or something for one of the houses Dad was building. They bought me a beautiful white dress for the occasion.

Some time later, I saw another girl wearing the same dress. I could not believe it. They had bought my dress in Dallas which was about 120 miles west of us. How could another girl have the same dress as I did.

Nevertheless, I was headed for Senior High School, which was across town and a completely new life for me.

CHAPTER 21
SENIOR HIGH SCHOOL – AT LAST

Longview Senior High School had a football team and a basketball team which played against other schools. I learned to like sports then because I could watch them play and I didn't have to participate.

In those days everyone went to the football game on Friday night. That was the big entertainment for the week in our town, as it was in most all of the towns around us. Our Senior High School was large enough that we had a regular football team, eleven men. Some of the smaller towns had what was called "a seven man team" because there wasn't enough students to have an eleven man football team.

My Step Mom took me to school every day because it was too far for me to walk. If I rode the city bus, I would need to transfer in downtown to get to Senior High School on the north side of town. School Buses did not take city kids to school. Students must live in the country before they could ride the School Bus.

One morning, we were running a little late. I got out of the car on the opposite side of the street from the school. I started to run and stumbled and went sprawling across the pavement.

I was holding my books, which put them in front of me, and that seemed to help break my fall. My Step Mom had driven on and did not see me fall. I went to the Nurse's Office to let her check me out because I felt a little banged up.

I was wearing a long sleeve white blouse which did not tear, but my arm was scraped from my elbow to my wrist. I don't know why my blouse did not tear but my arm was scraped. The Nurse doctored me and sent me on to class. We were not the type of kids that cried over a few scratches.

Senior High School was a completely different life for me. The building was three stories tall, which meant we had to hurry from one class to the other. Especially if one class was on the first floor and the next class was on the third floor.

My Step Mom decided she liked football and would take me and my girlfriends to the game on Friday Night. We always had a "Pep Rally" at School on Friday afternoon to get us "primed up" for the game. And believe me, we sure were "Primed Up." I didn't like to sit down at the games, and would stand up at the fence that separated the crown from the ball field. The fence was to keep us from "wandering or running out" onto the field.

One night I was yelling and jumping up and down and caused a crick to come in my neck. It sure did hurt, and did hurt all the next week.

But come Friday Night, the crick was gone. That night I was standing at the fence jumping up and down and yelling again, and – YES, another crick came in my neck. It was very painful and stayed in my neck all week. But come Friday Night it was gone and never came back. Thank God.

One of my classes was with the Mixed Choir. We had choices in Senior High and I loved to sing so I chose Choir. We sang at some of the churches in town, and also traveled to compete with other choirs in the nearby towns. My Step Mom would take us to the competitions. I think she still had a little bit of her teenage desires in her. She liked to laugh and have fun and so did we.

Senior High was three grades, 10th, 11th, and 12th. School started on September 10, 1947 and my best class was Study Hall. There sure was a lot of nice looking boys in Study Hall. In my Sophomore year, 10th, I took Algebra and learned to love it because it fascinated me. In English Class we learned to diagram a sentence. That also fascinate me. These were new experiences for me.

I attended my first football game the first week of school on Friday night, and on Saturday I attended my lessons playing the Hawaiian guitar. I was also working some at night at the Malt Shop. I made pretty good tips, nothing like what people get now, but things didn't cost as much then as they do now.

I was able to buy all of my school clothes, shoes, and supplies with the small salary I received, plus my tips. The

Malt Shop sold ice cream, sundaes, and malts. If a person got a nickle tip for waiting on a car, that was a good tip. Some people would leave only pennies. I learned what it meant to have a job and have someone depend on you to come to work. I learned to smile and be polite no matter what the circumstances. Those qualities would follow me all of my life.

When you respect your employer and that employer treats you well, if you need to leave that employment for any reason you will have a good recommendation. Dad taught me those ethics, plus, give your employer nine hours of work for eight hour of pay. Always do your best, smile and be polite. Address everyone with "No Sir or Mam, or Yes Sir or Mam, no matter what their age.

I have had many young people ask me why I call them Sir of Mam. I always say, "That's what I was taught." You may be surprised at the reaction you get, and it's always a nice one. People like to be treated politely.

I started dating in High School. Some of them broke my heart, and I broke some of theirs. Nothing was serious at the beginning of High School. It was a new kind of life with many adventures, and lots of growing up to do.

In Junior High there was a High School Band from up north that came to our school to perform. I thought the trumpet player was just "marvelous." I wrote a letter to the band director of that school up north and told him to congratulate the trumpet player for an excellent performance. He did, and I got a letter from the trumpet player. His name was Jerry and we corresponded from then and all through High School. It would later be "sort of a problem" for me.

I was sixteen years old and had a date with a young boy who knew how and loved to skate. I borrowed a pair of skates from someone and went to the church a few blocks from our house to practiced skating on the sidewalk before my date There wasn't much to do or see in our little town, but at that time skating was what everyone did.

I never could master the art of skating. I could go around the rink, but starting and stopping were not easy for me. I loved to go skating because everyone else went and that's where you could see all your friends and meet new ones.

Small things were made big events. Sitting outside and counting stars was very entertaining. All of the kids congregated at one house. We were not afraid to sit outside and watch the clouds roll by or count the stars. We didn't know about TV or Cell Phones or Computer Games or the Internet and Facebook. Those things had not been invented yet, and we were very happy without them.

If you wanted to talk to your friend, you just walked over to their house and visited for a while. Life was calm, pleasant, slow pace, and joyful. It wasn't unusual for us to run outside when we heard an airplane flying overhead or the sound of a blimp. In those days we could hear the planes flying by. Now, you very seldom hear an airplane because they fly too high and fast and the sound never reaches the ground before the plane is out of sight.

When we arrived home from Church this past Sunday, I could hear an airplane overhead but could not see it because of the trees. It was loud enough that we could hear it, but could not see it. Also, it was too hot to stand outside and try to find it. Our temperature was supposed to hit 100 degrees plus on that day, and I believe it did and has every day since then. We don't stand outside looking up at the sky for an airplane when the weather is that hot.

In my Junior Year of Senior High on November 14, 1949, most everyone from school attended the funeral of our classmate James Crawford. It seems his Dad had taken him and some others hunting. James was twirling a gun around and it accidentally went off and he shot himself. It was a very sad occasion for everyone. His Dad was our Sheriff. That's why he had a gun with him.

Then on November 15, 1949 our neighbor and father of my friends Margaret and Anita, was hit by a car as he was getting off the bus and was killed. I was cleaning up the kitchen when my friend, Margaret, came running into our house crying and saying, "Daddy was killed. Daddy was killed."

She had said many times how she hated her Dad. I knew she didn't mean it, but was only angry because he made her do some chores or made her stay at home. She took his death harder than any of the other five children.

Dad would sometimes buy some groceries for them. He probably helped them more often than I knew of. Dad was a very generous person. Once he told their mother to let him know what all she would need to make enchiladas for her family and our family. She came to our house and made the enchiladas and brought all six of her children. There were ten total in our family, plus her six, and herself, which made seventeen people to cook for.

I don't know how long it took for her to cook those enchiladas, but they sure were good. She never cooked anything else to go with them. As each enchilada was ready, it was served to whoever was waiting patiently at the table.

Years later when I was living in Dallas, I decided I wanted to go to a Mexican Food Restaurant and have some good Mexican food. Much to my surprise, that food was nothing like what our neighbor had cooked. I was so disappointed. I have never seen or eaten enchiladas like she cooked and probably never will again because she has gone on to heaven now.

On Sunday May 1, 1949, I started my day going to church with my cousin Bill and my friend Margaret. Then some of my friends and I went on a picnic at the lake. Then early that night Margaret and Anita and I were sitting on their front porch and just passing the time when a car pulled up in the driveway. The car had three people in it. They were Gene and Bucket and our once neighbor Charles Edward who had moved to White Oak.

They had been out "cruising around" and stopped at my friend's house. Charles Edward, and his sister Laverne, had lived in the house between mine and my friends' house. They had moved to White Oak a few months earlier.

Many years later, I told them they had been out "looking for girls" and Charles Edward told them where three girls lived. Naturally they came to "check us out."

The remainder of this story, which is very lengthy, is told in another part of the Book. I hope you'll enjoy it.

CHAPTER 22
JACKIE PRESTON HOOPER

Jackie Preston Hooper, Sr., was the youngest of the five children born to Samuel George Hooper and Bonnie Faye Ellis on March 7, 1941. I don't know why his name was shown as "Jack" on The Texas Birth Records. His name was always given as "Jackie."

Now that I and my Step Brother Tommy are the only two living relatives of our family, I will elaborate more about Jackie. Some may have disagreed or actually did not know the true story, and some may have had their feelings hurt by knowing the truth before, but I will tell you the truth about my Baby Brother Jackie as I lived through it.

Most of the children were named after a relative. Where the father's name should have been listed shows "DO NOT ISSUE" on the Texas Birth Records for Jackie. I have been made to understand that our Mother tried to claim that our Father, Samuel George Hooper, Sr, was not Jackie's father. Everyone knew that was not true.

That's hard for me to believe, because I have my Daddy's picture, my Grandfather Peter Preston Hooper's picture, and Jackie Preston Hooper, Sr.'s pictures hanging on my bedroom wall side by side and look at them every day. They all look alike!! But, if her claim were true, that would mean she was having an affair in June 1940 for her to become pregnant with someone other than our Father.

His name "Preston" was from my Grandfather, Dad's father, whom we never knew. Peter Preston Hooper died of pneumonia, caused when he was plowing in the rain at the time when he had the measles. My Dad was about three years old when his father died.

Peter Preston and our grandmother, Ida Mae Pettey, knew each other growing up but did not live very close to each other. She told me once that she was sitting on their front porch, as a young girl. Her Mother came out of the house and asked why she was sitting alone on the porch. She told her mother that she was waiting for Peter Preston, because he was coming to ask her to marry him. To me, that was such a sweet story, but she did not tell me – when, where, or how – they married.

She said that he had told her earlier that he was going to marry her someday. He must have told her which day he would come to ask her to marry him. She told me about Peter Preston and how he worked hard on the farm for his family. Our Father was only a baby himself, and our Grandmother was pregnant with her second child, a daughter who would be my Aunt Kate.

The weather was bad, but Peter went out to plow the fields while he had the measles. It rained on him, the measles went in on him, and he developed pneumonia. My Grandmother said that he coughed so much "he seemed to cough up his lungs." He never lived to see his only daughter born.

Another little known fact, of which I may be the only one living to know about, our Father, Samuel George Hooper, Sr. knew about women's minstrel cycles and when they were most likely to become pregnant. That's why most of our birthdays are so close to each other. **As for March –** Our Mother, Bonnie Fay Ellis was born on March 16, 1912 and our sister, Della Mae Hooper, was born on March 6, 1938 and Jackie was born on March 7-it seems he was pretty far off from Bonnie's birthday on those two guesses.

I guess, after that "bobo" he may have decided to try for a baby to be born on Della's birthday. Then he only missed by one day because Della was born on the 6th and Jackie was born on the 7th. of March. To me, that coincidence should not have happened if she was having "an affair." The birthdays could have been farther apart or even in another month.

I wrote a "Memorial Story" for Jackie's two children, Jackie, Jr. and Jennifer. They are the only living children of Jackie Preston Hooper, Jr. His daughter, Lisa, has already gone on to heaven.

I omitted some of the details before because I didn't want to hurt anyone's feelings or get into an argument about the things that happened. That will explain why there may be a difference in the "original stories" I wrote and this one.

So, continuing with our birthdays. Daddy was born on October 15th, then Sammie was born on October 14th – missed again. I, Betty was born on October 18th – still missed. Charlie was born on February 5th – Mamaw's, Grandmother Ida's birthday was February 2nd – he missed on that one, too.

Sandra was born on July 25th – don't know where Daddy got that date, but I think it was a date he **didn't** plan on. Lynn was born October 20th and our Step Mom's birthday was October 21st. She was cooking our Birthday Dinner when the labor pains began. Dad almost got it right that **last** time. I think Lynn was born close to midnight. If he had waited only a few minutes or hours, Lynn would have been born on our Step Mom's birthday.

Jackie Preston Hooper, Sr., who was the youngest of the five children born to Samuel George Hooper and Bonnie Faye Ellis on March 7, 1941. I don't know why his name was shown as "Jack" on The Texas Birth Records. His name was always given as "Jackie."

Most of the children were named after a relative. Where the father's name should have been listed shows "DO NOT ISSUE." I have been made to understand that our Mother tried to claim that our Father, Samuel George Hooper, Sr, was not Jackie's father. Everyone knew that was not true. If she had succeeded, she and her new husband could have kept Jackie as theirs. But, she did not.

That's hard for me to believe, because I have my Daddy's picture, my Grandfather Peter Preston Hooper's picture, and Jackie Preston Hooper, Sr.'s pictures hanging on my bedroom wall and look at them every day. They all look alike!! But, if her claim were true, that would mean she was having an affair in June 1940 to become pregnant with someone other than our Father.

His name "Preston" was from our Grandfather, Dad's father, whom we never knew. Peter Preston Hooper died of pneumonia, caused when he was plowing in the rain at the time when he had the measles. Our father was about three years old when his father died.

Peter Preston and our grandmother, Ida Mae Pettey, knew each other growing up but did not live very close to each other. She told me once that she was sitting on their front porch, as a young girl. Her Mother came out of the house and asked why she was sitting alone on the porch. She told her mother that she was waiting for Peter Preston, because he was coming to ask her to marry him. To me, that was such a sweet story, but she did not tell me – when, where, or how – they married.

She said that he had told her earlier that he was going to marry her someday. He must have told her which day he would come to ask her to marry him. She said that Peter Preston had worked hard on the farm for his family. Our Father was only a baby himself, and our Grandmother was pregnant with her second child, a daughter.

The weather was bad, but Peter went out to plow the fields while he had the measles. It rained on him, the measles went in on him, and he developed pneumonia. Mamaw said that he coughed so much "he coughed up his lungs." He never lived to see his only daughter born.

I wrote a "Memorial Story" for Jackie's two children, Jackie, Jr. and Jennifer. They are the only living children of Jackie Preston Hooper, Sr. His daughter, Lisa, has already gone on to heaven.

There is no question in my mind that our Daddy was Jackie's Father. Even now when I look at Jennifer's son Preston, I see the same resemblance with the eyes, ears, and mouth, not the nose. Maybe as he gets older, we can see the resemblance.

My Mother, Bonnie Fay Ellis Hooper, was having an affair with one of Daddy's friends, William, Bill, Otto Sullivan. Bill was married with 7 children, and was about ten or fifteen years older than my Mother.

Dad was also about ten years older than Mother. They had married when she was 13 or 14 years old, which was not uncommon in those days. Daddy told me once, "If I had known how young she was, I wouldn't have married her." But, I don't think it made any difference. In my opinion, she was much too young to marry whether she was 13 or 14 years old.

Two of Bill's children were mine and Sammie's age. Wesley Sullivan, about 12 years old, was Sammie's age.

Naomi Sullivan was 8 years old, and my age. They lived on the North side of Longview, therefore we did not go to the same Grade School. But, by Junior High School and High School, we were in the same grades and going to the same school because there was only one Junior High School and one High School in Longview.

When you're eight years old, you do not always understand what is going on and what is happening in your own home. Their "Get Away" must have been planned for some time.

School was out in June 1941. I had gone home with Mamaw Ida and Grandpa Jim to Jefferson in East Texas to stay with them for a week or two. Daddy had taken Sammie and Charlie to get their hair cut. Daddy's Sister, Aunt Alpha, took Della to the Beauty Shop with her. Mother was alone at home with Jackie, who was now about 3 months old. She could not abandon Jackie because she was nursing him.

I have no idea what happened when everyone came home that day and found her gone. I don't know if there was a note or not, because I was at Mama's house. Bonnie had left four small children at home without a Mother. Otto had left seven children at home without a Father. I remember that his oldest daughter was about 24 years old.

I don't know exactly when Daddy built the First Assembly of God Church on the corner of Fourth Street and Marshal Avenue in Longview, except that he said God told him to build it. During the construction of the Church may have been when and where Bonnie and Bill met, or it could have been that Bill and his family started going to the First Assembly of God Church after the construction was completed. Our family also went to that church that Dad built.

Some time after they left, could have been days or weeks, I really don't know, but I do remember Daddy taking me with him when he went to the Sullivan home to talk to Bill's wife. He may have gone to to see her more than just that time, to discuss their situation, and how all those terrible things had happened to our families, but I knew of only the one time.

Jackie was born in March and sometime in June, 1941 they "Ran away together." They may have waited until school was out for the summer so that we kids would be away for the day, or for some reason of which I have no idea. It's hard to understand what they may have been thinking and how they plotted to leave their children behind.

The Divorce Papers were filled out on September 1, 1941. I presume my Dad filed for the Divorce because he was listed as the Plaintiff. Mother did not need to be present for him to file Divorce Papers.

The Divorce was granted on October 31, 1941, 30 days after the papers were filed. Mother had to be present because she had to surrender all of the children before the Judge would grant the Final Decree and for the Divorce to be Final.

I had heard Daddy say that he would give her a divorce on the condition that he be given custody of all five of the children – that included Jackie. She did not want to give up custody of Jackie because she was still nursing Jackie, but Daddy would not give her a divorce without custody of all five of the children. So she agreed.

At that time, Aunt Alpha, Daddy's sister, was living with us to help Daddy take care of us children. I can remember the day the Divorce was granted. It was a cloudy, dreary, and a little cold since it was the last of October. Bonnie had missed all of our birthdays – Daddy, Sammie, and me because it was our Birthday Month.

There was an artificial fireplace in the living room that had a gas heater in it. I was curled up in Aunt Alpha's lap trying to understand what was happening. Aunt Alpha tried to explain it to me. I had heard my Daddy say that he would let Mother come and live with us and he would live somewhere else if she wanted to, and he would pay all the bills. That did not happen, so I guess she turned down his offer. We **did** get our baby brother, Jackie, back.

I don't remember too much about Jackie growing up except that it was my "job" to rock and feed the babies when they were young. I guess that's why Jackie and I were always very "close." He did not have a Mother so I had to take her place by feeding and rocking him.

All of his life, whenever he had a problem – no matter what it was – he would always come to me and talk about it.

I guess it was the "Mothering instinct" in me that kept us so close. I will say, I loved my Baby Brother Jackie very much!

We were now without a Mother, housekeeper, cook, laundry person, etc. We were in need of someone to help take care of us. Daddy hired several maids, but we were a "wild bunch" without a Mother and they would not stay very long.

One day Dad asked me to take a ride with him to Greggton to a Beauty Shop. It may have been a week or more later that a woman came to live with us and be the "maid." Dad explained to us that he told her if she would come to work for us and live with us, that she could bring her son, Tommy, She and her son were living with her parents on their farm, which had been their home. We were all very excited because we now had another playmate.

We all followed Tommy into the house one afternoon and into the kitchen. His Mother was there working and he asked her to make him a "Sugar Sandwich." Those were the days before lunch meat was in every refrigerator. In fact, that was before refrigerators as we know them now.

We had Ice Boxes and the Ice Man came by each day to sell us ice to keep those Ice Boxes cold. We had a cardboard square that was put in the window each day and on each corner there was a number for pounds. That let him know how much ice to bring us without asking first – five, ten, fifteen, or twenty pounds.

Daddy came home about that time. It seems we were all calling her Mama as Tommy did. Later he sat us all down and asked if we would like to have her for our Mother. We all agreed that we did. Her name was Mozelle Estelle Brasher and she was a dear sweet lady. Daddy had asked us the same question about other ladies he knew, but then, our answer was always, No."

One day she told me to sit down and let her fix my hair. I did and it probably was the first time it had been combed in a week. The other kids were just as bad because we didn't have anyone to teach us. I don't know how long she worked for us, but one day she and Daddy told us they were going to get married.

I went with her to the bedroom and watched her put on a beautiful dress and some make-up and comb her hair. Then they went to get married.

I'm sure she loved and took care of the others just as she did me. She saw us through all of our aches and pains and changes from childhood to adulthood. But, then there was another girl and boy added to our family, making eight children and two adults, for a Grand Total of ten.

I left our home in Longview in June of 1951 to seek employment in the Big City of Dallas and make my fortune. I did not leave my home because I was unhappy with my family or the home we lived in. On the contrary, I loved my family and our home, but there was not a job to be had in those days. I was now 18 years old, had been to college for a year, and wanted to have a job and make my own way. Daddy didn't have any "left over" money to give me.

I went back home to visit as often as I could. At first I had to ride the bus because I did not have a car. After I had worked for about six months or more, I went home so Dad could help me buy a car. I knew nothing about buying a car. We picked out a green, two door, Dodge sedan, about a 1938 or 1940, and he took me to his bank to get it financed. I sure was proud of that car, and drove it back to Dallas.

Sometime after that, I had my own apartment, a good job, and a car, but I missed my family. I asked Dad if Jackie and Sandra could go back to Dallas with me for a week and he said, "Yes."

I don't remember too much about that week, except our trip "up the elevator to the top floor of the Magnolia Building." I was still working for the finance company that hired me when I first came to Dallas. I was the Head Cashier and had to greet the customers as they came in to pay on their loans.

There was a very nice customer of ours, a black janitor, that worked as a janitor at The Magnolia Building, who would come in and visit with me whenever he was passing by our office. I told him about my younger siblings being in town. He said if I would bring them to the Magnolia Building on Saturday, he would take us to the top of the building in the elevator and they could see the Red Pegasus Horse on top of the building that turned 24 hours a day.

The next Saturday the three of us went to the Magnolia Building and my friend, the janitor, was waiting for us. He took us up in the elevator to the top of the building. Note: Sometimes I would often forget that I was afraid of heights, but when I stepped out of that elevator into the blue sky, I froze. There was fencing, like chicken wire, all around the edge of the top, and a step or two that went into the belly of the horse.

Sandra and Jackie ran up inside with my friend following, while I was glued to the elevator door and could not move. My friend was so nice to them. He showed and told them everything about the horse. The horse turns from the air that comes up from the elevator shaft.

He told them how much it weighed, etc. He was one of the nicest people I met in Dallas, except for the Police Officer that worked on the corner from our office. He also came in to talk and visit with me most every day.

After that week, it was time to take them back home, which I did. But I certainly did enjoy their visit and hated to take them back home.

It could have been around this time that Jackie came home from school and told Mother Mozelle that some boys told him that she was NOT his Mother. He went home crying and asked her. She told him, "she was the only Mother he had ever know."

This was partly true and no one in the family bothered to tell him the truth about what had happened to his Mother.

Remember this, I believe this is what haunted him all of his life. He had heard what the other children said, and he believed that his Mother went away and left him when he was a baby.

Daddy was having a very hard time financially and the bank foreclosed on our home. He was still building houses and moved them into one that he had finished.

I don't think I gave him any money at that time or not – that was a long time ago!!

I believe he managed to move them back into our home for a short time. That may be when I gave him some money and he used it to pay the house payments for six months. He told me I had given them back their home for six months.

He was a contractor and built houses – big beautiful homes. But like the shoemaker whose children don't have any shoes, now my family had no home to live in. This may be the time he took out – or – renewed his loan at the bank to remodel our house. That way he could move the family back home while the work was being done.

He bricked it and paid himself as contractor, which gave them some time to live in the house while it was being remodeled. But again he was not able to keep up the payments after the work was completed and the remodeling money was spent.

They had to move again, I believe to Spring Hill. It wasn't the best of places. I helped him by giving him the money to pay the house payments so they could move back to our home. I may not have all these "moving back and forth" correct but I know Daddy was having a hard time financially and it affected the children, too, including Jackie and I was very concerned about it.

When he finally lost the house for the last time, his sister, Kate, told him to come to Galveston and he could get a job where her husband worked, Uncle Artis, at the wharves, docks, where the ships came in. **THEREFORE,** he packed up the family and moved them to Galveston. That's where they lived from them on.

That was in 1956 and Jackie was now 15 years old. I don't know how long he went to school in Galveston, but following in his brother's and sister's footsteps, he joined the Army. I don't know how old he was or what year it was when he joined the Army, or the year he got out. I think, in those days the enlistment was for four years.

If Jackie joined the Army when he was 17 or 18, he would have entered the Army in 1956 or 1957. If he stayed in for 4 years, he would have been discharged in 1960 or 1961 at the age of 20 or 21.

Our Brother Charlie and his wife, Deanna, told me about the time when they were all stationed at Fort Hood, Texas and how they did things together. They all seemed to had a lot of fun with the three of them together.

I had married for the first time and was still living in Dallas. Then I was married for the second time when Jackie got out of the Army. He had met a girl named Maxine who was from the Gilmer area north of Longview. He called me to ask if I would come to their wedding in Gilmer.

This had to be around the last of January or the first of February. I had to decline the invitation because I was expecting to give birth to my second baby, my son Michael, any day and did not think I should be that far away from my doctor. They were married and his son, Jackie Preston, Jr., was born at the same hospital in Arlington where my son Michael was born.

Several years later Maxine called me one night and wanted me to come over because she and Jackie were having a "fight" and he had pushed Preston down. Preston was about two years old. I went over, but when I got there, there did not seem to have been any kind of a "fight." Preston was not injured, but they had been arguing.

Jackie was probably telling Maxine that he wanted a Divorce, or he was getting pretty close to telling her he was leaving, or something like that. The next memory I have is that they did get a divorce and he had a new girl friend. (I hope I get all of His Wives straight – if not – forgive me.)

The problem with Jackie was that he always seemed to find a "New Girlfriend" where he worked – and all of his wives knew that and did not trust him because he was around other women all day at work.

It may have been a year or two after he divorced Maxine that she came to my "little girl's dress shop" I owned in Euless. She had a baby girl with her. We talked for a while, then she asked me if I knew who the Father was of her baby girl. Of course I had no idea.

She said that just before their Divorce was final, Jackie came to visit her, they had sex, and she got pregnant with Anna Lisa Hooper who was born January 3, 1969. (Information obtained from Texas Birth Index 1902-1997. Note, her name **was** shown as "Hooper") She said Jackie would never claim Lisa as his daughter because he would have to pay Child Support, and he didn't want that. He was already paying Child Support for Preston. Lisa knew who Jackie was, but never knew him as her Father.

His second wife was Norma, she was maybe ten years or more older than Jackie. Age doesn't matter if two people really love each other. Norma seemed to be a very sweet and nice person and had grown married children, who had children.

Norma had gone through breast cancer and had one, or maybe both, breasts removed. During their time together she did not seem to be suffering or sick from the cancer. Several years after their divorce, Norma died.

They had a nice home in the south part of Arlington with a two car garage. Jackie started to dabble in repairing and painting damaged cars, and seemed to be doing well at it – that is in addition to his "day job." He was still working at Tex Star Plastics in Arlington. He worked there for many years. I believe he retired from there or planned to soon.

It was while he was married to Norma that he had the "paint shop" in his garage, and when Theresa had a wreck in my car. She had her drivers license and had been working at Baskin Robins in Wilshire Mall in Euless, not too far from our home.

I'm not sure, but I think it was Thanksgiving, and we had finished our dinner when Theresa asked if she could take my car and go pick-up her pay check at Baskin Robins. To get to the store, she had to cross Highway 183, which was a very busy, divided highway.

She picked up her check and was coming back across the divided highway making a left turn and pulled out in front of an oncoming car in the far lane. She had Denise and Krisha (our neighbor) with her. The other car had two young girls in it. I thank God to this day that no one was hurt.

There is a little side story here about our car insurance. You see, my husband, Buddy, needed to get his Drivers License renewed, but **would not.** To renew your Drivers License at that time, they were requiring everyone to take an eye test. Buddy had very bad eyes and said he could not pass the eye test. I told him he could not say that unless he tried.

We had some bitter arguments over the fact that he would not even try to take the test. I told him that if one of the children came home and told us they got a failing grade because they would not take a test at school because they knew they would fail anyway. **That means they did not even try – That's what he did not do – even try.**

That's one of the reasons I got a divorce, because we could not get any insurance on our cars. Without car insurance, we put our future and the future of our children in jeopardy every day.

Theresa called me to tell me what had happened. I think Sammie and Alene and Jackie and Norma were at our house for Thanksgiving Dinner. I asked if anyone was hurt, and she advised that no one was injured. Jackie took me to where they were and we looked at the cars. We saw that there was only some crumpled (crushed) fenders – nothing really major.

Jackie told the two young girls that he would fix their car – repair the fender and paint it – and would not charge them anything. There would be no need to call the Police. He fixed their car and mine, too. That's the way my Brother Jackie was. If I needed help, he would always help me. I was always there for him when he needed me and he was always there for me.

I don't know exactly where this part of the story fits in, so I'll put it in here. It was Christmas and Michael was about 7 or 8 years old and wanted a bicycle. We got the bicycle for him and took it to Jackie's house. For ten years we attended the Presbyterian Church in Euless, which had a candle light service on Christmas Eve each year. I always enjoyed those services.

I told Jackie to bring the bicycle to our house while we were at church and put it in my bedroom and cover it with my bedspread. A person could see it while walking down the hallway if it wasn't covered up. I knew the kids searched all over the house for Christmas Presents when they were home for the Christmas Holidays and we were at work. I had to think of new ways and places to hide the gifts each year because they always seemed to find them.

No one saw the bicycle when we came home from the Christmas Service because everyone was tired and ready for bed. The next day Michael was trying to figure out how we got it in the house under the tree without anyone seeing it. I never told him until he was grown.

It was probably around this time that Jackie decided to get rid of Norma and take a new wife – Beverly. They wanted me to be at their wedding and I was. Her parents, the Williams, lived just around the block from our house in Euless. They had a minister come and perform the ceremony in their home. That marriage brought baby Jennifer into our family.

I don't know how long that marriage lasted. During that same time I was getting a Divorce from Buddy. One night, while I was still living in my house in Euless, Jackie came over to see me. He told me that they were having some problems in their marriage. I asked him to keep a check on my car and keep it running because I was also having problems and may need to leave my home at any time.

He asked me if I was going to get the "Party Boat" in the settlement. The "Party Boat" was a boat Buddy thought he just had to have. He always kept a boat in the garage – That's right, "in the garage." I think we took the "Party Boat" to the lake twice, but Jackie borrowed it quite often. I told him "No." He was disappointed because he would miss using that boat.

I thought it was better for Jackie to use the boat, rather than let it sit in the driveway and "rot." The boat was a large deck type boat and it took two men to put it into the water. Buddy and I tried to do it when we first got it, and it took us several hours to unload and load it.

In June 1975 my Daughter Theresa graduated from Trinity High School in Euless. The graduating class was very large so they gave out tickets to the graduation. Each student was allowed only two tickets per family. Since my husband and I were divorced, and I didn't want to go with him, I asked Jackie if he would go with me. He was delighted and we had a very pleasant time together.

Jackie and I were sitting at my kitchen bar one night talking and headlight flashed in my driveway and brakes squeaked. It was Beverly, she came to find out what he was doing. I had the door open to the garage because it was a warm night.

They did not separate at that time, but were still together when my job with the Texas Department of Public Safety transferred me to Mineral Wells. My job was to call on all the Police Departments and Sheriff's Offices in forty counties. One of the Police Departments I contacted was the Euless Police Department in the town where we had lived.

On the day I was to visit the Euless Police Department, I would go by to visit Jackie and Beverly in their apartment in Euless. Jennifer was just a baby and Preston was about five or six years old. Beverly would ask me what I wanted to eat and I would tell her, "Just a peanut butter and jelly sandwich." She said Jackie would get mad at her if that was all she made for me to eat for lunch. But I explained, that was all I wanted.

I would wait for Jackie to come in for lunch so we could visit. I'm not sure, but I believe it was about that time when they moved to Royce City, just outside of Dallas. Jackie was still working at Tex Star Plastics in Arlington and commuted each day.

Years later he showed up at my place in Mineral Wells with his clothes loaded in his truck. I had re-married to a retired Army helicopter pilot named Pat. We had our house trailer parked behind a Restaurant and Bar we owned. We had over an acre of land on the highway going into town. At that time, all of my children were grown, some married.

This time it was different. He didn't have a new girl friend. He told me he just couldn't take it anymore. Beverly had locked him out of the house many times and accused him of all kind of things and affairs.

When a person lives a life of cheating on their spouse, and they cheated to be with the one they are married to now, then that marriage starts off with "lying and cheating" and it would be very hard to build any confidence and trust between the two people.

We decided to let Jackie stay with us and take the spare bedroom in our trailer. He wanted to file for a divorce and I helped him with the paper work. I did not tell him what to write in the divorce papers, only the spelling and grammar. That's when I found out that he could not read or spell very well. I asked him how he ever held a job without knowing how to read or serve in the Army.

He was a foreman at Tex Star Plastics in Arlington and had been working there for almost twenty years. When he was a teenager he worked at a grocery store as a stockier. He said he learned to stock the shelves by looking at the pictures on the cans. I never did understand why he could not read. He had gone to school and then into the Army and could not read?? I believe he could read!!

All of the other children did very well in school as long as Daddy could keep them in school. Sandra and I are the only two, out of eight who graduated from High School. I don't know about Sandra, but I did not think that I was "brilliant," but I did graduate from High School and attended one year of college at Stephen F. Austin in Nacogdoches and always made passing grades – not excellent – passing.

My third husband, Pat Malone, and I had bought a Restaurant and Bar in Mineral Wells which was on an acre of land and were living in a two bedroom trailer we had purchased and parked on the back of our lot. I don't remember all of the details, but Jackie did had custody of Preston.

Our sister Sandra and her husband Don, and Shannon and Donnie, their teenage children, were living just north of Mineral Wells and were attending school in Mineral Wells. He made some kind of agreement with Sandra to let Preston live with her and go to Mineral Wells High School. Jackie lived with me.

Every day after school was out, Preston would walk across the field to the restaurant and I would give him a snack. Then he would play some of the game machines until Jackie came home from his job in Arlington. Then they would play pool or Air Hockey. The two of them always had a lot of fun together.

They would also play the games on the weekend. Once three ladies came to have a night out and met Jackie. I believe they were sisters. Jackie and Lillian seemed to get along well – so they got married after Jackie's divorce. They went to a Justice of the Peace this time and I was not invited to the wedding. I didn't mind, I had been to enough of his weddings. Besides, who knew about how long this one would last.

Jackie and Lillian bought some property at Alvarado, Texas, which is south of Dallas and put a trailer on it. I don't remember if it was a double wide or single wide. He still had one of those long commuter drives to work, about

50 miles because he was still working at Tex Star Plastics in Arlington.

I went to visit them once and he showed me all around the trailer and the property and seemed to be very happy and pleased with his new life. One reason I did not go to see him very often, actually, this was the only time, because we worked at the restaurant seven days a week, and the other reason was that it was quite far from Mineral Wells to Alvarado.

Preston was still living with Sandra because he was in his Senior Year at Mineral Wells High School and did not want to move before graduation. He graduated from Mineral Wells High School on May 31, 1985. After his graduation, he joined the Navy but stayed in only several months. When he was released from the Navy, he went to stay with Jackie and Lillian.

Lillian came to see me at my home on the Brazos River in Mineral Wells one after-noon in the fall of 1985. She wanted to talk about Jackie's childhood and his life and relationship with his birth Mother Bonnie.

She told me that Jackie was very disturbed because his Mother had left him when he was a baby. I explained to her that our Mother, Bonnie, did not leave Jackie, but took him with her when she left with Bill Sullivan.

She left the four of us, but took Jackie with her because he was just a baby, about three months old, and was still nursing. Bonnie fought to keep him and did not want to give him up. Actually, Jackie was the only one of us children she ever asked about. I guess that was because he was her "Baby."

Jackie called me on Friday night, November 1, 1985 while I was working at our restaurant and bar. He was very disturbed because he felt like he had made a mess of his life. His other marriages had failed and he felt like this one was failing also.

"After all, my mother left me, I've made a mess of my life, and I might as well kill myself," he told me. I told him that his mother did not leave him, but took him with her and fought to keep him. I tried hard to convince him that he had lots of people who loved him, his children, me and all of his brothers and sisters. and not to think about "killing himself anymore." He had a big family who loved him very much.

I felt I needed to go and talk to him, but it was late at night and Alvarado was a long drive from Mineral Wells. I thought about him and worried about him all the next week. I will always regret for the rest of my life for not going and talking with him. The next part of the story is what I have been told.

Monday, November 11, 1985 was Veterans Day and a Holiday for most working people. It was a week after I had talked with Jackie. On Saturday night, the 9th, Lillian and her sisters wanted to go dancing. Jackie had "two left feet" when he tried to dance. He did not go with them. It is my opinion, which I am entitles to,

I do not approve of a married woman going dancing without her husband.

Preston had left the Navy a month or so earlier and was now living with Jackie. He told me that a man had called to speak to Lillian, then Jackie found a Phone Number either in Lillian's purse or coat pocket. Naturally, Jackie being a "cheating" husband jumped to conclusions and accused her of "cheating." He was naturally suspicious because he had been a "cheating husband" many times before.

The details are so painful for me to remember that I don't try very hard. It seems Jackie confronted Lillian and they got into an argument. He went to the bedroom and was getting the gun down when Lillian came into the room. She tried to stop him by grabbing him around his arms to try to hold him down. She was a nurse and knew how to restrain "violent" patients.

BUT, Jackie managed to get the gun down and shot himself. Preston was some where in the house – I don't know where. I only know they called an Ambulance or something. Preston called me and said, "Dad shot himself and they are taking him by helicopter to Harris Hospital in Fort Worth." My thought was that he had accidentally shot himself, maybe in the arm or leg.

Pat and I dropped everything and left immediately for Fort Worth. When we got to the Hospital, we went in to the desk and asked where Jackie Hooper was. The person at the desk said, "the family is in a room just down the hall."

I still thought this would be a simple case of an accidental shooting. I opened the door to the "Family room" and saw Lillian sitting on the couch and some of her family with her. I don't know exactly what she said to me, but my knees buckled and I fell down with my face in her lap. I could not believe what she had just said – My Baby Brother Jackie was gone. Even as I write this now, that pain still surges through me and the tears flow again. I loved my Little Brother so much!!!

I guess the Devil had such a hold on him from all of his cheating, that his life was over now. I don't remember anything after that moment at the hospital. The services were held at Harbison Cole Funeral Home in Fort Worth. He was still working at Tex-Star Plastics in Arlington and we knew his co-workers wanted to come to the services. I helped with the obituary information because Lillian did not know anything about our family.

I told the Funeral Director that all of our family was buried at the Gum Springs Cemetery outside of Longview and we wanted to bury him next to his mother. He then asked about living relatives and I named off his brothers and sisters and that his "Mother" was living in Arkansas. He looked at us with a blank stare, but proceeded on with the list. I didn't explain to him that Jackie's Step Mother was buried at Gum Springs, and that his Birth Mother was alive and living in Arkansas.

After the Funeral Service, we had a long drive from Fort Worth to Longview, and on to the Gum Springs Cemetery. Our half-Sister, Patricia, brought our Mother, Bonnie, to the cemetery for Jackie's burial. I would like to state here that I do not remember her going to any funeral for anyone else in our family, except Jackie.

It had been my duty to list all of the "living" and "deceased" relatives of Jackie. I had been under so much pressure and sorrow throughout the whole thing that I forgot to mention Lisa. She was the daughter that Jackie and Maxine had just after their divorce was final and Jackie never claimed her as his own, but I knew who she was. Jackie was very selfish for not claiming her. He did it only because he did not want to pay Child Support. Lisa also came to the burial at Gum Springs cemetery When the Director read the obituary and there was no mention of "his Daughter Lisa," there was a very loud scream and she ran out across the cemetery. I ran and caught up with her. I tried to explain that it was my fault her name was not read and that no one else was at fault, only me.

Lisa had a terrible car accident on the way to work one morning which paralyzed her from the waist down. Then she had "bed sores" for being confined to the bed and a wheel chair, which caused her death.

Her Mother, Maxine, buried her ashes in their family cemetery. I hope Lisa and Jackie are finally together and having a better life now than the one they had here.

James Terry Hooper, Sammie's Son, had said to me when we were gathered for my Step Mom, Mozelle's, funeral, "Why is it that we only get together now at a Wedding or a Funeral. Why can't we have some good times together." I decided then that I would have a Family Reunion for our Family at my house in Mineral Wells on my 3 ½ acres on the Brazos River. That would leave us with happy memories and not sad memories of saying "Good-by" to our loved ones.

Lillian came to our first Reunion and brought each of us a picture of Jackie. It was the last picture of him. She did not stay long, and I haven't seen her or heard from her since that day. No one asked her to do that, and I don't know if anyone thanked her or appreciated the picture but me.

However, it hurt me so much to look at his picture that I took it immediately into the house and put it in the top drawer of our Hutch upside down. It took me four years before I could take his picture out and look at it.

That terrible pain has left me now, only sadness and tears remain. Jackie's picture is hanging on my bedroom wall with my other family pictures and I can look at it every day if I desire. He was "Our Baby." "My Baby," and I still love him very much and miss him. I don't think the pain will ever leave me.

CHAPTER 23
THE MEETING OF BETTY AND GENE

It all started on Sunday, May 1, 1949. I was finishing my Junior Year at Longview High School. The weather was typical Spring weather, very nice. My Cousin Bill, my friend Margaret, and I had gone to Church for the Sunday Morning Service.

I started the afternoon with Bill, Margaret, her sister Anita and Anita's boy friend Ernest, and Crazy Brother Charlie by going on a picnic at Merrill Lake. That was our favorite swimming and picnicking spot at that time. I guess we had too many close calls at the River, so we found a new place to spend the day.

Merrill Lake was on Camp Switch Road in White Oak. It was large enough that you could ride your boat there or have boat races. It was shady and had some nice picnic areas, but nothing fancy. You had to bring your own table and chairs. This was 1949 and the government had not up-dated all of the lakes and camping areas.

Margaret, Anita, and I were sitting on their front porch enjoying the cool breeze and moonlight. There was a large, bright moon that night. A perfect end to an enjoyable day.

Then headlights appeared in their driveway. There had been a family who lived next door and between my house and Margaret's. There was a girl, Laverne, who was our age, and her brother Charles who was a year older, who we had made friends with. Then their family moved to White Oak.

I found out later that Charles had made friends with some of the boys at White Oak High School and they were out riding around and ended up at Margaret's house. It was Charles, and his friends, Gene and Bucket. They seemed to be very nice boys.

We sat on the porch and talked for some time, then they asked if we would go riding with them. Which we did. I sat next to Gene. We all did our usual teenage things, telling jokes and laughing. In 1949 there wasn't much else to do, but we always found a way to have fun and just enjoy ourselves.

Some of the boys were enlisted in The National Guard and had training on Tuesday Night. The training place wasn't too far from my house, so some of them, Gene, Charles, and three other boys came over to my house after National Guard training to sit around and talk. Then Gene phoned me on Wednesday night.

On Thursday night Gene came over and took me, Margaret, Anita, and Ernest to White Oak to see Charles and Laverne. In the middle of this, and for some time, I had been corresponding with a boy, Jerry, from up north. I received a letter from him this same day.

Much to my surprise, my Dad was observing all the things I was doing and who I was seeing and who I was writing to, etc. Children think parents don't pay any attention to what they are doing. Listen and Beware. They know everything you are doing, who you are with, and where you are going, how long you've been gone, and when you are coming back.

On May 27th, Anita and Ernest were married. This may also have caused my Dad to take a closer look at Margaret and I and who we were going out with. Gene came over almost every day, but he usually came with two or three other boys. On Tuesday, National Guard night, he would always have several boys with him.

As I stated, my house was close to the training area, so they stopped off at my house before they made the longer drive back to White Oak. There were other boys in my life beside these that came to see me. Some I dated and some I was just good friends with.

I had taken typing in school and Dad wanted me to help him with his office work. I thought that was really something, working for Dad in his office. He showed me how to make out the payroll to pay his men. I had also gotten a job at the Lunch Counter at M. E. Moses in town.

In June each year, Gene and his friends had to attend National Guard training for two weeks.

On July 1, Sammie, Alene, and I went to Galveston for the weekend. We did all the usual things we had done for years, ride the Ferry, swim at the beach, and go to the amusement park and ride rides. Sometimes we rented bikes to ride along the beach. We came back home on the 4th of July because we had jobs.

Around July 14th someone started a rumor about alligators in Merrill Lake, but that didn't keep us away. We still went to the lake, but did not go swimming. By the 17th the scare was over. Everything was back to normal and everyone went swimming every time they got a chance. That's the way we cooled off in the hot summer time. Our homes were not air-conditioned.

Sometime in July, Sammie bought a boat. That increased our activities at the lake quite a bit.

Around August 4th, I went with Gene to visit his grandfather in Tatum. His grandfather was a whittler and had whittled out some very pretty pieces which were to go on belts. He gave me one of those. He also gave me a rolling pin he had carve out of a solid piece of cedar. I still have it and am very proud of it.

By August 16th my boyfriends found out about me, that I had been dating others and was not theirs exclusively. Jerry, the one I had been corresponding with from up north was now at my door. I was trying to date him, perhaps in the afternoon, then date Gene at night. Then one August 26th, Dad had a talk with Jerry and I.

The next day, Dad and my Step Mom left for their "first vacation" to Colorado and around that area. That same day Jerry and I had an argument and he left. Later that day,

I had a date with Gene. But, the day after that, I went to church with Gene and his parents to their church.

Through all of this, Margaret and I had been going to church almost every Sunday. You see, I was not quite the heathen you might have thought I was. I was just a teenager, doing what teenagers do. But unlike some teenagers, I was also going to church.

On September 2nd I had a talk with Jerry and Gene together. I told them that I had chosen Gene for my boyfriend. Naturally, Jerry left brokenhearted and angry, but kept coming back for different reasons.

A week later, my Step Mom's friend, Dorene had a wiener roast at her house for me and all of my friends. She lived in the White Oak area with a small pond on her property, but not large enough to put a boat into. We had a very nice time sitting around the fire, roasting wienies, and chatting.

A couple of days later Gene walked to my house from White Oak. That was what we did because none of us kids had a car. Later Sammie took both of us to Gene's house. Then Gene and I went to church that night at White Oak.

It was Registration time for my Senior Year at High School on September 12th and things would be changing because of schooling. School actually started on September 14 after Labor Day. Now school starts early in August, which means that about a month is taken away from the student's vacation time.

Gene and I spent many Friday nights going to the White Oak football games and other activities at his school. His Dad was letting him drive his truck now. White Oak played all of the nearby schools which meant we could drive to the games because it wasn't too far. They had a good football team that year and won almost all of their games. Usually some of Gene's friends would go with us to the games, and also my cousin Bill and uncle Junior.

I had a part time job working on the weekends at M. E. Moses Lunch Counter. Many times I walked from High School to downtown to the Moses' Lunch Counter for lunch. The lady in charge was also the cook and most every day she had chicken and dressing on the menu. That was, and still is, one of my favorites.

The lunch was served on a large plate with two other vegetables and cost twenty-five cents, and was delicious! She also made homemade pies every day. When you got a slice of her pie, it was ¼ of the pie for a dime. Today, a person is lucky if you get 1/8th of a pie for $1.00 or $1.50 which was made somewhere in a factory. They are never homemade.

On October 4th my Mother came to see us for a short visit. Gene's Dad called to let me know Gene had been sick for two days. I had hoped he would get to meet my Mother, but he didn't.

Gene's birthday is October 11th and mine is the next week on the 18th. He is one year and one week older than I am. That was one of his sayings which I never forgot and would be reminded of many, many years later. I had gotten him an ID bracelet for his 18th birthday.

The next week, on October 13th, Gene came to my house and then took me to his house and gave me my birthday present. It was an engagement ring. I guess he couldn't wait five more days. I was very thrilled to get it, even if it was early. We were now officially a couple, engaged.

The next day, Gene and I, along with my Step Mom and her Mother and friend Dorene, and my Uncle Junior, and Della all went to the Texas State Fair in Dallas. This was like an annual event for us to go to the Fair. We would leave early in the morning, drive the 120 miles to Dallas, ride the rides and see the exhibits, then start back home very late that night. We usually arrived home about 4 am. That day would always be a "rest" day for everyone.

My 17th birthday was on Tuesday, which was the night Gene and the other boys had to go to National Guard training which was mandatory. He did manage to come by to see me on his way home.

We had our big Birthday Dinner on Sunday the 23rd and everyone was able to come, including Gene and my cousin Bill. My baby brother, Alfred Leonard "Lynn" had his third birthday that year.

Then came Friday, October 28th when Dad bought a new green Studebaker pickup truck. No one else had a pickup like this one. Not many people had ever seen a

Studebaker. There were several new styles of automobiles coming on the market.

The country was still being revived from World War II and new things were coming on the market every day. The soldiers had been coming home from the war, getting married, and needed new houses and everything that went in them. The world and the times we knew were changing fast.

One night we drove to East Mountain to find the church where Aunt Kate was preaching. We drove around for a while, and then gave up looking for her church. The next Sunday, I went to church that morning and then went to Gene's for Sunday Dinner. Later, Gene and I, and Sammie and Alene, and Charlie went to Aunt Kate's church Sunday night at East Mountain. This time we did find the church. Aunt Kate was very happy to see all of us.

We went back to her church the next Sunday Night, Nov 20th, and Aunt Alpha, which is Aunt Kate's sister, and her husband Bob were there. Thursday was Thanksgiving.

Gene, Margaret, and I went to Aunt Kate's church that night. After their stay with Aunt Kate, Aunt Alpha and Uncle Bob came back to our house to visit. Then they went back to Galveston the next week.

Our Senior High School Choir was now performing at different churches and functions during the Christmas Season. Christmas Day came on Sunday that year. I received lots of nice gifts. Then Gene and I went to visit his

Grandparents at Tatum. That night we took my Cousin Bill and Uncle Junior to church with us.

I was working during the holidays to make some spending money, but also to buy the clothes and supplies I needed for school. I worked New Year's Eve, but we managed to squeeze a movie into our busy schedule. New Year's Day was on Sunday, and that night Gene and I took my brother Charlie with us to Church.

Dad and my Step Mom went to Galveston to see Mamaw on January 7th. The next day, Gene was at my house and took ill. Uncle Junior, my Step Mom's brother, was there with us and drove Gene home. He was "under the weather" for two more days – could have been the flu.

A few days later, my friend Charles who had moved to White Oak, came to see me to tell me he was going into the Air Force. I hope he does well. I will miss him.

Gene had made a cedar chest for his Mom in Shop at School and I went with him to get it and we took it to his Mom. He sure did do a good job on it. He's good at woodworking – must take after his Grandfather.

On January 22nd Gene and I, along with Dad, Aunt Alpha, Uncle Bob, and some more of my family went to Aunt Kate's church that night. Aunt Kate is a very good preacher. I really like going to her church.

I am now driving fairly well after some lessons from Gene. Dad lets me take the car occasionally to run errands and shopping. That pleases him because it gives him more time to do his work which is designing and building homes for people.

Gene took me with him and his family to Troup to see his sister, Edna, and her husband, Cotton. They are such nice people. I sure did enjoy the visit.

These were the days when most people didn't have a telephone. Gene's parents did not have a phone, and neither did most of their neighbors. There were times when Gene would not come to see me or call me for several days. They lived out of town and away from telephones. No one thought about it because that's the way things were then.

By February 12th, we were still going to Aunt Kate's church on Sunday night to hear her preach. She even gave me a present this time. For whatever reason I don't know. Maybe it was just because she loved me. That's what I'll think the reason was. She was a very dear person to me, especially after my Mother left us. She did what she could to help us.

I remember she had taken me and Charlie over to her house to spend some time. It was probably during that first summer when our Mother left. Charlie had a long pipe, like a water pipe, he was playing with. He accidentally hit me in the head with it.

It really did hurt, so I told Aunt Kate thinking she would give out corporal punishment or something like that. Instead, she said, "Charlie, you shouldn't do that. Put the pipe down." Then she walked away. She was doing her laundry and I suppose she didn't have time to "mess" with two little kids quarreling.

By the 15th I was coming down with whatever Gene and the others had been plagued with and was sick off and on for several days. I missed some school and work at Moses Lunch Counter.

Gene had made friends with J. H. and he had met my new girl friend Jerry. They were now an "Item," going steady and went with us very often. Gene's Dad was letting him drive his truck more, and now we always had transportation. My Dad even lets me drive the Studebaker truck occasionally. The truck is for Dad's men to drive to pickup supplies for the job, not for pleasure.

My sister, Della's, twelfth birthday was nearing, so our Step Mom gave her a party on Sunday, March 5th rather than wait until the next day which was a school day on March 6th.

After the big party, Gene and all of our friends went out to the Airport to watch the planes take off and land. We also took our baby brother, Lynn, with us because we usually took him wherever we went. We treated him like a little doll.

The things we did probably seem strange or silly now, but you must understand, swimming and going to the movies and church was the only daily or weekly activities we had. There wasn't any miniature golf or regular golf for kids, game rooms to go to, hobby shops, dirt bike races, or car races for us to go to see.

There wasn't any TV yet, and cell phones, Lap Tops and computers were still about forty to fifty years in the future. We had old tires we could get inside of and roll down the hill, or get a piece of cardboard and slide down the hill. We had lots of fun and made our own fun. That was much more exciting.

We never went to a movie until after Dad married our Step Mom. It was forbidden by our religion. But, after Dad finally found someone to stay with us, and that person became our Step Mom who liked to go to movies, that part changed. My Aunt Kate and Mamaw did not approve of us going to movies, either.

I believe Dad was so happy after he found someone who would put up with us and our rowdiness and all the crazy things we did, he was willing to do anything to keep her with us. One of her favorite things was to go to the movie on Saturday night. That would also give them some time away from the kids, the final count was eight, and some much needed peace and quiet.

It was my job to stay home on Saturday night and take care of the kids. I have already told of some of the exploits that occurred. It may have been enough to drive an ordinary person crazy. The Arlene Theater had, what was called, the "Midnight Show" on Saturday night which started at 10:30 to 11:00 pm.

Because I was required to stay at home on Saturday night, as soon as Dad and my Step Mom came home from the movie, then I was allowed to go to the "Midnight Show" on my dates with Gene.

Now that you have your breath back and have said, "Oh, Jesus" at least three times, I will say that I never heard of anyone getting into any kind of trouble from going to the "Midnight Show" on Saturday night. No one was shot or knifed or killed after the Midnight Show. I never heard of any girl being raped or anyone being robed.

After the show, everyone went to one of the restaurants (we called them "cafes") to have coffee and a piece of pie. If anyone had gotten into any kind of trouble, everyone would have heard about it at school the next week. If not a school, surely at church.

I don't know about the other kids, but I had no idea what "drugs" were. My crowd didn't drink alcohol. The worst thing we ever heard about was when some of the boys, not my group, put someone's Renault car on top of the railroad ties at the train station. They had a hard time getting it down. No one would admit to doing "that cruel deed."

Another excitement in my life was when my first niece was born to my brother Sammie and his wife Alene. Linda Diane entered our life at 4:15 pm. on March 16th. Gene and I, and our friends J. H. and Jerry (Geraldine) were going to see Aunt Kate to tell her the news, and we ran out of gas on the way back home. That's the truth, not something we made up.

On March 26th, Dad and Mom returned from their Dallas shopping trip. Dad went to Dallas quite often to purchase "things" for the houses he was building. Sunday night Gene and I took our friends, J. H. and Jerry with us to church and got caught in a terrible rain storm on the way home.

Our High School Choral Class was entered into a Competition on April 21st in town. We won Second Place. I'm very proud of our Club.

Whenever possible now, the four of us go ten miles to the next town, Kilgore, to a theater there which is showing a Superman Serial. We all like Superman and don't necessarily notice what movies are showing. Being silly kids that we are, we would go over there every Friday night to see the serial. Yes, that was silly, but the truth is, I still like Superman.

We were just being teenagers, but on Sunday night we usually went to Aunt Kate's church at East Mountain. Maybe that made up for our "silliness."

Gene and I have now had our first anniversary. May 1st is the day we met one year ago. We didn't have a big party. The truth is, I was ill for three days. Terrible!!

A couple of days later, our friend, J. H. got a car. That was Good!! We now had wheels!!

The end of school was nearing, and the end of our Senior Year. On Saturday, May 6th was our Prom Night. The four of us went to the Banquet and Prom together. We were beginning to receive some nice presents for our graduation.

Gene and J. H. were students at White Oak High School, and Jerry and I were students at Longview High School.

That meant we had activities at both schools which we were supposed to attend. Also my Uncle Junior was graduating from Hallsville High School. During this time, our friend Charles was home on leave from the Air Force. This was a very busy time for all of us.

It's May 25th and Gene has gotten his "new" "used" car. Things are really moving fast now. The next day, Gene graduated. On, Sunday, the 28th, my school had our Baccalaureate Service. My Graduation Service was held June 1st with a party following.

The Student Union had obtained a building where the students could have parties and dances. That's where we had our party. The Student Union Building was named "The Roundup Club" and was open for the students the year round.

Summer is upon us. Aunt Alpha and Uncle Bob have moved here from Galveston. They are living in our Garage Apartment that Dad built with their little girl, Katie Sue. I will be her baby sitter for the summer.

The local Radio Station has a contest every day and gives away tickets to the downtown Arlene Movie Theater. The first person to call in when a song is being played and can tell them the name of the song, wins a free pass to the Theater. I am very good at remembering the names of songs and have won quite a few free passes. By July 1st I had won six passes and was able to treat everyone to a movie.

Our spare time is now filled with going to car races and boat races. Our neighbor, Herman, who is also Dad's Foreman, lives in the house Dad built on our property next to our house. He has a new boat and takes us boat riding at the lake occasionally. Him and his wife are very nice people.

I had been babysitting with Katie Sue the morning of July 13th. That afternoon we received the sad news that Aunt Kate's husband, Uncle Herbert, had died. Gene came over and we went to East Mountain to Aunt Kate's home to be with her. Uncle Herbert was lying on the bed because the Funeral Home had not come yet. He had died of a heart attack. It was a very sad time for our family,

He and Aunt Kate had not had any children, even though they had been married for many years. She told me once that if God wanted her to have children, He would have given her some. I know that's why she cared and love us so much. We were the children she never had.

Uncle Herbert did not go to hear Aunt Kate preach. He was a member of a Lodge and went to their meetings. He had told her that when he reached the highest rank in his lodge that he wanted to be, then he would help her with "her church and preaching." I believe he finally reached that rank.

A few weeks before his death, Gene and I had gone to Aunt Kate's Church, and much to my surprise, when we went in, there was uncle Herbert standing up and singing a hymn with the other church members. We had never seen him there in church before and especially singing. I didn't know he could sing.

His funeral was held in Aunt Kate's one-room small church. There were men from all over the state that came to his funeral. All of them would not fit in that small one-room church and were standing outside all over the yard.

At the end of the funeral, the procession started to the cemetery. As far as I could see up the highway and down the highway were cars and more cars. I have never seen so many people and cars in one place before. These were men, without their wives, that belonged to the same Lodge as Uncle Herbert and were from all over the State of Texas. They all wore nice suits and drove fine cars.

I know my uncle loved my Aunt and they had a good life together. I also believe that my uncle went to heaven because I'm sure he accepted Jesus Christ before his death. Aunt Kate would have seen to that. The only comment I can make is that he was "cutting it pretty close."

I started my first day at work at Leonard's Sweet Shop on July 24th. This is the same bakery that has made our annual October Birthday Cake for years. His son and I were also classmates.

Gene went away to National Guard Camp for two weeks which is mandatory for his training. He calls me and writes me most every day. One Sunday night, on their way back home from Tatum to visit Gene's grandparents, Gene's Dad and Mom decided to stop by my house to meet my Dad and Step Mom and my family.

We had all sat down to eat our Sunday Supper when they knocked on the door. I went to see who it was and asked them to come in and sit in the living room. I told my Dad they were here and wanted to meet them. I thought he would leave the table and go talk with them, but he did not.

I could not understand why Dad was acting the way he was. I finished eating and went in to tell them that Dad and my Step Mom would be out shortly. They said they needed to go and left. I was very embarrassed over the way my parents had treated Gene's parents. I could not believe it!! I did not question them or say anything about the situation, and they did not tell me why they treated Gene's parents the way they did. I thought it was just plain RUDE.

The last of August, Dad talked to me about going to college at Stephen F. Austin State Teachers College in Nacogdoches where he went to college. Years later the name was changed to Stephen F. Austin University.

Dad and Aunt Alpha took me to Nacogdoches to check out things. We went to see Uncle Jessie, who is actually Dad's uncle and my Great Uncle. Dad asked him to take us to his bank. I wasn't sure exactly why at the time. We all went in to see the president of the bank and Dad told him he wanted to open a checking account for me. That was a surprise for me.

The Banker asked Dad how much he wanted to put in the account, and Dad said, "One Thousand Dollars." I remember there was a long pause in the room while they all got their breath and the blood rushed back to their brains. A thousand dollars would have bought a new car in those days. When we were finished at the bank, we went back to Uncle Jessie's to visit and then back home.

When we were back at home, Dad told me that he would need for me to sign some blank checks for him before I left for college. It wasn't until forty-five years later that I found out the real truth. I had been talking to Sammie about me and Gene and how we had broken up.

At that time, God had answered my prayers and I was back living in Longview with Sammie and his new wife, Marie and sharing an apartment with them. Sammie asked me if I really knew what had happened back in 1950. I told him that I had no idea so he told me.

Dad had become partners with a man that owned some property in the Pine Wood Addition in Longview. They were doing very well building and selling houses. That is until Dad and my Step Mom went on their first vacation. It seems there had not been any check or money set aside before they left to pay the plumber.

Friday and Payday came around and the plumber was not paid. In case you don't know, if the person doing work for you is not paid, that person can go to court and file a Mechanics Lien against you. That means that your bank account is frozen until the Lien is paid. No money can be taken out of the account.

Since Dad was, I believe in Colorado and knew nothing about this. It was a week before he returned home. I don't know how it was all settled. I only know it ruined my Dad's business, threw him into Bankruptcy, and nothing was the same after that. One little rock can roll down a hill and cause a landslide, and that's what had happened.

Sammie, was living with his family in the house Dad's workers had helped him build and could not help Dad, or it would have pulled him into the mess. My brother, Charlie, just younger than me was too young to help. I was now eighteen and the only one old enough to help.

The trip to Nacogdoches and to Uncle Jessie's bank was to keep some money out of the Bankruptcy and provide money for Dad to buy groceries and pay the utility bills and any other household expenses that might occur.

During all this time in the summer of 1950, I was living in my own little world and oblivious to what was going on around me.

Sammie had been working as one of Dad's Foremen and knew everything that happened and when it happened.

I understand now why Dad wanted me to go to college at Nacogdoches. I would be living out of the county where the bankruptcy had been filed and no one could touch the money in the bank except me. I was eighteen years old and the bank account was in my name only.

Dad was trying to protect his family and furnish them with food to eat and a place to live. He always did provide them with food, but the bankruptcy would take their home away from them. Dad never did confide in me about financial matters, but he did concerning other matters.

He was not trying to break Gene and I up, he was trying to save our home and feed his family.

CHAPTER 24

THE BREAKUP AND OFF TO COLLEGE

I had been at Gene's home on Sunday afternoon before I was to leave for college. His Dad and Mom were going to church, so Gene and I went with them. I did not know then that it would be the last time I would go to church with them. That would be because my life would be changing fast.

I had decided I would go to college because that is what Dad said I should do and needed to do – get a good education. I was not aware of all the financial problems Dad was going through.

Gene was not too happy with my choice. Dad took me for Registration on September 15, 1950. I started college on Monday, September 18th. It's a new place, new people, a new town, and a new life. Change does not come easy for me. I was among strangers now.

The house I was to stay in was a two story house with lots of bedrooms because Mrs. Mitchel had raised twelve children. They were all grown now and had moved away. She was a widow and a very, very nice woman, kind and sweet. My roommate was Sue. She was a Sophomore and could stay anywhere, but she liked Mrs. Mitchel's place.

By the second day, I was already getting homesick. It was probably because I didn't know anyone there. I was late registering and could not stay in the Dorm. The college told Dad about a large home that was run by a widow mother and was on the list of acceptable places for Freshmen to stay. We were not allowed to stay anywhere else except in "approved housing."

I did know my Uncle Jessie and his wife, so after classes, I decided I would walk to their house to visit. They lived on the opposite side of town from the college. They couldn't believe I had walked all that way. The fact is, I was accustomed to walking because that's what we did at home. We didn't always wait for someone to take us places. We just walked.

I met their son, my Cousin Harry Gordon and his friend Dorothy, that afternoon. After visiting for a while, they took me to the College Inn for a bite to eat. The next night Uncle Jessie and his wife and niece Lana took me to the Fair. We had a marvelous time. The following day Gene came to see me. He and I took my roommate Sue and two other friends and went to the Redland Theater to see a movie. My roommate, Sue had been engaged to a young man. He was driving through Oklahoma and a horse ran out and he hit it.

The horse slid up the hood of the car, came through the windshield, and landed in his lap and killed him. I'm sure it was a very bad experience for her. She is a very nice, quiet person. After she told me what had happened, she never mentioned it again. That's not something we would want to talk about, but it did teach me something I did not know. If your car hits a horse, deer, or anything large, it might slide up the hood of your car and into your lap and kill you. I have never forgotten what she told me.

We have Lab work on Saturday morning at College, which means I cannot go home until after noon. My Step Mom came and got me and took me home. My Step Mom will be transporting me back and forth to and from college for the entire year.

After school, I sometimes would go to Uncle Jessie's. His son, Harry Gordon, and I are very good friends now. Harry shows me where to go and things to do, also helps me with my studies and how to find things around campus.

I go home every weekend. Sometimes Gene comes to see me on one of those days, and sometimes he doesn't. The weekend of October 7th, Gene came over to see me. We were sitting in his car when he broke our engagement because he was angry with me. He said, "You just want to do what your Dad wants you to do, and don't want to do what I want you to do." I had told him I would be home every weekend, but that didn't seem to please him.

He wanted us to get married. I had said we could wait until college was out in the summer. I guess he didn't want to wait. I cried for a week. My heart was broken. He had asked me to marry me on October 13th and less than a year later, October 7th our engagement was broken and was not to be mended. He did not ask for his ring to be returned. I kept the ring in my jewelry box, in plain sight, for fifty years.

The next weekend I went home on Friday. Gene came to see me and we went to the Longview-Texarkana football game that night. We are still on speaking terms.

We can't seem to let the past go, or each other.

Early Saturday morning my Step Mom took me, her mother, Junior, Della and her friend Jane to Dallas for our annual trip in October to the Texas State Fair. We always take that trip around our birthdays. This year my birthday, the 18th, was on Wednesday and I was 18 years old. Gene came to see me after we returned from our trip to Dallas.

The next day, Gene came to see me at college and stayed for only a short time. I was very glad to see him. I guess things are okay. I was supposed to have a date with someone else, but went with him to the movie instead.

The next day, Sunday, we had our Big Birthday Dinner for the family. After dinner, I went to see Gene and his family. Then we went to a movie that night.

When I was at home for the weekend on October 28th, I saw Gene with a girl at the movie. He came over on Sunday afternoon and we are now "officially broken-up."

November 3rd was Home Coming at college. Everyone went to the football game. Afterwards my Step Mom came to take me home for the weekend. My Step Mom's mother is in the hospital, so I went to see her. Junior was home also wearing his new Army uniform. He sure looked good.

He and I are almost the same age, we liked to do the same things and are actually very good friends.

His mother, Big Mama, had married a very nice man years prior, that we all call Daddy Bill. Daddy Bill has one glass eye. Sometimes if he rubs his eye too hard, his glass eye will turn around. Whoever notices it will always tell him, "Turn your eye around, Bill." Big Mama and Daddy Bill have always treated us as though we were part of their family.

They lived on their farm all of their married life and are just plain, simple people. When Daddy Bill wanted to dress up, he would put his overalls on with a nice white shirt and a tie. That was his "Sunday Best Dress."

On Saturdays, they would start out for town early in the wagon to buy groceries and anything else they needed for the week. In the afternoon they would go to a movie. It was always one of the old-time cowboy movies with lots of shooting and horse riding. That would be their entertainment for the week. Then they were ready to go back home.

A few years later, Daddy Bill gave up farming and got a job at Kelly Plow Works in Longview. At that time I was living in Dallas. He also bought a car because it would take him too long to ride a horse into town to his job. I know that he worked there long enough to earn vacation time.

I'm not sure, but I do know he and Big Mama had gone on a vacation and he had returned to work. It was noon on Monday, and the men were gathering outside the plant to go and eat lunch. One of his friends, slapped him on the back and said, "Bill, how was the vacation?" He fell onto the sidewalk on his face.

A Doctor told me that when a person falls on their face while having a heart attack, that person is dead when he touches the sidewalk. In 1959 Big Mama died also. They didn't have much money, but they sure had a lot of love and kindness to give.

The days are passing fast. Thanksgiving has come and gone without any special events. The Sadie Hawkins dance was held at college on December 1st on Friday night. I had a date with Jack. He's a nice guy and plays the trumpet in the band.

I am learning to understand and like basketball. At least the games are held inside out of the cold and rain. We do have a good basketball team. With Christmas and the Holidays drawing near, there are a lot of activities. On December 9th I went with a friend, Ben, to the Freshman Dance.

But, by December 20th, all the games and dances are over and everyone is headed home for the Holidays. I decided to go home with my friend Evelyn who is from Beckville. That's a very, very small town south of Longview. Beckville still has a telephone switchboard which her aunt operates. I had never seen one before.

I only stayed one night, then my Step Mom came to take me home. We did have a good visit and I learned some things about small towns.

On December 20th Gene came by and took me to see his family for the afternoon and gave me a Christmas present. It seems we don't know exactly what to do about our situation. Are we "broke-up" or not???

Charles, one of the boys from college who lives in Henderson, came to see me on Christmas day. It seems I'm not the only one during the first year after High School that is "sort of lost" at home and don't know where our High School friends are or what they are doing.

We spent twelve years with people. We lived at our own home and were around familiar places and things. Then we were transplanted into a community with people we had never met before, and surrounded by things we didn't know or understand. We were trying to be "grown-up" but weren't "grown-up."

My Step Mom was ill during most of the Holidays, but recovered in time for me to go back to College. I remember when I first came here, one of my Professors told the class on the first day. He said that we could come to class and have "cake" with everyone else, or we could miss and try to catch up by eating the "leftover crumbs." That is very true about any situation.

There are no "do-overs" in college. Mom and Dad are not there to wake you up each morning. You are on your own. Pass or Fail, It's up to you and no one else.

In February there was a huge snow storm and everything shut down, even the college. All the roads were blocked and most everything in Nacogdoches closed. There was no transportation. Buses were not running.

I checked with the Train Station and there was a train that went to Longview that I could take and I did. It was a "milk train." That meant it would stop at every road or crossing to pick-up the milk.

I had not ridden the train in many, many years and was looking forward to it. I heard the Conductor come down the isle saying, "Tennaha, Timpson, Bobo, and Blair, next stop." That didn't mean very much to anyone else, but since my Dad grew up in the Nacogdoches-Center Area, he had heard that "Call" since he was a kid and had taught it to all of us children. I felt like I had just met an old friend.

The "shut-down" lasted for a week, then everything went back to normal and my Step Mom took me back to college.

My friend, Charles, from Henderson, had asked me for a date several times and I had turned him down for different reasons. Sometimes I was busy, or already had a date. He said, "Well, why don't I ask you to go with me to the "Flappers Ball" in the Spring before you make a date with someone else?"

I said I would but did not know what the "Flappers Ball" was. He told me that the theme for the dance was centered around the 1920's and the girls wore dresses with a slit up the side and lots of beads. I had plenty of time to make my costume since the Ball wasn't until May.

The last time I saw Gene was when he took me over to see his parents just before Christmas on December 21st. In March I was told by my Cousin Bill that Gene was getting married. All of my heartaches started all over again. I wrote him a long letter begging him not to do it.

Years later his mother told me that my letter had come the day of the wedding. She said he sat for a long time on the back porch reading my letter, but went through with the wedding. He had given his word and would not break it.

It wasn't like him to break his word. We would not see or hear about or from each other for five years. I finished my year at college and went back home. I had learned that if a person would go to college for three years without taking a vacation, that person could finish and get a degree in three years.

I approached my Dad and talked to him about it. He said, "No!" He also said he knew me and that I would make myself sick studying. He really didn't know me as well as he thought he did. I studied, but not that much.

I was still not aware of my Dad's financial problems or the bankruptcy. Now that I know, the reason for him trying to discourage me about going to college full time was because of his financial situation. I did not have a job while I was going to college and he was paying all the bills. Since I did not have a car, it would have been almost impossible for me to find a way to go to work every day.

Since I wasn't going to college during the summer, it was time for me to find a job. I went to all of the local places, even Dad's Bank, without any success. Someone suggested I go back to Leonard's Sweet Shop. I said, "No! I didn't go to college for a year to learn how to sell donuts and cakes." I was very disappointed. I told everyone that if I were to get a job in Longview, someone would need to leave it to me in their will. But, with my luck they would leave it to someone else.

CHAPTER 25

OFF TO THE BIG CITY TO SEEK MY FORTUNE

It was nearing the end of June and I hadn't gotten a job, didn't even have a "nibble," and no prospects in sight.

About the last of June, my friend J. H., whom Gene and I had known for some time and had double-dated with, showed up at my door. I think he felt like the rest of us, which is; after school we did not have that daily connection with people we had known for many years. Those people were also scattered and not to be found.

J. H. was looking for a friend and I needed one, also. We visited and I told him my plight. His answer to the situation was for me to go to Dallas with him and his Mother. His Father was somewhere in Canada working on a pipeline. They had moved to Dallas to be near his Mother's brother while his Dad was gone.

I was thrilled at the suggestion, but did not think Dad would let me go. I went into Dad's office to ask him, and much to my surprise, He said, "Okay." I ran to my bedroom, packed my bag, and off I went to Dallas.

Surely I had some money in my pocket. I don't remember Dad giving me any, but surely he did I couldn't go off to the Big City without a "dime."

J. H.'s Mom was a very nice lady and welcomed me with open arms. J. H. was her only son and since she had no girls, she treated me like I was her daughter. The apartment wasn't very large and had two bedrooms, with two beds. She insisted I sleep in the bed with her, rather than a couch. That was fine with me, since most of my life was spent sharing a bed with someone or sleeping on a couch.

Their apartment was on the second floor of a large apartment house on Second Avenue in Dallas. It was on the streetcar line and was very convenient for those who did not have or owned a car.

We arrived on Sunday night, and come Monday morning, I was at the streetcar stop waiting for my ride to the big city of Dallas. J. H. had told me how to get to the Texas Unemployment Office.

I was interviewed, tested, and qualified and sent out to a company that was downtown. It was United Finance and Thrift on Commerce Street. I was hired that day. If you don't think that made my "proud feathers stand up," you're loony. Must have been God at work!!

Within twenty-four hours of leaving my home I had a job and a place to stay. The streetcar stopped in front of the apartment and then took me to downtown to my job. I had been hired as "Head Cashier" which meant I had a job with a "title" and my salary was $35.00 a week. This may seem small to you, but to me it was three times what I had made at the Bakery.

Now I was able to pay my rent, pay my streetcar fare, buy my lunch, and buy my clothes and still had money left over.

I think it was several months later that J. H. and his Mom received word that his Dad had been killed. We were told that he was helping string some wires when one snapped, whipped back, and almost cut J. H.'s Dad in two.

J. H.'s Mom was kind enough to take me to see her brother's family who lived on First Avenue, just a block or so away, to ask if they would take me in. They were more than glad to, because they had a daughter my age. I could share a room with her. Their name was Fuller and treated me very well. I learned that their family was very large.

I now had a good job and a nice place to live. I thought it was time for me to buy a car. Naturally, I rode the bus home so that my Dad could help me pick out one and get it financed. It was a green, two door Dodge sedan. I never was sure about the model, but I think it was about a 1938. It was a good car and served me very well. Up until then, I had been riding the bus back home to visit my family. Now, I could drive my own car.

It was in the Spring when I bought my car and I had it until the winter. I did not know about Antifreeze and radiators freezing and no one told me about it either. The Dad of the family I lived with said something about "draining the radiator" that very, very cold night. I didn't know anything about that or how to do it.

You know what happened. The temperature dropped down below freezing and the radiator froze on my car and busted the block. It was ruined. I didn't even know what to do with it or how to dispose of it. I just left it where it sat.

One of their sisters, who lived nearby, had twelve grown children. The baby boy of thirteen children was my age. We became very good friends, dated for a time, and then got married. I insisted that we get married in my home town in the church my Dad built and so we did. All of his family drove from Dallas to Longview to attend the wedding of their "Baby Brother."

About six months into the marriage, he received his Draft Notice and was inducted into the Army. At first he was stationed at Fort Leonardwood, Missouri. He was a very smart man, so he was sent to Officer's Candidate School in Indianapolis.

With him away, I was welcomed into his parent's home to live while he served his enlistment time. He was sent to Japan for two years to work in the Army Post Office. When it was time for him to come back home and be discharged, I rented an apartment for us in the Oak Cliff section of Dallas.

I knew shortly after our marriage that I was not happy. My husband was a good and kind person and would do anything for me to make me happy, but I was still in love with Gene, and there was nothing I could do about that. Therefore; I got a Divorce. We did not have any children, but I knew if I had had children, it would have been very hard for me to break up that family.

I remembered the hurt I still carried from my Mother leaving, and would carry that hurt for the remainder of my life.

A few weeks later, I went home to see my family. I saw my Cousin Bill in town and told him what had happened. He was friends with Gene and naturally told Gene that I was home for a visit and Divorced.

Gene came to see me and told me he was separated from his wife and children and getting a divorce.

I always liked Gene's parents and went to see them before going back to Dallas. They were now living in the Pine Tree area in a very nice new home with large windows in the living room which let you see into the back yard.

While I was talking with his mother, she looked out the window at two small children playing in the yard. She looked at me and said, "Don't take those children's Father away from them."

Her words couldn't have hurt me any more than if she had shot me with a gun. I knew what she meant. I could see myself and my brother playing in our yard and unaware of what was about to happen when our Mother left us.

That was Sunday afternoon. I went back to my life and my job in Dallas. The next day, Gene came to Dallas to see me and to talk. I told him I could not take his children's Dad away from them. I knew what it would do to them.

I cried and he cried, but it was not our time to be happy. Maybe some other day.

I had a nice car that was left over from my marriage and was now working for an insurance company in Dallas. I was head of the typing department and had six women under me.

During one of my visits home, Dad asked me to take my sister Della back to Dallas with me because she had run away twice to Houston. I agreed and took her home with me.

I was very serious about my job and working, but Della did not feel as I did. We clashed one afternoon and argued violently because she didn't want to go to work. She left and did not tell me where she was going and did not come back. It would be years before we met again.

I was working two jobs because I had allowed two girls to influence me and had rented a house. Foolishly, I paid the first month's rent, the utilities, and deposit. Then they decided not to stay and moved out leaving me "holding the bag" and no money left for gas, expenses, or groceries.

One of the girls did not leave, but stayed with me. She had a job at a Hamburger Place as a carhop working days and part-time nights. I still had my day job at the Insurance Company, but needed "grocery money." I was paid every two weeks, and a person can "starve in two weeks." I had eaten my last piece of bread and made some gravy with flour and water.

She introduced me to the owners, they were partners, and I started working every-other night, sharing the night job with my roommate.

The first night I worked, after my day job, I was very hungry and was counting my pennies until I made enough tips to buy a hamburger and soda. When I ordered my food, much to my surprise, I was told that I did not pay for my food. They furnished my food.

Months later I told my bosses about how hungry I had been the first night and they laughed at me. They said that all I needed to do was to tell them and they would have fed me before I started to work. It never seemed to matter what my circumstances were, God always seemed to put me in contact with kind and loving people that always had a helping heart.

You may or may not notice that I haven't spoken about going to church since I left home for college. I was away from my family and friends that I always went to church with. No one that I knew now seemed interested in going to church and I didn't know a church to go to, so I didn't go. One day, that also would change, but not now.

There were three men that frequented the Hamburger Place and always sat inside. One night one of them got into his car and drove over to the carhop area. He talked to me and then he asked me for a date. Since I wasn't dating anyone, I thought, "Why not." His name was Buddy and he was a little older than me, and seemed to be a very nice person. He also had a good job and a very nice car. That's what a woman should always look for in a man, a good job.

He had served in the Army during World War II and had been married before, but was not married when I met him. After dating for quite a few months, he asked me to marry him, and I accepted. We took my roommate and her boyfriend with us to Ardmore, Oklahoma and got married on a Friday night.

He moved in with me and my roommate. A couple of weeks later, my roommate and her boyfriend were married, too. Someone, a nosy person, called the landlord and told him I had a man living with me. When I went to pay the rent, he told me about the situation. He told that person that he knew about the man living with me because I had told him that we had gotten married. Whoever that was, the "joke was on them."

We lived there for a few more months, then decided to move back to the Oak Cliff area into a nicer home and a nicer neighborhood. We lived in that area for several years until we decided to buy a home. Every weekend we drove to different areas looking for the house we would buy and call "our home."

During this same time, we were playing in several Bowling Leagues in Dallas. I was in a women's league from my office and he was in a men's league. In addition we were in a mixed league so that we could be in a league together. The mixed league was the one we enjoyed the most.

Our fourth anniversary was drawing near when he said to me, "If you don't have us a baby soon, I want to adopt one." I should have told him that it wasn't all my fault we were not having a baby. About that time, we finally found us a house that we dearly loved in Euless, which is half way between Dallas and Fort Worth and not too far from either of our jobs.

We were trying to move into our newly built home, when I was told that my Ladies' Bowling League from the office was scheduled to go to Galveston for a tournament in May. I went and bowled the best I could, but we didn't win any fabulous prizes. I did get to see my Dad and my family while I was there because they had moved to Galveston to live.

Mamaw and Grandpa had lived in Galveston during the war so that Grandpa could work in the shipyards and had remained there after the war was over. Aunt Kate's husband, Herbert, had died and she married a fine Christian man, Artis, from East Texas. I guess they moved to Galveston to be near Mamaw.

After Dad's business bombed, Aunt Kate asked Dad to move to Galveston with the family, because she knew he could get a job as a watchman on the wharf. He did move and he did get the job. That's where they were living when my team went to the Bowling Tournament at Galveston.

I had gone to Galveston for the Tournament instead of helping to move into my new home. I was also having some health problems and went to see my doctor after I returned home. He told me I was Pregnant. I now have a new home and a baby on the way. Who could ask for more. I was happy and my husband was happy now.

Our daughter Denise was born on Tuesday Night, our "Mixed League Bowling Night," December 15, 1959, and spoiled the remainder of my Christmas shopping. I told everyone they would have to wait until January to get their presets, but in the meantime, they could enjoy the new baby we got for Christmas that year.

Everyone at the Bowling Alley said they knew what had happened and only one reason would keep both of us away from our bowling night. They were right!

Some people had said they did not think I should be bowling so late in my pregnancy. I asked my doctor and he said he found nothing wrong with it. Since I was bowling when I got pregnant, there wasn't any reason for me to quit. It was good exercise for me. After she was born, that stopped my bowling.

I worked in Dallas and we lived in Euless. My babysitter lived in Euless. The Bowling League was in Dallas, also. It was not practical for me to drive to Euless after work and pickup my baby, then drive back to Dallas to bowl.

She woke up from her nap when she was 13 months old in January. It was a beautiful day so I put her in her "walker." It was a thing she could sit in and touch the floor and "walk" herself wherever she wanted to go. It gave her freedom. The weather was nice and warm that Sunday afternoon so I opened the sliding glass doors. She loved to look out at the trees and flowers.

The next morning we could not wake her, and she was breathing hard. I called her doctor and he told us to bring her in immediately. He checked her and said she had pneumonia, but there was no reason to take her to the hospital yet. He gave her some antibiotics and after a couple of days she was much better, but it had been a very bad scare for us because it was the first time and she was very, very ill.

My sister Della had given birth to a girl after she got out of the Army and before she was married. She had a beautiful girl named Theresa. Then she met and married Charles, and they had four more children. They had some very difficult times and Charles went to jail several times for writing bad checks. Della was also jailed for writing bad checks in Dallas and called on me to bail her out, which I did gladly.

When they were living in Galveston, Charles was put in jail, I believe for writing bad checks. Aunt Kate called the welfare to find out if they could help Della and the children. Instead of helping, they came and took the children and placed them into Foster Care. The Child Protective Agency didn't give much "help" then.

We were all devastated at the way the Welfare Department had handled their case. Dad called me and told me what had happened and that the children might be put up for adoption. Dad was heartbroken because he thought he would never see his grandchildren again.

Dad began calling the family to see if any of us could adopt any of the children. I told him I could take Theresa. Sammie said he already had three children and didn't think he could care for any more. Aunt Alpha and Aunt Kate were told they were too old and were turned down by the court.

That had happened in January. In May was the date for the Court Hearing. My husband and I, Dad and my Step Mom, Aunt Kate, and Aunt Alpha were there in May in the courtroom for the hearing. Della was there, but not Charles. The Judge told Della to get a job and a place for her and the children to live, and he would return the children to her in thirty days. She never did come back to court.

My husband and I were given custody of Theresa on May 30th. The other children were put up for adoption. We were told to pick up Theresa that Saturday at the Court House parking lot in Texas City where the Foster Parent would deliver her to us. We did and she did. We brought Theresa home with us that day to Euless and she stayed with us until she was grown and married.

The other children were all adopted out to different families. When Theresa was grown and learned how to check adoption records, etc., she started a hunt for her siblings and did not give up until she found them. That took years.

I was pregnant during that time and gave birth to a find boy in February, Michael. We now had two girls and one boy. I left my job with the insurance company after ten years and four months. I wanted to be a "Stay At Home Mother."

When Michael was 5 ½ years old, my husband and I and the three children took a trip to see my Mother. She now lived in Little Rock, Arkansas with her new husband D.C. in an apartment on the east side of Little Rock.

We had not planned it, but shortly after our arrival, the landing on the moon of Apollo 11 was being broadcast on the TV. It was July 20, 1969 in the afternoon. All of us sat down around the TV and watched the landing with my Mother and her husband. That was a historical even that I will never forget and I shared it with my Mother.

After we returned home, I told my husband that we should find a church to go to so that the children could be raised in a Christian church and home. After all, I had been away from the church and God for a long time, and I felt the need to "return to my roots." He said he would think about it and ask around and decide which church he wanted to go to. He said he definitely was not going to an Assembly of God Church with all those "Holy Rollers." I gave in to his desires, because I thought that any church was better than no church at all.

There was a new church forming in our community, a Presbyterian Church. The building had not yet been built and the congregation was meeting in the old school house. The floors had large cracks in them. In the cold winter time, we took plastic bags and tied them over our shoes to keep the cold out and our feet warm.

There were several heaters in the front of the room but they didn't keep the room very warm.

Everyone wanted to sit on the front row because of the two heaters. It's the only church I have ever been in that people "fought" to sit on the front row rather than the back row. That doesn't happen today. Most people want to sit in the back. But I still prefer to sit up front or at least near the front.

The new building was soon finished and we moved in. I don't remember having Sunday School in the old school house. That may have been because there wasn't enough room.

I was asked to be the First and Second Grade Sunday School teacher. I accepted, and continued in that position for ten years. I taught all three of my children as they grew and attended First and Second Grade. When I told my Aunt Kate about it, she was very proud of me.

The church needed a little help with the Secretarial Work and I volunteered to help.

The Bulletin, that's a list of the coming announcements for the next week, needed to be typed up each week as well as other reports and forms that required attention pertaining to a church. I performed those duties also for several years.

The girls were in school now and Michael was about four years old. I opened a "Children's Clothing Store" that

I named "Angel Fashions" which required my attention six days a week, Monday through Saturday.

I asked my husband to take care of the children on Saturday, but he refused and said, "I will not be the Babysitter on my day off." Sometimes I took them with me to the shop on Saturdays, or hired a Babysitter. They were all in school at that time and only needed someone to watch over them.

We had become well established in the church and accepted by the congregation. My husband and I and our three children were baptized which meant "sprinkling of water."

My three children had been invited to a Birthday Party for one of the children of the congregation. They were always included in any activity involving the church.

My husband agreed to take them to the Birthday Party, and he did. Later I found out that Denise had gotten sick at her stomach and threw up in the car before arriving at the party. In spite of that, my husband took them to the party and let them out. He did not wait to see if Denise was okay or not.

Several hours later, my Pastor's wife called and told me that Denise was very ill and had been sick at her stomach since she arrived. That particular day I was without a car. I don't know why. I asked her if she would bring Denise to the shop. I was renting space for my shop in a dress shop that the doctor's wife and a friend of hers owned.

When they arrived, the Doctor's wife was sitting in the back seat holding Denise in her lap. Denise was unconscious and not responding to anything. I went back into the shop and called my doctor. His office was just a few blocks down the street. He said to bring her and come in the back door of the office. He looked at her and stepped out of the room. He came back and gave her an injection without telling me what may have been wrong with her. He said to take her home and he would come by later and check on her.

Someone had wrapped up a piece of the Birthday Cake for her and gave it to me. They took me and my three children home and I immediately put Denise to bed. She still did not respond to anything. She was like a limp dishrag.

I sat by her bed not knowing what to do for her and prayed for several hours. She finally opened her eyes and said, "Can I have some cake now?" There aren't any words to express my joy at that moment, and I gave her the cake and thanked God.

The doorbell rang and it was my doctor. I told him that she was sitting up eating her cake now. I also asked him what had been wrong with her and what was in the shot he gave her. He did not answer me. He just continued checking Denise.

As the days passed, other people who were at the party with their children, asked him what was in that shot and what was wrong with her?. To this day, he has never told us or said what made her sick or what was in the shot he gave her. I just leave it at that and know God answered my prayers.

Later that day, my husband returned home not knowing what had happened. He had been gone most of the day and had been drinking. I was very, very angry with him because he had shown complete disregard for our daughter and her health and told him so. He had not been present during my cancer operation and now he had shown disregard for our daughter and her health. It was also the beginning of the end of our marriage

Our Pastor owned two cabins at Red River, New Mexico. Each year he would take the older girls and boys sixteen years old and older, with chaperons, to his cabins for a week. They learned to brush their teeth with snow and all the things a person does in cold, snowy country. The children had to earn the money to charter a bus to take them to New Mexico, and also money to pay for their food.

There was a family who lived next door to us and they knew how to make "Hot Tamales." I don't know how many dozens the children made, but they made many, then sold them to earn the money they needed for the trip.

One family in the church was from the North and had never eaten Hot Tamales. He said they had a good flavor, but "Sure were hard to chew." We all knew exactly what had happened and laughed. It seems no one had told them to take the "Shucks" off before eating them. Everyone laughed about that for years. We had good fellowship and good times during those years.

My husband was a Deacon in the church. The only problem we had was his drinking. I prayed to God for help, but no answer came. You see, in all my years of attending church, I had not been taught how to pray. I now know that we must pray Good's Word back to Him and ask for His Will to be done. I did not know what I needed to know about My God and My Jesus and nothing at all about the Holy Spirit and how He is always there to help us.

I needed a job and was Blessed with a job working in the office for the Texas Department of Public Safety, the Highway Patrol, on the Dallas-Fort Worth Turnpike. I had been working there for about ten months and began having some health problems and consulted our family doctor. He did the usual testing and prescribed medicine for me. I was not pleased with the way he diagnosed me.

I had a bad feeling about the way I felt and talked about it with one of the ladies in the office. Her mother had worked for a Gynecologist whom she respected and said perhaps I should consult him, which I did. He did the usual testing and when he got the results, he called me at my office. I answered the phone and when he told me who he was, I almost fainted. Doctors don't call their patients, the nurse always call. This was highly unusual and must be very important for him to call.

He asked me if I could come to his office that day. Of course I said I could and he asked me when? I said, "Any time you say." He asked me to be there within the hour, which was between noon and one. Naturally, I said, "Sure," and left for his office. Years later, I realized that not only was that my lunch time, it was also his lunch time.

He was waiting for me and asked about the PAP Smear testing my family doctor had done, especially about the "numbers," and that the stages of CANCER had numbers and that was my problem. I immediately went into shock. I was told I needed to have a hysterectomy as soon as possible. I don't remember much of what he said after that. He scheduled the operation for as soon as the operating room was available and I left his office.

I did not go back to work, but went home and waited for my husband so that I could explain to him what had happened. He seemed very sympathetic and we made plans for me to have the operation which was scheduled for the following week.

The next day I went in to work and told my Captain, who was the kindest and most sympathetic person I have ever known. He told me I could take off as long as I needed to recover from the operation, which was estimated to be about six weeks.

The afternoon before the operation, my husband took me to the hospital for my "Check-in." Blood work and other tests needed to be done before the operation which was scheduled for the next morning. They put me in a private room and my husband left.

The operation was scheduled for the next morning at five or six o'clock. That morning, I looked up about five o'clock and my Dear Pastor was coming in my door. He was there to console me and help me through this "trying procedure." He was also there to pray for me and with me. It's not every day that a person has a cancer operation, but my Pastor was there for me, and my husband was not.

A nurse came in to give me a shot and he said, "Okay, I'll step out." The nurse told him he could stay. I realized she did not know who he was. I explained he was my pastor and not my husband.

My husband did not come to the hospital that day. When I questioned him about it later, he said he did not have anyone to stay with the children. The truth was that he did not ask anyone. Why, I never knew. Anyone in our neighborhood or at our church, even the Pastor's wife, would have been glad to take care of the children. They were not babies and could actually take care of themselves.

My Pastor stayed with me and talked with me and prayed with me until time for the operation. Then he walked next to the gurney holding my hand until they pushed me through the double doors into the operation room and he was forced to let go of my hand.

I know God knew what was happening and had sent my Pastor to help me through the situation. God led me to the lady I worked with who told me what Doctor I needed to see. God sent my pastor to pray with me and prepare me mentally for the operation. Then God guided the Doctor's eyes and hands through the operation and all of the cancer was removed.

I was only 37 years old at the time, but there were things I did not understand until I was in my 80's. That's when I realized, with another Doctor's help, that I was not told I needed to take any type of radiation or chemotherapy because the Cancer was gone, removed. No one told me about "follow-ups" after a cancer operation. I was trusting God and knew everything was okay. Praise God for His mercy!!

After the operation, I was free from Cancer. I never lived in fear that it might return or that I would have any more problems. I did not realize why my Doctors had run tests on me all these many years, until recently. They were checking for Cancer. I was not worried about Cancer, because God took care of everything. I am now 87 years young and still free of Cancer.

When I was able to receive visitors in the hospital, three of the Sergeants came to visit me and sort of "circled my bed." A nurse came bounding in the door and stopped abruptly. I quickly said, "It's okay. We work together." She thought they may have been there to arrest me.

When I left the hospital, two large double tiered carts were need to carry all the flowers I had received. The Captain told me to stay at home as long as I needed. Then when I returned to work, he told me that if I began feeling bad, I was to go home. If I worked only half a day, that would be fine.

The Captain and all the Troopers gave me "high priority" treatment. One day after lunch, a very dear Trooper, John, appeared at my office door holding my coat. He told me that the Captain had told him if he noticed I was getting pale, it was time to take me home. He was there to take me home.

I explained that my car was in the parking lot. He said not to worry. He would be at my home in the morning to bring me back to the office. And that's exactly what he did. I don't have words to explain how kind and helpful those Troopers were. I did not know at the time they were "watching me."

Once when my brother, Charlie, and his family were coming from California to visit, I went into the Captain's office to ask if I could leave early. He was writing a check in his personal checkbook. He never looked up, but said to me, "If I ever find out you are here working when you have sick children at home, I Will Fire You." That's the kind of person he was. He always tried to protect and help those who worked for him.

My marriage was going downhill after my operation, but I didn't want to make my children go through what I had gone through when my mother left us. I coped for as long as I could, until the day I could not anymore. I talked with a Marriage Counselor. He said my husband needed to come with me to the meetings. He came to one meeting. The Counselor told us that his father had been an alcoholic and had died an alcoholic drinking Beer.

My husband did not believe he was an alcoholic because he drank only Beer. He argued with the Counselor saying drinking Beer did not make him an alcoholic. Anyone who drinks alcohol of any kind or form, beer or wine or hard liquor, in excess, is an alcoholic.

Buddy had gotten worse. He had a ride to and from work, which made him free to drink on his way home each day. Then he would always finish at least one six pack after Supper and then fall asleep in the middle of the Den floor watching TV.

Many things happened which I will not describe. But one of the things he did was to fall asleep while smoking a cigarette and caught our bed on fire. He could have burned the house down with us in it. That was the time my brother, Charlie and his family, were visiting from California. They personally saw the situation.

I decided it was time, and after they left, I filed for a Divorce. I knew what it might do to our children, but something had to be done. The Divorce was granted on December 31st after 18 years of marriage. I did not want our marriage to end while our children were still young, but I felt I had no other choice.

I was now working as the secretary in the Warrant Office when an opening was posted for a "Field Representative" with the DPS. I had no idea what it would be, but decided to put in my application for the job. After all, it paid a lot more than I was making as a Secretary. I said, "Why not?"

The interviews were being held in Austin. One of the Dispatchers I worked with also applied for the position. Our Captain was very proud that two of his people had been chosen from the State of Texas to interview for those new positions.

Only five people would be selected from Texas.

We had to furnish our own transportation to Austin for the interview. One of the Sergeants was going to Austin Headquarters on business and said he would take us with him.

I was interviewed by the Chief of Identification and Criminal Records and his Assistant. One of the questions they asked was, "Would I feel comfortable talking to the Police Chief of a large city, the same as I would talking to a Sheriff of a small county who had just come in from feeding his horses." My answer was "Yes." That's when I realized I had applied for a special job that required five positions to be filled for a Special Department to be formed and would be connected to the FBI in Washington. Until then, I thought it was some type of regular job.

The job required me to move my children from our home in Euless to Mineral Wells, Texas which is west of Fort

Worth. I was assigned to work with 32 Police Departments in those 32 counties and the Sheriff of each of those 32 counties. The largest Police Department I worked with was the Fort Worth Police Department.

I was trained by and traveled with two FBI Agents from Washington DC for two weeks each. We traveled around those 32 counties giving seminars to the employees of each Police Department and Sheriff's Office. There wasn't anything secret about the job. The FBI and the Government needed for all reporting to be the same from each agency and my job was to teach them to all report the same.

That information was compiled from all of the other States to reach the statistics that appear in the newspaper and on TV, advising if "Murder" or "Auto Theft" or "Bank Robbery" and several other crimes were up or down that year.

The main reason I applied for the job, not knowing what it consisted of, was the fact that I would be making more money. I didn't know the job also included a "Company Car" that came with the job, an expense account, which was nice and traveling over a large part of Texas.

I enjoyed my job, but some of the Troopers in the different cities found out I was making more money than they did, and seemed to resent me and treated me a little cool. This was not the usual reaction I received working with Troopers in the past. My thoughts were, they could have applied for the job just the same as I did.

Theresa had already graduated from High School when we moved. Denise and Michael attended school and made friends easily. One of their friend's Mother was a widow and wanted me to meet her. Her husband had been stationed at Fort Wolters, which was the Army Base at Mineral Wells. It was a Training Base for helicopter pilots during the Korean War and Vietnam War.

We became acquainted and she asked me to go with her to a "Special Place" which was someone's home that had been converted into a cafe and bar. The garage was now the pool room with three pool tables. The living room had a pinball machine in it in front of the fireplace. The "sun room" across the back of the house had a shuffle board in it. The kitchen was still a kitchen where they cooked Bar-B-Q for sandwiches and lunches.

The owner of this house had been in the Army and was one of the helicopter instructors. They were the type people that drew others to them. There was always a crowd at their home. Someone suggested to him, after he retired, that he should make his home into a "Special Place" and charge everyone for eating and drinking there. He did just that and named it "The Blade and Wing."

The word "Blade" stands for the blade of the helicopter. The word "Wing" stands for "Fixed Wing" which means an airplane with wings. There was an Officer's Club at the Army base in Lawton, Oklahoma with the same name. That's why he chose that name.

My friend and I stayed and talked with the owners because she and her husband had known them for a long time. Everyone that came into the place was a retired Army Officers. It was very nice and quiet and friendly.

We decided to try some Shuffleboard. I had never seen the game played, but I tried. Two gentlemen came in and asked to join our game. We did and had a nice evening playing Shuffleboard. I did not do too well. The two gentlemen were brothers. One had been a helicopter pilot and was retired from the Army and lived in Mineral Wells. The other was a carpenter and lived in Austin.

My job required me to travel every day of the week and contact four or five of the Police Departments and Sheriff Offices in my area. Therefore, come Monday morning, I was on the road again. I always came home off the road on Thursday if possible and contacted some of the local police departments on Friday.

The next Saturday night I decided to go back to The Blade and Wing and maybe play some games since I did not know anyone and did not have any friends in town. The brother that lived in Mineral Wells, Pat, was there and we played some games together.

Our friendship grew and he took me out to eat and dancing. As a Major in the Army and a helicopter pilot, he had been in two tours of Vietnam. He had also been stationed in Berlin, Germany for about twelve years.

While in Berlin, his duty was to patrol the American border of Berlin along the Russian border. American helicopters were not allowed to cross the border into the Russian zone. He said he knew he had NOT crossed into the Russian zone, but suddenly there were two Russian Migs, one on each side, waving for him to land.

He knew if he did not land, even though he was not in the Russian area, they would shoot him down. He was taken captive by the Russians and held for three months. Our government finally came to terms with the Russians and they released him and sent him back to Berlin.

We dated for quite some time, then he asked me to marry him. I accepted, not knowing what he had planned. Several months later he told me he had accepted a job in Tripoli, Libya to train their soldiers how to fly and maintaining helicopters.

He and several of his Army buddies left in November for Tripoli and I remained at my job with the DPS. He called me several times and wrote many letters to me. In June 1977 he returned for our wedding. Then we both flew away to Tripoli.

My two girls had finished school and had jobs. Nearly a year earlier, my son, Michael, told me he did not like living in Mineral Wells and asked me if he could live with his Dad. I did not want to force him to live with me, even though I had legal custody of him. Nevertheless, I granted him permission to live with his Dad in Euless where all of his friends were and the school he had attended.

My new husband, Pat, was making "huge money" working in Tripoli. I did not know he had talked to Dexter, the owner of the Blade and Wing, about selling it to him. Dexter was in bad health and needed to sell out and retire completely.

We returned to the States on January 1, 1978 and went back to Mineral Wells to buy the cafe and bar. That's not exactly what I had in mind to do, but he had set his mind to buy it, and did. I was naive and could not see what was in store for me.

Because he had not been a resident of Texas for six months, the license had to be put in my name. I had lived in Texas from the day I was born. With the license in my name, it meant that I would be responsible for making sure all the laws and regulations were kept. If not, I could be arrested, fined, and go to jail.

Ii was not long before my "dreams" were soon shattered. The restaurant and bar was open seven days a week. His only interest was sitting with his "old Army Buddies" and re-living the wars they had fought together. It was my job to take care of the business. After all, He Was Retired.

He began drinking very heavily which was against the law. The owners and the people serving the customers were not allowed to drink. He could have been arrested at any time, and I would have to pay the fine and whatever else the law required because the license was in my name.

His family lived in Kansas and was having a Family Reunion about a year after we opened. Naturally, he wanted us to go. I hired a man to be in charge while we were gone, thinking he could take care of everything. That was wrong!! There was a "Bad" fight on Friday night. I guess it's always the same. "When the cat is away, the mice will play."

They didn't play, they fought which is also against the law. I sure did have a surprise when I came back from Kansas. I was required to go to the office of the DPS Liquor Control Agent. He was in charge of issuing and canceling the liquor license. He was very stern and informed me that whatever occurred in my establishment was my responsibility.

It did not matter if I was in the vicinity or in another state. It was up to me to see that everything went according to the Law. I could be sentenced to "jail time" if it didn't. BUT, because nothing like that had ever happened before, he would let me off with a warning. Next time it would be different. Next time could have meant "Jail Time."

That was just the beginning of some very difficult times for me. I could not believe that I had left a marriage with a drinking husband, and walked into another with the same problems. I sure did need some help and guidance from God. The only problem with that was, I never asked Him. God lets us do whatever we please. He does not force us into anything.

Pat did not want to take any responsibility for running the business, and left it all up to me. I was also in charge of all the cleaning and moping, the cooking and serving the meals. He did take charge of barbecuing the meat and taking out the trash, and a few other minor details.

However, that did not work out too well. One night he drank too much and fell asleep and when he woke up, the $120 dollars worth of meat on the pit was ashes. That mean we had just lost $120 and there was no Bar-B-Que for the lunch menu.

We had not been in business for 6 months yet, and it was disastrous. We had to buy more meat and cook it.

The end of our first 6 months in business came on a Sunday. When I awoke that morning, I noticed he did not awake. I shook him and he still do not wake up. We had a man working at the club cleaning before we opened. I called him and he told me to call an ambulance.

I was in complete shock. I had never known or been around anyone who had those problems, not even my ex-husband. He had gone into the DT's from drinking too much vodka. He recovered from that time, but that would not be the last time. It would happen seven more times in the next sixteen years. My other husband had not caused me problems like this.

The business was doing well despite everything else. But after eight years we had to close. The economy and the city were going through some hard economic times, and so was our country. Several of the factories closed that we depended on for our "lunch runs." I cooked pinto beans and potato salad and sauce to go with our Bar-B-Que and was ready for the lunch run.

Then, one Monday in January 1988, I had everything ready for lunch and not one person came for lunch. It was not until Friday when one of our regular customers from the "lunch crowd" came in and I asked what had happened. He told me that their factory had shut down and so had another. They were without jobs.

We kept open until March and then we did not restock anything as it was sold out. We wanted to get the inventory as low as possible before we closed for good. That day did come and we sold the building (house) to a car dealership because the property had a very large parking lot and was on the main highway into the town.

During that eight years, we purchased a beautiful house with 3 ½ acres on the Brazos River, with a mortgage. Pat had his retirement pay, but that wasn't enough to pay the mortgage and all of our other expenses. The money we received from the sale of the business was applied to the mortgage, but it did not pay it in full.

We decided that each of us would look for jobs, and whoever was employed first would go to work and the other would stay at home and take care of the property. There were no available jobs for us in town.

My sister, Sandra was living in Mineral Wells also. She had gotten a job with the Government Office in Fort Worth. She told me they were hiring and filling different kinds of professions and that I should apply for a job. I did and got a job.

I worked for General Services Administration for three years. That meant a drive of 1 ½ hours each way to and from work. During the winter I left home while it was dark and returned home after dark. I did have a good job that paid well and worked with some very fine people.

The building was fourteen stories tall. Sandra and I did not work together, but we had lunch and had our coffee break together in the cafeteria. The cafeterias in all the Federal Buildings are leased to and operated by "The Blind." The law had been passed many years ago that allowed only "Blind" persons to lease the cafeterias.

My office was on the twelfth floor. I worked for Design and Construction. Our Department built all the Federal Buildings and repaired the Federal Judge's Offices in all Federal Court Buildings. Sandra worked on the fifth floor in the Accounting Department paying the bills. My daughter, Theresa, also obtained a job working there in the office where I was.

In January we talked about and we decided we wanted to have a Family Reunion on July 4th 1986. I knew our house on the Brazos River and all the acreage around it would be the perfect place for it. That's one of the reasons we bought it.

My nephew Terry, Sammie's son, had made a statement to me at the last funeral we all attended. He said that it was a shame we only got together at funerals and weddings and something should be done about it.

I thought it was time for our large family to get together and have a lot of laughs and enjoy each other. At that time, the family was scattered all over the States. Della was in Texas City, Sammie was in Houston, Charlie was in California, Sandra was in Fort Worth, Lynn was in Galveston, and Tommy was in Longview.

We made our plans for the 4th of July weekend and everyone came. Denise came from Colorado and brought her son, my first grandson Ryan, who was about 6 months old. We all had a wonderful time for about four days just playing games, telling jokes and stories. In fact, we had so much fun, we decided to have it again the next year and for several years thereafter. I had this beautiful home and land on the River, and my grandchildren could come and spend time with me in the summer, also in the winter.

My daughter Theresa was expecting her second child and had me to be on stand-by. I remember they took Emily, her first child, with them to the hospital and then called me. I did not live very far from the hospital and met them there to collect Emily.

I waited for the baby, Cynthia, to be born so I could see her, and also to let Emily see her. It was very early and was also Emily's school day. We were both tired and decided to go to my house and take a short nap.

Then I took her to school and told her teacher that if she fell asleep in class, "Please excuse her. She just received a new baby sister that morning." Now I had three grandchildren, Ryan, who was born on Halloween in 1985, and Emily in 1986, and Cynthia in 1991. Everything was good.

It was in April 1989 that my Mother died in Lonoke, Arkansas. She and her husband D.C. had been living in an "Assisted Living Apartment." My half sister, Patricia called me in January of that year to tell me that our Mother was in the hospital because the Alzheimer disease had gotten much worse.

It was earlier that same year that Sammie and Marie came to stay with us and help put the finishing touches on our house. They went with me to her funeral. After the funeral, we all went to Patricia's house and looked through many old pictures she had of Mother's family. All of Mother's children were there that were born to her and Bill Sullivan except for J.D.

They didn't know very many of the people in the pictures, but Sammie and I did. We had a nice time visiting with our siblings from the other family. We had only seen most of them occasionally as we all grew up.

After my husband, Pat, had the first encounter with the DT's, and would not stop drinking, he would go into the DT's about every two years. The Doctor had told him that the next time would possibly kill him. But, that did not stop him.

Those were horrible times for me, because I never knew when the next encounter would come. And it did come. The second one came on the 4th of July and I was told by the hospital attendant in Mineral Wells to take him to the hospital at Shepherd Air Force Base at Wichita Falls because he was retired military and they would treat him with no charge. Since he did not have any other health insurance, I knew that would be the best thing to do.

When we got to the emergency room at the Base, he was able to walk in and was fairly coherent. The attendant told me to take him around to the Lab and let them do his Lab Work. At the military hospitals, you take care of yourself. Anything you can and are able to do, you must do yourself. They don't cater to you.

I took him around to the Lab and while we were sitting waiting for the Technician to take his blood, his body stretched out like a board and he slid out of his chair onto the floor.

It was July 4th and the Lab area, and most of the Doctor's portion of the hospital, was deserted. I yelled for the Technician and he came to see what was happening. He was a very young man, probably in his first year in the Air

Force, and did not know what to do. He rang the emergency bell and it took only a second or two, and I saw the nurse from the Emergency Room running "full gallop" toward us and her attendants following behind her with the gurney.

They put Pat on the gurney and took him back to the Emergency Room. Then they put him in an examination room. I was there with him and he kept looking at me with a weird stare. Then he asked who I was. He did not know who I was, who he was, or where he was. That's what the DT's do to a person. The alcohol fries their brain and kills their body.

This was only the second time, the next six times would get progressively worse. He was tied in the bed because he was belligerent and they did not want him to hurt himself or someone else. Each stay got longer and longer and worse.

The seventh time would come in May 1995. We were planning a visit with our friends in Oklahoma and then continue on to Missouri to visit his sister. We had talked with both parties and made plans to leave the next morning.

He seemed okay that night, but around 11:00 pm. he went into the DT's. He was talking, but not coherently. He thought that Vietnamese helicopters were landing in our yard. He got out his pistol and was waving it around. That's when I really got scared. He was going to shoot those "helicopters in our yard" and called the police to tell them about it.

He had been on two tours during the war in Vietnam and all of those horrible experiences were coming back to him. I think he was trying to aim or load the pistol when it went off and he shot himself in the hand. At that instant, I ran out of the house and stood where I could see him through the windows, but he could not see me. The front of our house was all windows that gave a beautiful view of the Brazos River. But, this night, nothing was beautiful.

I was standing in the driveway, but still able to see into the house, when two bright headlights started down the driveway. It was a Deputy Sheriff responding to the call Pat had made, because the law required them to respond to any situation that might be violent.

He asked me what was happening and I tried to explain the situation to him. He asked me if Pat had any other guns in the house, and if so, where were they. I said there was a rifle in the pantry, and that Pat had put the piston into the kitchen sink. Pat was sitting on the kitchen floor and leaning against the cabinet holding his bleeding hand with a towel wrapped around it.

The Deputy asked me if I thought I could sneak into the house and retrieve the pistol without Pat seeing me. I said I thought I could and proceeded to do so and retrieved the pistol.

Now the situation was under control. The Deputy went in ahead of me to question Pat. He asked him how he got shot, and Pat answered that he was trying to shoot those helicopters landing in our yard. I'm sure the Deputy understood then what was going on. An officer does not go into a place where there has been a shooting without trying to "disarm" the situation. I had learned some of the laws while working with the Texas Department of Public Safety.

Pat proceeded to tell him how the helicopters were "zapping" him on his bare head and hurting him. The Deputy asked me if I thought he would be okay. I said,

"Yes" and the Deputy told me that he was leaving.

I was instructed to take him to the hospital the next day to have his hand X-rayed. I did, and there weren't any bones broken in his hand. They bandaged him and let him go home. Several months later, I tried to wake him one morning. I didn't know just what to do because he looked like he was sleeping. A friend of ours came to see us and I asked him to look at Pat and tell me what he thought.

While we were deciding, Pat rolled off the bed onto the cement floor. He was a bit too heavy for us to put him back in bed. I put a pillow under his head to make him as comfortable as I could.

He had fallen on the far side of the bed and a short distance from the closet door. That made it difficult to reach him. At that point, I called the ambulance.

When the ambulance attendants went into the bedroom and saw him on the floor, one asked me why I didn't get him up. I told him that Pat was not a large man but was too big for me to pick up. Then they tried to figure out how to get him up and out of that narrow space. I told them to roll him over on a sheet, and drag the sheet out into the open area where they could lift him up onto the stretcher. They did, and took him out to the ambulance.

I followed them to the hospital and when I entered the Emerge4ncy Room, I could hear him yelling. He was awake and "full into the D.T.'s" I called my daughter Denise to tell her the situation. I asked if she could hear him yelling over the phone and she said she could. That's how loud he was yelling. She came to the hospital that night. Later she returned home because there was nothing we could do for him now. He was in the hospital and they would take care of him.

The next day he was put into a room and restraints were used to tie him into the bed. If not, he would have gotten out of bed and hurt himself or someone else. He was completely incoherent now. He could not talk, only jabbered because the alcohol was now effecting his speech. Nothing about his body functioned properly now.

I went to see him on Sunday afternoon but did not stay very long because of the condition he was in. His eyes did not appear that he could see anything or anybody. He did not react to anything.

About 4:00 am Monday morning. the hospital called me to say that he had passed away. That seventeen years of my life were now ended. I had a funeral to plan. It was May 25, 1995. He was retired military and that meant everything needed to be done military style.

After the news spread about his death, one of the dearest memories I have was that I looked up from my chair in the living room and saw my Banker and his wife at my front door with a dish of food. I'm sure other people came, but the one I did not expect, came.

Later I told my banker what that meant to me. My Banker had always tried to be a friend to me, but now he became someone special to me. I don't think he ever knew how much that small gesture meant to me. It's not always the big things people do for you that you remember. It's the small gestures of kindness during a bad situation that stay in your memories. All these many years later, I can still see him and his wife coming through my door. Several years later I called him and told him how I appreciated him.

It was a little easier for me because Pat had decided back in January to be buried in Texas at the cemetery where several of his military friends were buried, instead of at the military cemetery in Kansas. Even though he was Catholic, the funeral service was held in the funeral home and was a standard service.

I know his family did not approve of the service, but I had no one there to help me plan a Catholic service. The service at the Cemetery was conducted by the Army with Taps blown and the rifles fired. All of his military friends who lived in the area were there. One of his very dear friends helped me with the military paperwork. He looked and saw that Pat had not added me to his military benefits which meant I would not receive any of his retirement pay or anything else.

Some of the men he served with called me long distance to find out if there was anything they could help me with or anything I needed. The military was taught to "Take care of their own."

I had the only person that I needed and the one who could help me to get back on the road God had set before me. Long after the friends and relatives are gone, the most important person in anyone's life is JESUS. It was for me and I thank You Father for Jesus. He has been with me ever since because He said He would never leave me or forsake me. I love You, Jesus.

CHAPTER 26

THE DEATH OF SAM THE CHURCH BUILDER AND HIS LADY

Many years go Dad's business had failed and at the prompting of his sister, Kate and her husband, he moved the family to Galveston because they told him they were sure he could get a job at the wharves where Uncle Artis worked.

I know my Aunt Kate and her husband Uncle Artis, and because they had told my Dad to come to Galveston, they were praying for him all the time and were sure God would answer their prayers. Dad did what they advised and packed up the family that was left and headed for their new home in about 1956.

I believe the only children still living at home were Tommy, Jackie, Sandra, and Lynn. The other four children were grown, married, or in the military. Dad got a job as night watchman on the wharves, with God's help, just as Aunt Kate had told him.

I'm not sure of the date, but I believe it was about 1972 or 1973 when our Step Mom started having stomach pains and problems in her lower abdominal area. She went to the doctor, and after many tests, the doctor told her she had stomach cancer and Hodgkin's disease.

Hodgkin's disease is cancer of the lymph glands. Since we all have lymph glands all over our body, the diagnosis was that she had cancer all over her body. The doctors began radiation treatments and chemotherapy on her immediately. Those treatments made her terribly ill and only extended her life about 3 or 4 years.

She had a "rally" as the doctors called it and was without pain for a year. During that time, Jackie and his wife Norma took her on a vacation with them. They went to New Mexico, Colorado, Arizona, and California. I know they wanted to do something special for her because she had been so good to us. She had a grand time, but it would be her last vacation.

Shortly after their return she began to have the same "old symptoms" again, but worse. This time she would spend most of the time in the hospital. This happened while was employed by the DPS. Sandra's husband, Don was in the Army and stationed at Fort Richie, Maryland. Charlie was in the Army and stationed at Fort Ord, California. Jackie was working for Tex Star Plastics in Arlington. Sammie was working as an Engineer in Houston. Tommy was a barber in Longview.

Both Sandra and Charlie decided to take a leave and come to Galveston to see her before it was too late. Jackie and I would travel together to see her and stay with her at the hospital on weekends. Tommy would come from Longview alone.

In the final year of her life, while taking the treatments, she would be admitted into the hospital for one week while they built up her body and strength and then she was given the treatments for one week.

After the treatments she would remain in the hospital while they built up her strength again in order for her to go home for one week. Then the process would start all over again.

During the last stages the doctors did not think she would make it many times, and Dad would call us. We would immediately leave our jobs and head for Galveston. She was in the John Sealy Hospital, which is one of the best Cancer Prevention and Research hospitals in the United States. We knew she was getting excellent care.

Since Sammie and his wife Alene lived in Houston, Alene would go to the hospital and stay for a week at a time. The rest of us would go for only a day or two at a time because we had our jobs and could not be away for more than a couple of days without taking leave. She would seem to get better after a day or two, but that never lasted long. Then it was the same thing again.

I returned home after one of those hasty trips to the hospital. I was still married to Buddy at that time and living in our house in Euless. He was out on the patio, so I went out to tell him I was home. He looked up at me and said, "I hope you're not planning to do this every week-end." He was upset because I had depended on him to take care of our three children while I was away.

His words cut me to the bone. I could not believe that anyone, especially him, the father of our children, could be so inconsiderate and unfeeling. We would be divorced before her death. But, he did come to her funeral. When I asked him why, he said, "I did love her, too." That was hard for me to believe considering the way he had acted while she was in the hospital.

Sandra and Charlie both decided they had used up their leave after a month and made plans to go back home. Charlie was studying to be a Doctor and asked for a consultation with her head doctor to discuss her condition. The Doctor told him it was very difficult to predict her condition at that time, saying she might live for a week or a month or longer. It was very hard for him to say. Therefore, Charlie and Sandra decided to go home. Charlie flew to California and Sandra flew to Maryland on Friday, July 27th.

I had already made plans to be at home on that July 29th weekend. Sunday, July 30th was Dad and our Step Mom's thirty-third wedding anniversary.

The next phone call I received from Dad was on Monday, August 1st when he told me she had died. I was very disappointed at myself because I was not there. But that wasn't the worst of the situation. Charlie and Sandra had spent all of their money for plane tickets home.

Sandra called me and I sent her the money for a ticket to come back. Charlie called the Red Cross and they provided him with a ticket because he was in the military and he had a death in his family.

The funeral home made arrangements to bring her back to Longview for the services which were held at the Gum Springs Baptist Church east of Longview. Her mother and father, and her stepdad, were buried in the cemetery there.

I believe all of my brothers and sisters were there. I did not take count of who was there. I only know that the little church was full. She was buried next to her mother and stepdad.

The Red Cross had also paid Charlie's fare back home. Sammie's son, James Terry, had driven down from Washington D.C. where he was stationed in the Army. Sandra rode with him back to Maryland, which was on his way.

The children who had moved with Dad and her to Galveston were all on their own now. That meant Dad was now living alone at age 73. He traveled around and spent time with his children. He went once to California and stayed with Doctor Charlie and helped him "fix-up" his new Clinic.

My Dad had suffered with asthma all of his adult life, but it did not kill him. I would call him occasionally and wait for him to answer the phone. The only thing I heard on the other end was "gasping." Then I would say, "Dad, just sit back and let me do the talking. When you are able to talk, then you can join in."

I would tell him all the things that were happening with me and my children, and how they were doing in school. As they grew older, I would tell him about their marriage and their children. He always loved to hear about his grandchildren.

Our youngest brother, Lynn, and his wife were living in Dallas near his wife's family. Dad sold the house in Galveston and went to live with them in Dallas. He spent most of his time in bed. He wasn't one who liked to exercise or fish or hunt. The only thing he really enjoyed was reading – encyclopedias or history books.

At one of our Family Reunions, he requested we have a meeting about him. He complained that Lynn and Linda would not let him have the cookies and ice cream in his bedroom like he wanted. We all agreed that he should have a small refrig-erator in his bedroom to keep his milk and ice cream in and to satisfy him.

Our family grew up drinking milk. When I was small, and even today, I still drink milk with my meals. Dad liked ice tea, but he still enjoyed a glass of milk with his meals sometimes and with his cookies.

I believe he may have lived with Lynn and his family for about ten years. Then Tommy and his wife, Shirley, came to visit him at Lynn's and said he was very welcome to come and live with them in White Oak.

After thinking about it and discussing it, he decided that was what he wanted to do. Tommy and Shirley both worked, which mean he would be at home alone in the daytime. They were quite active in their church and would take Dad to church with them to the night services and Sunday services.

They told me that they had left him at home alone one night while they went to church. When they returned home, they could not find him immediately. Then they heard him and found him wedged into a small space between the kitchen range and the side cabinet. They did not know how long he had been there.

He had also begun to eat strangely. Shirley said he had eaten half of two loaves of bread. It was becoming evident that Dementia was coming on him. The doctors told us that his brain was not telling him that his stomach was full.

It agreed that the best and safest place for him was in the Pine Tree Nursing Home. He would have someone taking care of him 24 hours a day. They would feed him, give him his medicine, and make sure he did not wander off alone. He would be safe there and well cared for.

At this time, I was living in Mineral Wells and Sandra and Denise were living in the Fort Worth area.

For his birthday, I don't remember which one, but it had to be in his late eighties, the three of us, along with Denise's son Ryan, decided to take him a Birthday Cake. Ryan was about four years old. The Nursing Home let us use the dining room to serve his cake. A lot of the patients gathered around to have some of the cake. The attendants were watching the patients because some of them were not allowed to have "sweets."

Dad sat and watched Ryan run back and forth across the room. He seemed fascia-nated watching Ryan and kept saying over and over, "That's my boy. That's my boy." The other patients were also watching Ryan. It seems they all loved to see little children.

On my next to the last visit to see him, I took him a pint of my home made plum jelly that he liked so well. He had finished his breakfast earlier and was sitting on the side of his bed. He had a tray next to his bed and reached for a spoon. Then he opened the jar and began eating the jelly from the jar without any bread.

I asked him if he would prefer to have some bread with the jelly and he said that it was okay just like that. He ate half of the pint. It made me shudder to watch him eat all that "sweet jelly" without any bread.

The last time I visited him, he did not know who I was. He thought I was the lady that lived down the street from our house in Longview. That would be the house he built for us to live in on Culver Street, which he had sold over twenty years earlier.

He said to me. "Kate (his sister) took Mama and Daddy Jim to my house and left them there. I don't know why she did that." I told him his Mama (Mamaw) had died long ago and so did Kate. His reply was, "Well, no one ever told me."

It broke my heart because he did not know who I was. I knew it was the Dementia working in him. I was living in Mineral Wells at that time and had driven about 200 miles to see him, but those days would soon be over.

He made that journey to see his Daddy that he had only known for a short time on 12 September 1991 from the Pine Tree Nursing Home at age 88 years. The nurse told us that he had eaten a good breakfast and lay back down to take a nap.

He had raised 8 children and taught them the ways of the LORD. He had many grandchildren and great-grandchildren. My grandson Ryan, who was about four years old at the time, was riding in our car after we left the cemetery. He asked me where great-granddaddy was going. I tried to explain that he had gone to heaven. Ryan began to cry and said, "I want to go with Great-granddaddy."

I told him he couldn't go, because where Great-granddaddy was going, he wasn't coming back. Little did we know at the time that Ryan would go to meet his Great-granddaddy only twelve years later. Ryan was the "apple of his Great-granddaddy's eye and the pride of our family. He was my first and only grandson.

We laid him to rest at the Gum Springs Cemetery next to His Lady. That cemetery has become our Family's final resting place. We had already buried his son Jackie, my brother, there in 1985 and my "Uncle Junior," my Step Mom's brother in 1988.

As the years have pass now, and I have finished writing this book, we have buried or sprinkled the ashes of Sammie, Della, Jackie, Sandra, and Lynn all together around Dad and our Step Mom's grave.

CHAPTER 27

STORIES OF MY CHILDREN, STARTING WITH DENISE DIANE

Denise Diane was my first born, born to me and her father Buddy. Since we were addicted to bowling, it should not have been a surprise that she was born on our Bowling Night, Tuesday night, and at the same time our league started, 7:00 pm.

Actually, I had been to a Bowling Tournament in Galveston, Texas and began having some bleeding. That was in May of 1959. The weather was rainy and cold for May so I contributed my problem to the weather.

When I returned to Euless where we were moving into our new home, I went to my doctor. Much to my surprise, he told me I was pregnant. That was something Buddy and I had wanted and were very pleased to hear. The doctor advises me to cut my bowling back to only one night a week.

The people in my bowling league said I should not be bowling at all. I asked my doctor again and he said that anything I was doing when I became pregnant was okay for me to continue in moderation.

I was Secretary of our Tuesday Night Bowling League at the Cotton Bowling Palace in Dallas, Texas, so I decided I would discontinue my membership in all of the other bowling leagues except that one. We were living in our new home in Euless and I was working in Dallas. That meant I had a 30-45 minute drive one way each day.

I went to work that Tuesday morning, and had a terrible back ache that caused me to double over my typewriter. I had no idea that the back ache was a sign my baby was getting ready to be born because no one had told me about it. My baby wasn't due, according to what my doctor said, for about four or five more weeks.

By ten o'clock that morning the pain was getting worse. I called my doctor and he told me to come to his office immediately. His office was in Dallas and across from Baylor Hospital and was about twenty minutes away. When I arrived, he examined me and said that I was in the first stages of labor and for me to go across the street to the hospital.

Then I told him I was there alone. I called Buddy from the doctor's office and told him what was happening. He said that he had ridden to work with Pete Moore and could not come until after work that night. He was working in Arlington, Texas.

My doctor said for me not to worry, but to drive across the street and park my car in the parking lot of the hospital and go in by the Emergency Room Entrance.

The attendant in the Emergency Room had the funniest look on her face when I told her I needed to be admitted. She asked me about my husband and I told her he was at work, but would be along later.

I was admitted and when the doctor came in later with his nurse to examine me, she laid her hand on my thigh and looked at the doctor and said that I had very strong legs. You see, that was from all the bowling I did.

Since we did not show up at our Bowling League that night, they presumed something was wrong – or good. She was born at eight o'clock on Tuesday night of December 15, 1959. Our Bowling League always started at eight o'clock on Tuesday night.

This was ten days before Christmas. I had done most of my shopping, but that had to come to a stop. I finished my shopping in January. No one complained because they were excited about the new baby.

It was in January, on a Sunday, when she was 13 months old and I had put her in her roll-a-round walker. The weather was fairly nice that day. She loved to sit at the sliding glass doors that led onto the patio and watch the wind blow the trees. There was a slight breeze and I had opened the sliding glass doors.

On Friday, I had taken her to the doctor for her check-up, and everything seemed to be okay. On Saturday she was watching the wind blow the trees in our back yard. But, by Sunday morning she did not respond when I tried to wake her up. I contacted her baby doctor in Arlington and he told us to bring her into his office at one o'clock and he would meet us there. This happened on a Sunday. Doctors don't go to their office on Sunday.

She was running a fever of 103-104 degrees. The doctor said she had pneumonia, but he did not think it necessary to admit her to the hospital because her breathing was normal. We took her back home and watched her very carefully while I prayed. She came through that ordeal okay after several days.

I have already told you about her experience at the birthday party when she was five years old. It was the one that one of the mothers from the church was having for her child and the one that their Dad, Buddy, had taken Denise, Michael, and Theresa to and left them there. Denise had thrown-up in the car before arriving at the party and after she arrived.

When she was 2 ½ years old, we welcomed another daughter into our family. She was the daughter of my sister Della. Theresa Joy was her name. We picked her up in the parking lot of the Court House in Texas City on Friday, July 31, 1962.

I was also pregnant with my second child. It would be a boy, Michael Dennis and would be born to us in February of 1963.

Christmas came around in 1962 and while I was shopping with Denise and Theresa, and had slightly overdone it, I began to feel faint. I had waited in the check-out line too long. As we were walking toward the door of the store, I tried to hurry so I could sit down in my car, but I didn't make it.

I crumpled into a big ball on the floor. When I opened my eyes, Denise and Theresa were standing over me crying, "Mother's dead! Mother's dead!" The store manager was leaning over me also and asking if I was okay, or should he call an ambulance? I assured him I was okay and just needed to get on home.

As the girls grew older and were in school, I would make them nice lunches and put them into pretty polka-dot bags. Months later while I was working around the Holly bush bed, cleaning out grass, I saw some pink and green things behind bushes. I pulled them out, and much to my surprise, they were Denise's lunch bags with the sandwich and cookies still in them.

When I questioned her, she said she didn't like the sandwiches, but took out the fruit to eat. She didn't tell me until many years later that the smell of the bologna made her feel sick. If she had told me, I would have given her something else.

Denise would be the child that would get sick on vacations. My brother, Sammie's daughter Brenda was getting married in Illinois on Valentine's Day. My Step Mom had come up from Galveston to go with us.

We had traveled through Springfield, Missouri when I noticed some "white fluffy stuff" in the fields. I thought it was cotton that had fallen on the ground. BUT, much to my surprise, it was SNOW! Then my Step Mom looked back at Denise who was laying in the back of the station wagon on a quilt. She looked at me and said, "I think Denise has the chicken pox." But, upon closer observation, we decided it was the three-day measles. Since we were over half way, we decided to go on to the wedding. During the remainder of the trip she was okay.

She couldn't be having the chicken pox, because she had them when she was only six months old. Buddy and I had gone with his Mother, Step Dad, and Aunt Nellie to visit his sister Dorothy and her husband, Ken, and children, at Fort Walton Beach, Florida.

Ken was in the Strategic Air Command Branch of the Air Force. He was required to live on the base for seven days and then he could go home for seven days. Their duty was to keep some of their planes in the air around the clock.

We were there for a week and on our last day the youngest of their daughters came down with the chicken pox. All of the girls had been playing with Denise on a quilt pallet on the floor. I was concerned that Denise might get the chicken pox also. Everyone said that she was too young to catch anything.

When we returned home, I called Denise's doctor. He advised that most babies are immune until after they are six months old. Naturally, she would turn out to be the exception and broke out with the chicken pox. The doctor said that since she was as young as she was, it would be to her advantage. She did not know how to scratch and scratching leaves scars.

Then there was the three day road trip to California to see my brother, Charlie, and his wife, Deanna, and their three girls. We were ending our first day when Denise began to complain about her ears hurting. We stopped at several pharmacists along the way for medicine or ear drops, but nothing helped.

Once we arrived at Charlie's, I told him what had happened. He said he would take her to the hospital where he worked the next day. He did and registered her as his daughter. The doctor there gave him some medicine for her, and after a day or two she was fine again.

When she was in her "Teens" she graduated to "Hair Dos." She asked Theresa to give her a little "feathering" or the "wispy look." Then she asked her cousin,

Shannon, to give her a "spiral perm" either right before or right after she graduated from cosmetology school. That turned out to be an "Afro do."

Then there was her cousin, Wesley, the hair stylist, who could have been a stand-in for Johnny Depp. He asked her to be one of his models at a hair show in Dallas. He needed ten models. Her Cousin Shannon would wash their hair.

Denise and Theresa both volunteered to be models for him. Denise's hair looked great – short on one side and long on the other. She said she never could make her hair look like it did when Shannon or Wesley did it.

In spite of everything, she did grow up. I got my promotion with the Texas Department of Public Safety and moved my family to Mineral Wells, Texas on the west side of Fort Worth. There she met Alan Lewis and they were married at a little Baptist Church. Alan's Mom and I both attended the wedding.

Alan's Dad was a retired Army helicopter pilot who was now working in Colo-rado, so they decided to move to Colorado. One of the reasons was that after our vacation to Colorado, Denise decided that was where she wanted to live.

She became pregnant and I received the phone call on Halloween night that I was Grandmother to a beautiful baby boy whom they named Ryan Alan Lewis. I had wanted to be there, but it wasn't possible because I was working. When he was a year old, I did make the trip and stayed for a week. Denise was separated from Alan by that time, so I stayed with Ryan during the day while she worked.

Denise was asked to do a Television Commercial for one of the Clothing Stores there in Grand Junction, Colorado. I took Ryan with me to watch the filming. I knew that if he saw his Mother, he would cry for her. I kept his stroller pointed in the opposite direction so he could not see her or hear her.

In the commercial, she was supposed to be shopping with "Her Dad" at the Store. He seemed to be a very nice man. The commercial turned out well. I have a copy of it.

Everyone told her that she needed to return to Texas so she would be near her family and we could help her take care of Ryan. Finally she did move back. She took Ryan to an eye specialist to have his eyes checked because it appeared he could not see – or at least very well.

I believe the doctors explained that the nerves that controlled one of his eyes was very weak and caused him to have a form of "lazy eye." The operation helped him to see better.

Occasionally he had to wear a patch over the "good eye" forcing him to use his "weak eye.". He did not like that at all, because he still could not see well out of his "weak eye." He would cry every time he had to wear the patch.

At this time, my husband, Pat, and I were living in Mineral Wells at our home on the Brazos River. On weekends, and whenever she needed me, I would keep Ryan for her. One day my neighbor called me on the phone to tell me that "a little boy was standing in my yard crying." It was hard to hear the outside noises from inside my house.

I looked out and there was Ryan standing about ten feet from the back door crying. He was wearing the patch over his good eye and could not see which way to go. I felt so sorry for him, but it was necessary for him to wear the patch over his "good eye." He knew when we put the patch on that he would not be able to see as well.

One Summer while he was staying with us for a week, we decided to have "siding" put on our house. Theresa's daughter Emily was also staying with us for a week.

The man who was putting the siding on was named Dave. I noticed that he would stop his work quite often and play cars with the children in the sand pile where I was building my patio. I complained to Pat that Dave was "goofing off" when he should have been working. He spoke to him and found out that Dave was not paid by the hour, but by the job.

After Dave finished for the day, sometimes he would come in and talk with me. I found out that he had been raised in a Christian home and I was very pleased. I told Denise, one Friday afternoon, that I was cooking spaghetti for the kids and the "siding man" was going to stay for dinner. I wanted her to eat with us also and meet the "siding man." Denise and Dave both lived in Fort Worth, and she wasn't dating anyone at that time.

She did, and they did, and he asked her for a date. I was told they went "mudding" in his jeep. Denise said she really had a good time. The next weekend, when she came to get Ryan, he asked her what she had been doing. She told him she had been "mudding" with Dave in his jeep. Ryan got very angry and said, "Dave is My Friend." We all knew then that Ryan approved of Dave, so later when they got married the day after Thanksgiving in 1998, Ryan was very happy. He had the Father he had never known.

Dave said he had always wanted to be in Scouts, so he enlisted Ryan in Scouts and became one of the Den Fathers. Dave went with them on every expedition. Dave became the "Perfect Father" for Ryan. When Ryan was old enough to pick up "scraps of metal," Dave would take him on his jobs as helper and pay him.

Ryan said one day that he wanted a sister or brother. Denise's Dad, Buddy, was living with them now because he had a stroke and could not take care of himself very well. He could barely talk. Denise said she was not ready to have another child because she already had her hands full taking care of the three of them.

Eventually her Dad died and Denise decided it would be a good time to have another baby. Haleigh Michelle Tober was born February 3, 1998 in Fort Worth, Texas. This time I was there for the birth and helped Ryan welcome his new baby sister. We were all happy to welcome our new baby girl. Ryan was twelve years old now and loved his baby sister very much. He hurried home from school every day to play with her. He would swing her around like a rag doll.

At the end of his Junior year in High School, he had his picture made in May for his Senior year in High school that would begin in August. He had been enrolled in "Auto Mechanics" which taught him about repairing cars. He was also working part time while going to school at the Blockbuster Movie Rental Store.

He was now wearing Contact Lens and no longer needed to wear a patch over his "good eye." He was in his second week as a Senior in High School and spent the afternoon of August 24, a Sunday, with his family watching a movie. He took the movie back to Blockbuster and saw a friend of his while driving home. I presume they motioned to each other "to race." and they did. That's just what boys did at that time – race up and down the streets. This was in North Richland Hills in Fort Worth on Ruff Snow Drive. I am sure they were both going pretty fast when Ryan's car ran into so loose gravel on the road where there had been some construction. This caused his car to be "air born" and when it stopped it was wrapped around a utility pole that had a cement base. He was killed instantly.

He had brought great joy to our family on October 31, 1985 and departed too soon on August 24, 2004. The service was held at the Baptist Church in North Richland Hills where he had been Baptized a short time earlier in May. His best friend, Steve's Grandfather, was pastor of the church and performed the ceremony.

The church was full and overflowing down the street. Everyone that came could not get into the church. All of his classmates were there, as well as his family and friends. He was well loved and respected.

God's Word tells us in Mark 10:19 "The devil comes not, but for to steal, kill, and destroy." He killed my Grandson and destroyed our happiness. But I do have joy in knowing that Ryan is with his Great-Granddad now. That's where he told me he wanted to go that day after his Great-Granddad's funeral and we were leaving the cemetery.

Even with that comfort, the grieving is still there today because we miss him so much. He was a jewel to us and we will never know what he might have accomp-lished in his lifetime if he had lived longer. He was very smart and on the National Honor Society roll in Senior High School.

Denise was having some health problems as well as problems at her job when they decided to move to Kilgore to be near me and my husband Gene. By doing that, we were able to see our Granddaughter, Haleigh, grow up next door. Thanks Denise for sharing Ryan and Haleigh with us.

I would name my children, but either they or friends and relatives would put an alias name on them. Denise's names were D. D., De De, Nisey, or Aunt Nisey.

THERESA JOY

I will start my story about Theresa Joy by relating to you what she wrote to be put in our "Big Family Book" that I put together several years ago. I asked each of my family to write something for "The Book" and this what she wrote. She titled it "Coming Home."

I don't remember the exact date, but I do remember the day. I remember pulling into a parking lot and seeing a lone car parked in the middle of the lot. It looked very lonely sitting there all by itself.

I don't remember the exchange or the going from my foster home to my new home. I just remember the image of that big car siting in the parking lot all by itself.

My Mom said I had some questions when I got in the car with them. She said I asked her, "You're my aunt, aren't you?" She told me, "Yes" and I called her Mom from that day forward. That was the beginning of my new life. A new Mom and Dad and a new sister.

"A Surprise Visit" My Birthday is July 15th. Every year my Mom would take me and a friend to Six Flags for my birthday. It was always a fun time. When I turned 16, I decided that I wanted to do something different that year for my birthday. I asked my Mom if we could go to Grandma's for my birthday. Of course she said, "Yes we could." I remember hearing her call Grandma and telling her we were coming and asking if she would order a cake for my birthday.

If we were going to Galveston, we would always leave on Friday night after Mom got off work. This was no different; we left when Mom got home and arrived in Galveston about 10:30 pm. I am sure.

Grandma was always waiting up for us when we arrived, and this trip was no different. The next morning we got up to cinnamon rolls and Mom and Grandma had coffee. As we were sitting at the kitchen table, there was a knock at the front door. Everyone was still in their pajamas. I told

Grandma I would get the door. I thought it was the kids from next door wanting us to come over and play.

I walked into the front room where Grandma's bed and dresser were. I could see the front door from the mirror on the dresser, and when I looked up there was a man and woman coming in the door. I immediately turned around and told Grandma I didn't know who it was.

When she appeared in the doorway to the kitchen, my Grandma asked, "Della, how are you?" You could have knocked me over with a feather!!! There stood my birth mother that I had been thinking about and searching to learn about for years.

My Mom made me get a bath and get ready to run errands. We went to pick up my birthday cake and to visit Mamaw and Aunt Kate. When we got back to the house, Della and her friend were still there.

I remember later that evening asking my Mom if I could spend the night with Della and she said, "NO!!" I didn't understand that at the time and was very angry. I was not able to spend the night, but today I am very grateful for my Mother and Father.

Author….Theresa Joy Llewellyn Welch

It had been on a Friday, July 31, 1962, 16 days after her fifth birthday, when we parked in the parking lot of the Court House in Texas City and waited for the foster mother to bring Theresa to us.

We were not allowed to go to the foster parents' home. She had all of Theresa's clothes in a box and put them on the back seat. She told us that Theresa was easily scared. We were instructed to never raise our hands up over our head because she would think we were going to hit her.

Immediately upon arriving home, I inspected her clothes. I found that the hems of all of her dresses had been let out to hang below her knees. The family she had stayed with were very religious and believed that girl's dressed should always cover their knees. I love the LORD, too; but I think this was a little too much. I immediately raised the hems to strike above the knees. After all, she was only five years old.

In February of the next year, our family was enlarged to three with the birth of my son Michael.

By the beginning of the next school year, Theresa was six years old and ready to start in First Grade. I was a little concerned because Della now knew where she lived. I thought she might come and try to take her away with her. I was not working at the time and took her to school each day and picked her up afterwards.

She did very well in school. In First Grade the students invited their parents to come and have lunch with them and stay for the afternoon session. I went and after lunch was Story Time. Much to my amazement, her teacher let her read from the "Big Book."

Afterwards, I asked her teacher why she was allowed to read from the Big Book because it was very clear that she didn't know all the words. The teacher said that she read very well and the words she did not know, she would "slur" over them. The other children in the class did not notice this, and after all, it was after lunch and most of the students fell asleep while Theresa was reading the story.

She came home from school when she was about 15 or so years old, and informed everyone that she did not want to be called "Theresa" anymore. She now wanted to be called "Terry." You might note that I always called my children by their birth names, not nick-names. That's just the way I am.

It was during a visit from Sammie's son, James Terry, that he noticed she was being called "Terry" now. He quickly informed her that "Terry" was his name and she was trying to "steal" it.

We all went through some very trying times with our children growing up. At Christmas, I believe it was during her senior year of school, she came bounding through the door and told me her boy friend, Tim, had given her a "promise ring." I almost fainted, because I thought it was an engagement ring. Later, I was told the difference.

She graduated from Trinity High School in Euless. After she graduated from High School I received my promotion with the DPS and we all moved to Mineral Wells. She immediately found a job and went to work. It seems she would come home every few weeks and tell me she had quit her job. Then she would immediately get another. I told her that pretty son she wouldn't be able to get a job in Mineral Wells because she would have worked at every establishment there and no one would rehire her.

During her childhood, she was very afraid of thunder storms, as were Denise and Michael, also. One night, while my husband was away on business, the thunder was very loud and the three of them came running down the hall and jumped in the middle of my bed. What a surprise!!!

After Theresa was married and living in Jacksboro, she called me one night because she was afraid of the storm. I don't know what she expected me to do because she was thirty miles away from me. I don't know if she ever grew out of it or not, but she didn't call me during the storms anymore.

She had married Emil Kaster who lived in Mineral Wells, and then they presented me with a beautiful granddaughter, Emily Diane Kasten. But that marriage was not to last and they were divorced.

One night, while they were waiting for the divorce to be final, Emil came to see me and my husband Pat. Emil told us that they were getting a divorce and he had a big concern about Emily. He asked if we would watch over and protect her as best we could. We said, "Don't worry. It will be our pleasure and duty. We will see that she is taken care of." That was a pledge I took and will honor it until the day I die no matter how old Emily gets.

Then Theresa married Ernest Welch who lived in Mineral Wells. They presented me with another beautiful granddaughter, Cynthia Denise Welch. I am very proud of all of my beautiful grandchildren and love them dearly. Theresa's alias is Terry.

MICHAEL DENNIS

Michael Dennis is my one and only son. He was born on the 9th of February 1963, at 6 am on Saturday morning.

The day before, Friday, I had been preparing dinner for Buddy's sister, Dorothy, and her husband Ken and their girls. They were coming in from Shreveport to visit Buddy and Dorothy's mother, who lived in Fort Worth. We were expecting them to stop at our house in Euless because it was on the way, but they did not.

I had cleaned house all day, because I thought my house should be spotless from top to bottom even if our company would be staying for just an hour or two. For some reason, for which I never learned, they did not stop, but went straight to her Mother's home in Fort Worth.

At about 9 pm my water broke as I was washing dishes. We did not have a dish-waster in those days. Everything was washed by hand. Euless was a small town and Doctor Warren didn't live very far from our house.

We called Doctor Warren and he told me to get into bed and await his arrival. He was going to come to our house and check me to determine if I needed to go to the hospital. After he checked me, he said it was time to go to the hospital, but there was no need to hurry.

We went to Arlington Memorial Hospital in Arlington because that was the nearest hospital, and also the one Dr. Warren used. About 3 am Saturday morning, Doctor Warren seemed upset because Michael was not ready to come on the scene, so he went into another room to lie down. Michael did arrive about 6 am.

Buddy had an Aunt Nellie who had lived with his mother in Fort Worth for many years. Actually, she was of no relation, but had been a friend of his mother for so long that she just seemed to be part of the family. She came to the hospital to see me and the baby. When she saw him he was sleeping on his stomach. She said "Hi," and he raised up his head and looked at her. She always remembered and spoke about that time and how astonished she was that he had raised his head and looked straight at her and he was only a day old.

Buddy's sister, Dorothy, and her husband never did came to see our new baby.

Buddy's mother's name was Dena. She and Tom Glink had been dating for about twenty years when they finally got married. She loved our children and came to visit and help me around the house when Michael was about six months old. She noticed that Michael had a terrible diaper rash. She asked me what soap I was using to wash his diapers. She thought the soap might have been the cause of his diaper rash because the rash imprinted the diaper on his bottom. I changed to a soap named "Dreft" which was especially used for delicate fabrics and the diaper rash cleared up immediately.

From then on I had to wash his clothes separately from the other laundry because he would break out all over his body if I used our regular laundry soap. I washed his sheets with the other clothes once and his cheeks looked raw because he was a little baby and rubbed his cheeks against the sheets.

After that, I always washed all of his clothes and sheets in "Dreft" and that solved the rash problem. This lasted until he was about seven years old when he finally outgrew the rash problem and I was able to wash his clothes with the other laundry.

He was about three years old, and it was on a Sunday afternoon, when he came into the kitchen where I was cooking, and I saw red on his face. I thought he had gotten into my purse and my lipstick and painted his face.

Of course, I was pretty upset and yelled at him all the way back to my bedroom and on into my bathroom looking for my purse. I saw the mess he had made in the bathroom sink with red smeared all over it. But upon closer inspection, I discovered it was red blood.

He had climbed up on the toilet seat and then into the sink and was able to reach his Daddy's razor in the medicine cabinet. He then proceeded to shave. I turned to look at him and almost had a heart attack. He had sliced the skin off of both cheeks and it was blood all over his face and in the sink, NOT lipstick.

I called to my husband and he said the best thing to use was after shave lotion. Of course that was the worst thing and set him on fire. He screamed and cried. We "doctored" his face the best that we could with him screaming all the time. That night, he was not able to lay in bed with his face touching the sheet or pillow.

Weeks later, when his face had healed, we would ask him if he wanted to shave again. He would yell, "NO." I did not want to be mean. I just did not want him to forget what happens when he sneaked and use Dad's razor.

His Dad moved his razor to the top shelf in the linen closet which was next to the ceiling. We were sure it was out of his reach now.

I don't know if he was curious or mischievous. My husband had brought a jar of carpet cleaner home for us to use. He put it on the window sill over the kitchen sink where it would be out of reach from the children, so he thought.

Much to our surprise, Michael pulled a chair up to the sink, got into the sink, and reached the jar of cleaning fluid. When we saw what he had done, he had the jar up to his mouth. We both yelled at him and he put the jar down.

We were not sure if he had drank any of the liquid, but we didn't want to take any chances. We made him drink raw eggs, and everything we could think of to make him throw up – but, he never did. We finally decided that he had not drank any of the liquid.

He also climbed up onto the cabinet and mixed my three canisters by putting flour in the coffee, coffee in the sugar, and sugar in the flour. The next time he climbed up onto the cabinet, he fell backwards off the cabinet and hit his head pretty bad. He really kept me on my toes, but I never was fast enough to stop him.

Once when my Step Mom came to visit us for a few weeks and we were cleaning up the kitchen after the evening meal, we thought we could smell smoke. On our vacation trip to California, we had stopped at a souvenir shop and bought him a horn that looked like a cow horn. It was supposed to be a powder horn like the settlers used to keep their gun powder in.

We went to find the source of the smoke. Naturally, we went first to Michael's bedroom and then to his closet. There was the "powder horn" stuffed with paper and smoking. We took everything that was on the floor of his closet outside.

Another day, he and one of his friends decided to put his tent up in the back yard that we had gotten him for his birthday. They put it up at the rear of the back yard under the mimosa trees. That was fine until they decided to build a fire in the door way of the tent while they were inside. We put the fire out so they could get out of the tent. It was about this same time that he went to the far side of the house and built a fire next to the rose bushes.

If I left him in the car while I went into the bank or store, when I returned I could smell smoke. If there was a pack of matches in the car, he would light them and watch them burn.

As he grew older, or because we threatened to kill him, he finally grew out of his "fire works" period.

I did need his help when I was living in my house in Mineral Wells on the Brazos River out in the country. It was after my husband Pat had died and Michael was separated from his wife Cindy and he was living with me.

We always burned our trash in a large wire cage because there wasn't any trash or garbage pickup that far out in the country. It was a nice calm day when I lit the first piece of paper. Then a gust of wind came down the driveway and blew it and several more pieces of paper out of the cage. They began to tumble over and over down toward the river. Each place they landed, the dead grass caught fire.

I tried to control it, but it was very quickly apparent to me that it was out of control. Michael was asleep because he was working the night shift at a grocery store in Fort Worth. I ran in and got him and when he stepped out of the door of the house, he turned and yelled, "Call the Fire Department."

My property was made up of three and one half acres with neighbor's houses on each side on large parcels of land. One of my neighbors was away on vacation. Of course, the water hose would not reach very far and the fire was spreading quickly.

We were in a "No Burn Area" and that also concerned me. I thought that I would probably be fined. Then the sound of the fire trucks coming down my drive broke my thoughts. It took a while for them to put out the fire. I was also bracing myself for the "scolding" and "fine" I would receive. But, much to my surprise, the fire chief said they had several fires like this one. They collected their equipment and left to go to another fire. My "Fire Bug" son had come to my rescue that day.

When Michael was in Grade School, he played in Little League Baseball. Natur-ally, I thought I had to go to all the games. They called me their "one person rooting section." The baseball games were played on Saturday in the summer.

In the winter, he played Pee Wee Football. His ream was named "The Longhorns" after the football team of Texas University. He was issued a "practice" uniform and a "play" uniform with all the padding.

Being the good Mother that I was, I thought his practice uniform needed to be washed every day because it was dirty. The coach told the mothers not to wash their uniforms until the end of the week, even if we could "stand them up in the corner and they would stay there." The boys needed to learn what it meant to get dirty. All of the games were played on Saturday. After the games we could wash their uniforms.

Michael's first job was with a new car dealer that was owned by the grandfather of his best friend, Warren. He was later promoted to Service Representative.

Michael's first marriage was to Cindy. She had worked at the new car dealership with Michael. Cindy's Father gave her a wedding with all the trimmings. Her father was a high ranking official with the FAA. After the wedding he was transferred to Alaska to be head of the department there.

Cindy's Father and Mother had just bought a new home when he was notified of his transfer. He decided that the best thing for him to do was to let Michael and Cindy live in his house until he returned to Fort Worth about three years later. Michael's Dad also lived with them because he had suffered from a stroke and couldn't take care of himself.

Michael and Cindy's marriage lasted only a couple of years and they were divorced. He also left that stressful job at the new car dealership and went to work for a grocery store chain in Fort Worth. Then all of their Texas stores were closed down and he went to work for another grocery store chain. He worked there for eleven years.

He met a girlfriend, Tammy, the wife of a friend of his and they seemed to get along quite well. She lived in White Settlement in the Fort Worth area and was separated from her husband and had a son named Scottie. Michael had no children which meant there would not be any jealousy between Scottie and Michael's children. That worked out very well.

Scottie was a very smart young boy and graduated from High School, then entered college. He earned his degree and graduated from college with a job waiting for him. We were all very proud of him.

We had our Family Reunion at my house on the Brazos River in the Mineral Wells area. At first, we always had it on the 4th of July, but later changed it to Memorial Day in May.

Since the first reunions were on the 4th of July, all of the boys – big and small – stocked up on Fireworks and put on a fantastic display for everyone. Sometimes there would be twenty or thirty of our family members there to watch it plus our neighbors could see it from their houses. Of course, you know who had the largest display – Michael. Those displays were as beautiful and fancy as any of the commercial ones we saw.

Michael is my son, my only son, and I love him dearly. I wouldn't trade him for a dozen more – even if they didn't like fires. Also, he likes his name and never wants to be called "Mike"-but always preferred to be called "Michael." I'm glad because that's the name I chose for him.

CHAPTER 28
ON MY OWN, JUST ME AND JESUS

I was on my own now. Pat had not done what he told me he would do all those years, "Don't worry, I'll take care of you." I did have my Social Security, but it wasn't enough to take care of my home and pay the bills that go along with it. Pat failed to sign me up to receive his Retirement Pay if he should die. Therefore I was not entitled to receive any of his Retirement Pay.

I had reached 65 years of age seven months ago back in October. The man who handled my claim to draw Social Security checked my background and found that if I filed against my husband Buddy, I would receive quite a bit more, than I would on my own or if I filed against Pat.

I did not want to file against Buddy because he was in very bad health from the strokes he had. I decided to file against Pat, but that didn't give me but a few dollars more each month. Pat had been in the military and did not pay into Social Security, except for the few years he worked before he joined the Army.

Pat and I had made out our Wills when we got married. That was something he was required to do in the Army and continued to do in civilian life. I would soon realize that I was very fortunate in that respect. Naturally, our wills made each other beneficiaries. Our lawyer, whom we both knew for years, prepared the wills for us and filed Pat's will for probation.

A month or so after Pat's death, I contacted a lawyer in Kansas to look into the property that Pat, his sister, and brother had inherited from their parents who had been deceased for many years. Since Pat was one third owner of two large acher-ages in Kansas in the Wheat and Milo producing areas, I needed to find out if I was entitled to his part. I was desperately looking for some income.

After a long search and months of waiting, the lawyer called to tell me that Pat's parents had set up their will in a way that as each of their children died, their part of the estate would go to the surviving siblings. Pat had never mentioned it to me.

A few days after my lawyer called to tell me the bad news, my sister-in-law's lawyer called to tell me that she wanted to and was in the process of probation his will in Kansas. She had given her lawyer an old will, dated years prior to our marriage, which made her and her mother beneficiaries of all Pat owned.

Their mother was now deceased; therefore his sister would inherit anything Pat owned according to the old will. When I heard what he said, I dropped to the floor on my knees. I could not believe what I was hearing. She had not contacted me about "her will" or asked if Pat had a current will, or anything. In fact, she had not contacted me since the funeral.

I advised her lawyer that Pat had a current will, and that his and my lawyer had already had it probated in Texas. I guess I was just too ignorant to see it and thought his family liked me. But, I guess, because I wasn't Catholic and may not have handled the funeral as they liked, they disowned me. I never heard from any of his family after that. We had been married seventeen years.

By September I had come to my senses and knew what I had to do. On Saturday night I looked in the phone book for churches and found a Methodist church I thought I would try. It was filled with very nice people and two of the ladies came to my door the next day with a fresh, warm baked cake. They declined to come in but stated they just wanted to thank me for visiting their church.

I had decided I did not want to go back to an Assembly of God Church, so I went to several other churches during the coming weeks. I had given my life to The LORD many years ago at the church my Dad had built, and knew The LORD hadn't let go of me. I could feel those strings drawing me back to Him more and more.

It was now October and I looked up the address of the Assembly of God Church and attended their service. I heard a wonderful sermon and met some very fine people. I felt that was the place for me. Years later, the Pastor told me that he said to his wife, after they shook my hand that morning, "She will not come back."

He said his wife stated, "Yes she will." I guess I surprised them all, because I did come back the following Sunday and the next. But, the following weekend was my High School Reunion for the Class of 1950. I had already planned to attend it in Longview, and did.

My Step brother, Tommy, was now the pastor of a small Pentecostal Church in my home town, so I panned to go to his church on Sunday morning, October 20th. My brother Sammie and his wife were in town and met me at the church, and some of my old friends. The two sisters I played with and double dated with, Margaret and Anita, were there.

We were all having a good time talking about "old times" when I felt a tug on my arm. It was my Step Brother, Tommy, who said to me, "Sis, don't you think it's about time." I knew what he meant as we both walked toward the altars. That day, God helped me turn my life around. He has walked beside me, helped me, guided me, protected me in every area of my life. I couldn't have made it without Him. Thank You Father. He was there all the time. He never let me go.

I followed Sammie and his wife after church to Tommy's house. I found out that our brother, Charlie, was wanting to move back to Texas from California. Sammie said that he wanted to move from Houston back home also. When my sister, Sandra, found out we were planning to move back, she decided she also wanted to move from Fort Worth back home.

There we were, the four Musketeers, going back home. However, it was easier to say than to see it come to pass. Charlie had his Clinic in California that needed to be sold, or leased. Sammie had a business in Houston. Sandra owned a home in Forth Wort and she and her husband had jobs there. All of our plans would take a few years, but we were determined to do it.

A few weeks later, Sandra and her husband went back to Longview and talked with Tommy. He knew of a widow lady that wanted to sell her home and it wasn't very far from his church. They went to check it out and liked it. Her husband called me that night after they returned home and asked if I liked flat ground with lots of trees. I said I sure did. The land my home was on slanted down to the banks of the Brazos River. All the land was "up hill" or "down hill" depending on which way you were walking.

The house was on seven acres and was positioned perfectly so we could split it up four ways. Sandra said she liked the house, and we all decided she could have it.

Charlie, Sammie, and I wanted to build our own homes. Since Sammie had helped our Dad's Construction business, he knew how to build houses. We were all set.

All we needed now was some money and people to purchase our properties.

I know that I wasn't depending on myself to do all of that. I was expecting God to help me do it, or He would do it for me. I asked Sammie to help me complete the things that had not been done to my house on the River and get it ready to sell.

My house was a "Bermed" or "Underground" house. Three of the outer walls were covered with dirt up to the roof. When the house was built, the walls were made by pouring cement into frames built for the walls. The "Rule" is that the cement must be poured in "One complete pour."

After living in the house for several years, the rear walls began to "seep water" especially when it rained. The problem got so bad that I had to hire a company to excavate the walls and waterproof them. This had not been done when the house was built and was quite expensive. However, my insurance paid for most of the cost for the repairs.

I had put in flower beds around the roof and had planted six shrubs. I knew the shrubs had to be dug up and replanted somewhere else, so I undertook that chore myself. I had to dig up the six shrubs, dig another six holes around the garage, and replant the shrubs there.

During all of this digging and planting, my right foot became tired. I switched from using my right foot for digging to my left foot. That was like using my left hand to write instead of my right hand. It doesn't work that way. My left foot and leg were not as strong as my right foot and it caused me to damage the sciatic nerve in my left leg from my hip to my toes and was extremely painful.

I went to three doctors in Fort Worth who could do nothing to relieve my pain. They advised me to go to therapy at my local hospital, which I did. After weeks of treatment, the therapist gave me the diagnosis by saying, "I'm sorry. We have done all we can for you. You will have to learn to live with the pain." Those were words I did not want to hear.

That was on a Tuesday. When I returned home, I realized that my Brother Tommy was having "Camp Meeting" at his church in Longview starting on Thursday. I made up my mind that instant that I would go and get my healing at Tommy's Church in Longview.

My Pastor and the congregation in Mineral Wells had prayed for me many times, and my pain had not gotten better. Therefore, on Thursday I was on my way to Tommy's Church. I drove up to the church and went in to see Tommy to tell him what I wanted and what I needed.

Tommy and his wife, and my childhood friend Anita, prayed for me and anointed me with oil that first night. Nothing happened. It was the same on Friday and Saturday night. Sunday morning I asked for them to pray for me again before I returned home.

After I returned to my seat, the young man that was sitting in front of me with his two children and wife, turned to me and said, "God told me to tell you that He is going to heal you on your Birthday."

That sounded wonderful until I realized my birthday was three months away. I suffered with the pain for three more months. The pain was unbearable at times. It was painful to walk, sit, stand, or lie down. Nothing seemed to relieve the pain.

My birthday finally came around on October 18th and was on Sunday. That morning when I got up to get ready for church I realized there wasn't any pain in my leg or hip. God had done exactly what He said he would. I was free of that pain in my left leg and hip and am still free of pain in my left leg and hip to this very day. That was over twenty years ago. God always keeps His Word.

After Sammie took care of his affairs, he came to help me do the same. My house had cement floors and needed carpet on them. The doors were missing the trim around them. Since I didn't have much (almost none) money, we had to "make do" with what we had and could find.

Sammie and his wife, Marie, were a comfort to me. They had been going to church regularly and had been taught many things about the Bible and were glad to go with me to church and help me learn about the Bible.

Sammie had studied the Bible and could help me with things I did not understand, one of which was Tithing. He explained that whatever comes into our hands is called "First Fruits."

Years ago when most everyone was a farmer, whatever was first picked or harvested from his fields, according to the

Bible, was "First Fruit." The "First Fruit," or one tenth of the harvest was the "Tithe" and it belonged to God.

It was to be taken to the House of Worship and presented to the Priest. It did not belong to the farmer, it belonged to God. If a person kept the "First Fruit" he was considered by God to be a thief. Sammie was very good to help me learn about the Bible. We would sit each morning drinking coffee and studying the Bible. I still remember those wonderful days.

Sammie picked-up some odd jobs here and there to supplement his income. He had worked on a house where the people replaced their carpet which was still very nice and we were able to obtain that. We installed it in the house. We bought and gathered the materials as we needed them.

During my prayers and study of the Bible, I found in Deuteronomy a verse that really spoke to me. Chapter 6 Verse 10 And it shall be, when the LORD thy God shall have brought thee intro the land which He swore (promised) unto thy fathers, to Abraham, to Isaac, and to Jacob, to give thee great and goodly **cities**, which thou buildest not.

We must study God's Word to know what He will and will not do. God's Word is very **plain** **and** **clear.** God has declared that we are the "seed of Abraham." And, as his seed, what God did for and to Abraham, He will do for us. Only Believe His Word. We may not live in Israel as Abraham did, but God is always true to His Word, and He will bring us to the Place He has prepared for us just as He did for our Father Abraham.

I expect to help make the city where I live now into God's Kingdom on earth. He said it, I believe it, and He will do it.

Verse 11 And houses full of all good things, which thou filled not, and wells digged, which thou digged not, vineyards and olive trees, which thou planted not; when thou shall have eaten and be full; Verse 12 Then beware lest thou forget the LORD, which brought thee forth out of the land of Egypt (Mineral Wells was not where my Blessings were; therefore, I had to leave), from the house of bondage.

If I stayed any longer in Mineral Wells after God told me to leave, things could have happened to me that were not in God's plans for my life. My Blessings were in Longview. That's where He told me to go.

There was a stair on the outside of the house that led up to another floor, but it was only accessible using the stairs on the outside. That floor was used for my Wood-working Shop and storage. It did not have water or heat or cooling. One morning, as I was going up the stairs and stopped to look out at all the flowers and fruit trees I had planted, I heard a very quite voice say, "You'll never be happy here." I knew it was God, because I had heard other words directed toward me in church.

On a Sunday morning, Sammie, Marie, and I were listening to Brother Scott as he walked over in front of the area where we were sitting and said, "You go where God tells you to go." After service, I asked Sammie if he heard what Brother Scott said. He said, "Yes, I sure did." Months later I asked Brother Scott if he remembered saying those words to the congregation. He had no memory of it. I knew who he was speaking to and that the words came from God.

I put my house on The Market. I was told that property on the Brazos River very seldom ever went up for sale and that my property should sell very quickly. For some reason, which I did not understand, I only had a few nibbles. I listed it with several Real Estate Agents and even that did not seem to help.

I was surprised when Sammie announced to me that he was going to help Sandra fix up the house she had bought that came with the property in Longview. I did not want them to leave, but I knew Sandra needed his help. He had helped me all he could.

People would ask me if I was afraid to live alone there in the country and I would always tell them, "I'm not alone. Jesus is always with me." Sometimes I enjoyed being alone. I did not have any animals to take care of, and furthermore, I did not want any. I had been given pets from time to time, but living in the country, they would die or mysteriously disappear. Without pets meant I could go as I pleased and stay as long as I desired. I did not have anyone living with me or pets to take care of.

One weekend I decided to go to Longview and visit Sandra and Tommy. By that time, Charlie had disposed of all his properties and was living at Sandra's in his travel trailer. He was waiting for Sammie to finish with Sandra's house, then he was to build Charlie and his wife a new house on the south side of where I was to build mine. Sammie was being kept quite busy.

On my way back home, I decided to stop off to visit with my daughter Theresa and her husband and their two girls. I was told about the High School that the oldest daughter, Emily, was attending in Fort Worth. It was also the largest High School in that area at that time.

Emily said she could not go to her locker between classes because of the size of the building. She had to carry her books with her during the morning classes and then exchange those books for the books she would need for the afternoon classes. She told me of things that were happening in the school that disturbed me.

My daughter's husband, Ernie, had always loved my house on the Brazos River. He made it clear that if anything ever happened to me or if I wanted to get rid of the house, He Wanted It!!! So when he asked me if I would consider selling the house to him without a down payment, I told him I would go home and pray about it and let him know.

When I left, I was very concerned about my two granddaughters going to that large High School in Fort Worth. I also thought maybe this is the reason my house had not sold even though it was "Prime Property on the Brazos River." I prayed for a few days until I felt sure that was what God wanted me to do.

During those years of living alone, God had Blessed me with good neighbors who were always willing to help me. It seemed that every time I could not start the lawnmower, my neighbor Earl would always appear coming down my driveway or riding his four wheeler toward my house from the river. He also knew what to do when my well pump didn't work right. He had a well of his own. He showed me and taught me a lot about my equipment and how to use it during those four years when I was there alone.

One year, before Sammie and Marie left to help Sandra, he plowed up all of his land across the road from me. He said he planted all the seeds he had been saving for several years. He planted peas, cantaloupes, and watermelons and said we could pick all we wanted.

There was a man, Lance, and his family that went to the church we attended, who had three small children and three teenage children. Marie and I picked boxes full of peas, cantaloupes, and watermelons and took them to Lance and his family.

That was also the time when my son, Michael, was living with me because he and his wife, Cindy, were getting a divorce. He worked for a large grocery store chain in Fort Worth and would bringing home large boxes of chips, cookies, and crackers that were outdated, but still good to eat. I gave all of it to Lance and his family. He told me they were most grateful to get it.

One day, Michael brought home ten bags of ten pounds each of potatoes. I called Lance and told him to come and get the potatoes. He came immediately and said to me, "Sister Betty, I promise you there will not an eye grow on these potatoes."

I never expected anything in return for how I helped his family. Several years later, I would be Blessed by Lance in a wonderful way. After all, God promised us in His Word, and Jesus quoted it in Luke Chapter 6, Verse 38 "Give, and it shall be given unto you; good measure, pressed down, and shaken together, and running over (that's a lot), shall men give into your bosom. For with the same measure that you meet (used in measuring anything) withal it shall be measured to you again."

It was now about December 1st and Ernie asked if he could start moving them in so they could be settled by Christmas. I agreed, but I did not have a place to go, so I stayed until February packing and preparing to move. I did have a good time with their family at Christmas. They put up a huge tree with beautiful decorations.

This is the time when I need to add a different tone to my story. Pat had been dead for 4 years now. I had decided after his death, and my previous marriages that had not turned out so well, that I was not very good in making my own choices. It was time for me to ask and trust God to lead and guide me.

My previous husband, Buddy, my children's father, had also died a year after Pat's death. He also had been a heavy drinker. He had several strokes that finally caused his death. My son Michael had been living in Fort Worth with his father in his apartment until he got married. Then Michael and his wife moved into a house and his father, Buddy, went with them.

My children were doing well. My two girls had children of their own now. I had decided I had made such a mess of my life that I never wanted to marry again. I knew after all those years that I would never be happy with anyone except Gene and that seemed to be an impossibility. Never underestimate the power of God and what He says and promises in His Word, and in what He alone can do.

My children weren't too happy about my moving back to Longview, but they had their own lives and families, and I and my brothers and sister, were ready to go back home. We were all getting older, with grown children and no ties. Now we were looking forward to a quieter life in our home town.

There are verses in Psalm 37 starting in Verse 3 that I read and prayed almost daily: "Trust in the LORD, and do good; so shall thou dwell in the land (the land God will show you), and verily thou shalt be fed".

To me this verse meant that I must trust God with my whole being and in whatever He brings my way. I was to do good by helping those who needed help and praying for those who needed prayer. The last part tells me that I will dwell in the land, my home land, and that's where God will now feed me and take care of me.

Verse 4 reads, "Delight thyself also in the LORD; and He shall give thee the desires of thy heart." I was delighted, glad, in serving and worshiping God and doing His Will because that was where I found peace and comfort. I knew exactly what the desires of my heart were, and that was to see Gene again someday.

I prayed most every night and asked God, "Father, please tell me or show me where Gene is now. Is he well or is he sick, or has he died in these long 50+ years. If he has died, please let me know where his grave is so that I might go and visit it. If he's in a Nursing Home, let me go visit him one more time."

Verse 5 reads "Commit thy ways unto the LORD; trust also in Him; and He shall bring it to pass." I had learned my lesson and was well committed to the LORD. I was not going to do anything stupid or dumb as I had done in the past. I put my life in God's hands to do whatever He desired. If He showed me where Gene was I would be more than happy. But, if He didn't, then I would know that it was not in my best interest or was not in God's will. God would now lead me **all the way**.

With all of that being said, it was now February and I was still in Mineral Wells. I was helping with the chores around the house and helping my two granddaughters with their chores.

It was Friday, February 13th when I saw a U-Haul coming down the driveway to my house. To me it was a glorious day. It was my sister, Sandra, and our nephew Preston and his cousin. This was a surprise to me and I told her I didn't have the money to pay her for the U-Haul, but she said, "Whenever, will be okay with me."

We loaded most of my things that afternoon and finished the loading Saturday morning. Then we headed for Longview and I waved good-by to all the fruit trees and flowers I had planted. It was a happy time, but also a sad time because I was leaving my home that I had worked on and decorated for fifteen years.

I had already broken the news of my leaving to my neighbor Earl, who had helped me whenever I had a problem. He was very upset at my leaving. We had been friends for many years. I know God was watching over me, because He would always send Earl when I needed help.

I was also leaving my church and friends that I loved. I lived at the end of a road, so I stopped to say good-by to a couple of my neighbors. They had all been very helpful to me while I was living alone. Then I was on my way to a new home and a new life, back where it all began. God is so good!!

CHAPTER 29

MY NEW LIFE, STARTING OVER

The date was February 14ᵗʰ when I crossed the Gregg County Line and the City Limits of Longview. At last, I was back home. What a good time to be back home, on Valentine's Day. I had been listening to my Gospel CD's and as I crossed into Gregg County, Kenneth Copeland began to sing, "My God Has Made A Way For Me." I had lots of dreams and promises to look forward to now, and I knew God had already prepared the way for me.

Sammie had finished the work on Sandra's house and was building Charlie's house now. He and his wife had found an apartment for us to share. With all of us to help it didn't take long to unloaded the Van. I found some clothes to wear the next morning for Church, Tommy's Church.

It made me sad to know that I had left my children and grandchildren behind, but I knew if I was to have a new life without all of the old memories haunting me every day, I must be in the place where God wanted me to be.

I felt at home and comfortable in church that Sunday morning. One of my child-hood girlfriends, Anita, was a member of Tommy's Church and was there to greet me and some other friends I had known for a long time.

On Monday morning I set out to take care of getting the utilities, phone, and TV turned on and the accounts in my name. By lunchtime, I was tired and went to Sandra's house to have lunch with her.

My nephew, Preston, was there with his little girl. I sat back in a recliner to rest before going out again that afternoon. I fell asleep with Preston's daughter in my lap. When I awoke, I still felt very tired so I decided to go back to the apartment.

I don't remember anything unusual about the way I felt that Monday, but I do remember that I didn't feel too well on Tuesday. I was running a fever and coughing. By Thursday, I felt horrible and was still coughing and running fever. I asked Sammie's wife, Marie, to make me a peanut butter and jelly sandwich.

When I don't feel well, that's the only thing I like to eat. I ate only half of the sandwich. I felt very bad and was coughing horribly. I did not normally get sick and knew something was very wrong. I coughed all Thursday night. Friday morning I waited for Sammie to get up and told him I needed to go to the hospital.

The doctors checked me and said I had pneumonia and started the antibiotics. I would remain in the hospital for a week. Each morning, about 5:00 am, I was wheeled down to the X-ray department.

I had not been that ill since I rode the bus all night going to my grandmother's house in Houston when I was about four or five years old.

I was also out of the jurisdiction for my Medicare Insurance. This was at the start of Medicare and it was not "perfected" yet. I was released after a week and tried to get my prescriptions filled, but could not because I was listed as living in the Fort Worth area.

Since my daughter, Denise lived in Fort Worth, I set out for her house to put me back in my jurisdiction. Also, remember, I had just been released from the hospital after being there for a week.

That was a long drive for me in my weakened condition so I did not try to get my prescriptions filled that night. I asked Denise to get me an aspirin to help me relax, keep my fever down, and go to sleep.

I hope you understand that Satan was trying to kill me now just as he had all of my life. Thank God, Jesus was on my side. I know now that God had a work for me to do and Satan was trying to stop me.

I felt terrible and could not relax. I paced the floor all night long in the dark. I did not want to disturb any of Denise's family. When it was daylight, I heard Denise and her family in the kitchen getting breakfast. I went in to tell her I needed to go to the Emergency Room. She looked at me and knew I had to go immediately. I was broken out in a rash from my head to my toes. I had not turned the light on in my room, but now in the light, I could see that I was broken out all over.

In the Emergency Room, the nurse started giving me shots of Benadryl. It took an hour or so for the Benadryl to work and for the rash to disappear, but then after another hour, it came back again. The nurse gave me another shot and they wheeled me off to the "Astronaut Medicine Area." I was fortunate to be in one of the largest hospitals in Fort Worth which was equipped to handle any type of emergency It had been very early in the morning when I was taken into the Emergency Room and remained in the hospital until late that afternoon while every test possible could be run on me. At the end of the testing, I was told that I was **very** allergic to Tylenol and that I needed to keep Benadryl handy at all times in case a had an allergic reaction from any medication.

Satan was trying to kill me, but God turned it around so that I had very important information about my health which would be very beneficial to me later.

When I returned to Longview, I was able to get my prescriptions filled in Longview because my "home base" had been changed to Longview.

I alerted the pharmacist where I had my prescriptions filled that I was very allergic to Tylenol. He would be my "overseer" and checked every medicine that was prescribed for me. The doctors don't always know what is in the medicine, but the pharmacist does. The pharmacist told me it could be the "binder" that I was allergic to. Later, the list of medications I was allergic to would grow. That was probably because of the same "binders" are in different types of medicine.

After my recovery, I started looking for a job because my Social Security wasn't quite enough to cover all my expenses. I filled out many applications and mailed some to different companies, but did not get even one reply.

About April 1, 1999, I was checking the ads in the newspaper and saw a job listed at the newspaper for a "telemarketer." That was a word I didn't know and neither did Sammie. I decided I would check it out and applied the next day. I am 68 years old and did not know if anyone would even interview me.

Much to my surprise, a young lady in her late twenties interviewed me. She asked me to read a script from a page in a book which began, "I'm Betty with the Longview Daily News." She stopped me immediately and told me to read it exactly as printed which I did, "This is Betty with the Longview News Journal."

I did not realize I had inserted "Daily News" instead of "News Journal."

I explained that I grew up in Longview when the name of the paper was "Daily News" and not "News Journal." So she hired me for a job I didn't even know what the word "telemarketer" meant but at a good salary. She never mentioned my age.

That had to be God at work, because it certainly wasn't the Devil.

There were seven or eight of us each day seated around and on each side of a long table with the lady who interviewed me sitting at one end. Her job was to listen to what we said as we talked to subscribers of the newspaper and potential subscri-bers on the phone. Naturally, I was the oldest at the table and a young male college student was the youngest.

Contrary to what some people believe, we did not dial or call anyone. There was a large "automatic dialer" located somewhere else in the building that had cost about $10,000.00 and it dialed the numbers for us.

We sat at a computer monitor with a keyboard for typing. The "dialer" dialed numbers until it made a connection, then it connected to the next person available to continue the call.

We had a script which was mandatory that we follow. Our Supervisor was listening to make sure we did not make any mistakes or deviate from the script. We could not begin or carry on a personal conversation with the person we were talking with.

We would asked the person if he or she were a subscriber. If they were, then we asked if they were satisfied. If that person was not a subscriber, then we told that person about a special subscription offer. It was a very simple job and it paid well. We were paid for every new subscription we sold in addition to our salary. I am proud to report that I sold more subscriptions than anyone else and received many bonuses.

No one spoke of or asked about my age. I must admit I always looked younger than my actual age. They were all very friendly to me even though they were at least twenty or thirty years younger than I. Most all of them had other jobs.

The only distinction I had was that I carried a small bag of candy which I usually put on the table each day next to my computer. Someone would usually say, "I'm hungry. Does anyone have anything to eat?" Someone else would reply. "Check with Betty. She's always got some candy or cookies." I guess you could call me the "Candy Lady" of the group. We had a lot of fun "wise cracking" to each other.

The Day shift worked Monday through Thursday and Saturday. During the week we came to work at Ten am and broke for lunch from Twelve until One. Then we worked until Five pm. I had been hired to work the day shift, but there was also an evening shift from Six until Nine pm.

On Saturday everyone worked from Ten am until One pm. Our time schedule was governed by the Law. No calls could be made before Nine am, or after nine pm. A company that broke that Law could have their license revoked. They were very strict about our obeying that Law.

There wasn't actually a Night Shift, so the Supervisor would ask each one of us each day if we wanted to work the Night Shift. That also meant we could make extra money. Everyone usually worked the Night Shift for the extra money.

The first time the Supervisor asked me about working the Night Shift, I told her I would except on Thursday night because I went to church on Thursday night. Each afternoon the Supervisor would ask each one if we wanted to work that night. When she came to me, on Thursdays, she would look at me and say, "Never mind. I know. You go to church on Thursdays."

She never seemed to resent the fact that I would not work on Thursdays, but would always smile at me. I knew I was being Blessed by God because of the way I was treated, and because I put God First, before my job. I was the oldest person there and made the most salary and bonuses. That was God Blessing me.

It was in June when I saw my monitor light up and the name of the person I was calling was "Gene Pittman." My heart dropped to the floor and I could hardly speak. The person I was talking to was a female. I asked the usual questions and since she said she was satisfied with the service, I thanked her and hung up.

I had no idea who I had been talking with, but I did have presence of mind to copy the phone number and address before my monitor turned off automatically. Now that I had the information, What Could I Do With It??

I took it home and told Sammie what had happened and asked him if he knew where the address was located.

He did not know because it was a Rout Number and not a street address, and it was in Kilgore. Also, he remembered Gene, but did not know I was still in love with Gene after all those years.

One night after work, I was talking on the phone to Sandra's husband, Don, and complained to him about my shoulder hurting. He told me to get some medicine like he was taking for his shoulder because it helped him very much.

The next night, I stopped off at K Mart, on my way home and got some of the medicine. I took it just as my phone rang. Denise was calling to inquire how I were doing on my new job. I was in my bedroom with my gown on and had been talking for about fifteen minutes.

My thigh started to itch and I scratched it. Then I noticed my leg was broken out with a rash and so was my body. I told Denise and she said, "Get the Benadryl quick!" I hung up and took the Benadryl.

I went into the living room where Marie was and told her I needed for her to stay up with me until the rash went away, which she did. It took several hours to disappear. During that time I was pacing the floor, waiting for the rash and itching to go away. I was very glad the nurse in the Emergency Room in Fort Worth had told me what to do if I took anything I should not have taken. Thank God, He was always watching over me.

Months had passed and it was now the last of October. I looked up and my monitor was lit up with the name "Gene Pittman" again. Since I could not speak anything personal with whoever answered the phone, I was very brief. It was a man. I asked if the service was satisfactory, and he replied, "Yes." I said, "Thank you" and hung up.

One of the Evangelist I had been watching every night on TV was scheduled to be in Dallas at the Reunion Arena on Saturday night, October 30th. Four of the ladies from the Church and I decided we wanted to go.

I had been praying that morning as I usually did. I'm sure I was praying about Gene. When I entered the bathroom to take my shower, I heard this "quiet, still" voice say, "I gave you two." I knew immediately who was speaking. God had already showed me twice where Gene lived through the phone calls at work. Now I needed to decide what I wanted to do with the information.

I took my own car to Dallas, and the other ladies rode in one car because I had planned to visit my daughter, Theresa, and her family living in my house which was only an hour and a half drive from Dallas Everything went well. I had planned to visit the church I had attended and was a member of while living in Mineral Wells. However, Saturday night I could not go to sleep thinking about Gene and I wanted to go home.

Driving back to Longview on Halloween Eve, I was listening to Gospel music when I crossed the Gregg County

Line again. And as before, I heard Kenneth Copeland singing, "My God Has Made The Way For Me." I knew He had made the way for me as I turned off the Interstate to go by Sandra's house.

When I drove into the driveway, Tommy and his wife were leaving so I just waved at them. I went into Sandra's house and saw her sitting at the Coffee Bar in her kitchen. No one knew about the "Torch or the Burden" I had been carrying for Gene all those years. I did not talk to anyone about my feelings or about Gene.

Sandra asked me what I was up to. I told her what had happened and that I had Gene's phone number and wanted to talk to him. She didn't know who Gene was. At that moment my upbringing kicked in and I knew that girls never called boys.

I was so nervous and frustrated I didn't know exactly what to do. I knew what I wanted to do, but was too nervous. Then, Sandra reached out and grabbed the note out of my hand and then the phone and dialed the number. As soon as someone answered, she handed me the phone and said, "Here!!" With my heart pounding, I said, "Is this Gene Pittman who graduated from White Oak High School in 1950." He said, "No," and my heart sank again.

I said, "I graduated from Longview High School in 1950." Then he said, "Betty Hooper, I've been looking for you for a long time." I knew instantly my search was over and God had answered **all** my prayers. Gene explained that he had not received a diploma for graduation, but a Certificate of Merit because he hated "Romeo and Juliet" and failed English II twice.

I briefly explained that I was living with Sammie and his wife in an apartment in Longview. He said he would like to come and see me the next Saturday on his day off, which was fine with me. I planned to ask for that day off when I went to work the next Monday. I did and my supervisor said, "Yes."

The days dragged by. It was finally Saturday morning at 10:00 am. and Marie and I were looking for Gene's arrival. Sammie was working on Charlie's house and would be gone all day.

Then the pickup pulled into the parking lot and a knock was on my door. I opened the door and we were face to face after forty-five years. Marie was standing behind me. Gene told me later that he wanted to grab me and hold me until he saw a woman behind me and he decided not to. He did not know that the woman was my sister-in-law, Marie, who was Sammie's wife.

I asked him in and we sat and talked for four hours while Marie sat in her bedroom waiting. Yes, we did kiss. We talked about all the things we had missed and all the things we had been through and about our families. We discovered we loved each other just as much at that moment as we did fifty years ago. The true flame never dies.

God had Blessed both of us by bringing us back together. Everything that had happened to me since Pat's death and the moment I realized I could do nothing without Jesus had been God at work. Of course, Satan tried to kill me with pneu-monia and Tylenol along the way, and discourage me at times, but I knew who to follow. And My Shepherd still knew my voice, even though I had not called on Him for a long time. He never gave up on me. He was always there.

Our work schedule was not alike, but with a little ingenuity we made it work. I worked late at night and he went to work early in the morning. Most of the time, he would bring me a Bar-B-Que sandwich or a hamburger for my break for my evening meal.

He worked on Friday, which was my day off, but he would come by after he got off from work. When my Saturday morning shift was over at 1:00 pm, we would be together in the afternoon.

Everything was working out fine, except for one thing. Gene was married. He told me about a friend he had for many years, and had died. Some time later, his friend's wife showed up at his door looking for a place to live. Being the kind person he was, he could not turn her away.

Gene said he knew the arrangement would be for some time and decided they could not live in the same house alone without being married. So they got married. That was about nineteen years earlier. She was also ten years older than Gene.

During one of her Doctor's checkups, they found that she had breast cancer. They operated and removed her breasts. At the present time, the Doctor was checking to find out if the cancer had come back, and was waiting for the results.

Gene said they never did live together as husband and wife, but since she was going through a hard time, he hated to ask her for a divorce. I don't know if it was God at work, but I suspect it was Satan trying to spoil everything again.

It was now Christmas and I gave Gene a beautiful card for Christmas. He put it in the glove compartment in his truck. I did not know that she was a nosy person and looked through the glove compartment in his truck. I believe it was in January.

Gene explained to her what had happened and that he wanted a divorce. He rented an apartment for her and paid for everything.

He even bought her a new car because she said she did not like the one she had. He tried to be very generous with her because of her health and her age. She was now eighty years old. Gene had owned his home for many years before she came to live with him and did not feel she was entitled to any part of his home.

Gene filed for the divorce and it was granted in April 2000. There is a thirty day waiting period in Texas before a person can re-marry. He asked the Judge to waiver the waiting period and he did. We were married on May 6, 2000. When we let God be in control, everything will work out beautifully.

CHAPTER 30
OUR WEDDING DAY

I had been baptized May 12, 1996 at my church in Mineral Wells, but I wanted us to be baptized together before our wedding. And so it was, Tommy baptized us both a week before our wedding, which was to be on Saturday, May 6th.

I owned the lot where we were going to build our house and thought it needed to be mowed – which I did. The weather was quite warm and sunny. I did not wear a low cut blouse, but just enough of my shoulders were showing so that when I was blistered that day my face, neck and some of my shoulders were quite red. That was going to be a nice contrast for my white wedding dress. By the way, I made my dress and veil.

Then finally the day we, and our friends, had waited so long for had finally come. We were married on May 6, 2000 at Tommy's Church with Tommy performing the wedding. The church was full of our old friends and new friends we had know all those many years. Some even said, "We've been waiting for this day for a long time." It may have been a long time for them, but it seemed twice as long for us.

The ceremony was beautiful. Sandra stood up with me as my Matron of Honor, and my Granddaughters Cynthia and Haleigh, were the flower girls. Gene's boss, whom he had worked with for forty years, stood up with him as his Best Man. There wasn't a dry eye in the church. Even Tommy cried while performing the ceremony.

My childhood friend, Anita, was there. She told Gene that he still had those pretty blue eyes she had remembered. Her brother, Eddie sang two songs for us. I picked the first one, "This is The Day That The LORD Has made" and Eddie picked one of his favorites, "The Ring." It was all very beautiful. Thank God!

Our Day had finally come. Everyone knew that we both had been through some bad marriages. Gene wasn't quite as smart a I thought he was, because he married his second wife twice. That's a little too much. At least I didn't go that far.

Gene's mother was living in a Nursing Home and in a wheelchair, but she was there. His Sister Edna and her husband were there. In the 1950's I saw a lot of them at Gene's home when I visited. One weekend, I had gone with Gene and his family to Troup to visit Edna and her family. Edna has been a very dear friend to me then, and was becoming my best friend now.

Tommy and his wife, Shirley, had said we could go to their cabin on The Lake of The Pines for our honeymoon. We didn't have any special place to go, so we took them up on their offer.

Tommy had been raised in a house full of Carpenters, but learned very little about the trade. Mr. "Fix It" Gene, saw some things that needed to be repaired and proceeded to do so. We even went to the lumber yard in Marshall and bought things to repair and fix the things Gene thought needed fixing while we were on our honeymoon.

Don't misunderstand. I didn't care what we did as long as we were together.

The front porch steps needed repairing, so Gene repaired it. Gene had a good heart and liked to help people. That's the way we spent our Honeymoon, repairing Tommy and Shirley's Lake Cabin and cleaning what needed to be cleaned. After all, they did not charge us anything for staying in their cabin.

We have now been married twenty years. I always thought God Blessed me so much just because He Loved Me and wanted us to be together because that was "my heart's desire." Well, that's half right. He does love me, but God had a Work for Gene and I to do for the Kingdom, and we could only do it Together. That makes me Love God even more, because He trusts us to do His Work. And that's what we will be doing for the remainder of our lives.

I have related some of my deepest thoughts and memories. Some were happy and some were sad. Maybe I gave the impression that I am not a Christian, but that is quite the contrary.

Maybe I did not always live my life according to your standards of a Christian, or even my own, but I did the best I could at the time and always tried to help and please others and Jesus the best I knew how. I never forgot my LORD and He has never forgot me.

When I was finally able to turn my life around, God was right there waiting for me and showed me how to do it and led the way for me. If we could only learn without going through the heartaches and pain our mistakes cause us, our life would be much more pleasant. But, I was hurt, and like a hurt animal, I cowered down and did not allow Jesus or any person to come close to me for many years.

I knew I needed my LORD Jesus, because I could not go on alone. He was there all the time, all I needed to do was reach out or call his Name. Thank You Jesus for answering my call.

CHAPTER 31
AFTER THE WEDDING

Gene had worked for Buster for forty years and also knew him as his friend. He and his wife never had any children, so in some ways they treated Gene like their son. Buster had given up all of his other businesses when Gene and I were married, except the Health Food Store he owned in downtown Kilgore.

He no longer had anything to do with the oil field business, and had sold all of the real estate he owned except for some property on the west side of town, and one small store in the downtown area. Since he had nothing for Gene to do, Gene had gone to work with another man helping him remodel houses and build flat bed trailers. That's what he was doing when we got married.

One afternoon, Gene and I went by to visit Buster and his wife. We were visiting with them in the sitting room when I heard Buster say, "The only thing wrong with Kilgore is that it has too many churches." He was of course referring to the property taxes. The churches in any town do not pay property taxes.

Buster was an official in the Rotary Club. For those who do not know about the Rotary Club, it is something like the Masons or Odd Fellows Lodge. They do a lot of charity work in their town.

It was in September that he took a young man to his house to discuss the affairs of the Rotary Club. The young man said they were in the Sitting Room sitting on the couch when Buster made a gesture with his hand toward his head and fell over in the floor.

Everyone was notified shortly afterwards that Buster had died. Gene and I went immediately to the hospital to be with his wife. He died on September 12, 2001 at the age of 83 and childless.

Buster had left everything he owned to his wife, Valura. I believe they had been married for about 50 or more years. Buster had prepared his will so that if his wife had died before him, everything he owned would be left to the Rotary Club. Since she was still alive, everything went to her.

The bad thing about the situation was that she was in the very early stages of Dementia and had a hard time remembering things. She wasn't completely able to take care of their business, and that's why she always asked Gene to help her.

She closed down the Health Food Store because she could not run it alone. She loved Gene like the son she never had, and Gene, I'm sure, loved her in return just as much.

Gene would make sure she had groceries and anything else she needed. I took her to her Beauty Shop appointments and Dental appointments. She would be very confused at times. She was having some trouble with a tooth or the filling, so I took her to my dentist.

While we were there, about every two or three minutes she would ask me, "Does Gene know we are here." I would always guarantee her that he knew where we were. I'm sure that was because she was not always sure where we were or what we were doing there.

The property they owned on the west side of town was "land locked." For those who do not know what that means, it means there was no way to get to the land without crossing another person's property.

Gene found a buyer for the land and helped her sell it. Gene collected the cash money for the property and took it to her. He asked her what she wanted him to do with the money, which was in a brown paper bag, She said, "Gene, why don't you just keep it."

Gene brought the money home and put the bag on my desk in front of me and said, "Here." I asked him what was in it, and he said for me to look. I did and there was ten thousand dollars in cash.

Years earlier when her husband was in the oil field business, he had told Gene to go to the Dodge Dealership and pick out a small truck for himself to use for work. He did, and drove that truck for many years. When Buster closed his oil filed business, Gene asked him if he could have the truck or buy it from him. He said no and parked it in a large garage on the property that was used for working on the large trucks for the oil field. In many ways Buster was very giving, but sometimes he was not.

The truck had been stored since Gene put it in the garage, except for when the landscape man was doing the yard work. He would use it occasionally. Gene asked Valura if he could have the truck to drive now and she told him to take it.

Since she had no children or living relatives, she put everything in Gene's name to avoid any legal problems after her death. She changed her will to show that Gene was to inherit all that she had. She had originally left everything to the Church of the Jehovah Witness where she was a member.

When I was living in Mineral Wells and trying to decide whether or not I should move back to my home town or not, God had spoken to me in many ways about leaving. He also showed me a verse in Deuteronomy Chapter 6 and Verse 11 that reads, "And houses full of all good things, which thou filled not, and wells digged, which thou digged not, vineyards and olive trees, which thou planted not; when thou shall have eaten and be full; Verse 12, Then beware lest thou forget the LORD, which brought thee forth out of the land of Egypt (Mineral Wells) from the house of bondage (all alone except for Jesus).

When God tells you it's time to go or move, you must go. God had blessed me and took care of me as a widow in Mineral Wells, but when He said for me to go, then I had to go. That also meant there would not be any more Blessings for me in Mineral Wells because that was not where I was supposed to be now.

All of my Blessings were waiting for me in my home town. That's where God would Bless me with a good job at the Newspaper Office and show me where Gene was and answer all my prayers.

CHAPTER 32
BUILDING OUR HOME

The day Gene and I had dreamed of, and waited for, all those fifty years had finally come true. Now we were planning our new life together. But, it seems that Gene and I have a small problem – too many houses.

I had given (sold) my house in Mineral Wells to my daughter, Theresa, and her husband, Ernie and my two granddaughters, Emily and Cynthia.

Because I was planning to move back to my home town of Longview, I had gone into "partnership" with Sandra and Don, Charlie and Deanna, and Sammie and Marie and purchased the property that Tommy had told us about. It consisted of a house on 7 ½ acres of land in the town of White Oak, which was adjoining to Longview.

All of us had decided to let Sandra and Don have the house and the one acre of land that it sat on, and we three would split up the remainder of the land. That left 6 ½ acres to divide between me and Sammie and Charlie on which we could build our houses.

Gene owned his house in Kilgore that he had lived in, and also his Mother's house. Gene and his family had built his Mother a house next to his which was also in his name. His Mother was living in a Nursing Home and was not able to return to her home. He listed the two houses for sale and they sold quite quickly because God was still working.

A lady in that area had seen the For Sale sign in the yard who had a sister that lived in Florida, but wanted to move back to East Texas. The State of Florida was building a new highway and her sister's house was going to be demolished. The State had purchased her property and she needed a new place to live. Actually she needed two houses and could pay cash.

God was always at work in my life and with Him in charge, it all went very quickly. Gene's two houses had sold very quickly and now we needed a place to live. He had a very dear friend who had a travel trailer we could borrow. The city did not allow travel trailers to be used for a residence inside the city limits. We found a Trailer Park where we could park it while we, and Sammie, built our home. That took us about eighteen months to complete.

The city "code" would not allow us to stay in the house until it was complete and livable. During that time, we lived in the travel trailer. But, Gene talked to some of the people at City Hall and found out we could put an "Office" on our property while building our house. So we declared the travel trailer "Our Office."

Another law and regulation that most people don't know about is the Homestead law. That means that a person who owns their own property has the right to build their own home and install the plumbing and electricity if that person knows the regulations about their installation. After each part is done, the owner must notify the City so that the Inspector can come out and inspect the work. All work must meet the City Codes that are being enforced at that time.

Sometimes those Codes will require the owner to "tear-out what has been finished and replace it according to the City Code." Then the repairs will need to be inspected again. The Laws cannot deny the man the right to build a home for his family on his own property but it must be built according to the Codes.

Thank God, our trailer now became our "Office." Living on the property meant we could work longer each day on our house. Sammie and his men had worked on our house until it was "In The Dry." Then we took over with all the finishing touches of the inside.

I mentioned before that while I lived in Mineral Wells and was a member of the First Assembly of God Church there, I met a family with three young children and three older boys. It's the family my son, Michael, brought things home for from the Grocery store where he worked. They are the ones that were very glad to receive the ten bags of potatoes, one hundred pounds.

I tell you about them again because they had moved from Mineral Wells and were living not too far from us now. They were also going to my Brother Tommy's church. The one we also attended. That's how I came in contact with them again.

Lance was now in the "Sheet Rock" business and he and his partner came to help us with our house. They installed all of the sheet rock for us. When they had finished, I asked Lance for the bill. He said I could pay his partner, but that he would not accept a dime from us because of how we, Sammie and Marie and I, had helped them with food back in Mineral Wells.

When I wrote about their family and us going to the same church in Mineral Wells,

I mentioned that I would tell more about them in the years to come. I always believe that when you help those in need, God will repay you in some way, in some time, and by someone you may not even know. I'm so glad God let Lance be the one to help us, because if it had been a stranger, I don't think it would have meant as much to me.

I thank God for Lance and his family and think of them quite often. They have moved again and I don't know where they live. I know their children are all grown now. Maybe, God will bring them across my pathway again some day.

I don't know why Gene decided to put out an animal trap near the rear of the "Office" trailer, but he did to catch wild animals. He caught about eight possums and about 24 skunks. One of the skunks was a baby. People will tell you that baby skunks will not "spray" you, but I assure you, they will!!

One night he caught a baby skunk in the trap and took it to be re-located. It was small and scared and did not want to get out of the cage, so Gene shook the cage until the skunk fell out. At first it started to run, then stopped, and YES, you guessed it. He gave Gene a good spray.

Gene liked to go to the Hamburger place early in the morning to eat breakfast, drink coffee, and read the newspaper. He thought, why should this morning be any different, so he went to the Hamburger place. It was still before daylight, and one of the ladies was sweeping the floors around the booths. She came over to the booth where Gene sat and backed away very quickly. They weren't very friendly, and asked him to leave, which he did.

He came home. I was in the center of the trailer which was supposed to be a second bedroom, but we were using it for storage. The weather was getting pretty warm every day, so we put a box fan just inside the trailer door and pointed it back toward the bedrooms – Where I Was Working.

It only took a second or two for me to Yell – GET OUT OF HERE!! I told him to go in the garage and take his clothes off and leave them somewhere on the other side of the garage – OR BURN THEM!! He thought that was very funny, but I didn't. He left his clothes out there for several <u>months</u> and the odor disappeared finally. Then and only them, I washed them.

He did not catch them to kill, just to relocate them. A small creek ran across the property to the rear of our house, which made it a nice place for all wild animals.

There were quite a few deer around. Gene had planted a small garden behind the garage and planted some okra and other vegetables. When the okra was still very small and tender, the deer ate it.

Gene would put some "bait" in the trap, usually peanut butter. One night about 8 or 9 o'clock, I stepped out of the trailer and glanced to the rear where the trap was and I saw something moving inside. I had never seen anything in the trap at night and it frightened me. I pivoted on one foot back into the trailer where I thought I would be safe. Then I watched the trap through the window.

It was the strangest thing I have ever seen and reminded me of a cartoon in slow motion. The trap was "full of animal" and it seemed to be gnawing at the side of the trap. The trap was a wire trap. It kept gnawing until it gnawed a small hole, but large enough to squeeze out through.

When it started coming out of that cage, it looked like it was in slow motion for sure. It started standing up – and standing up – and standing up – until it stood taller than the cage. It turned and ran off towards the woods behind our property. It was silver in color and looked like a silver fox, and I'm sure that's what it was.

We saved quite a large sum of money by doing some of the work ourselves. It helped because Gene knew carpenter work, plumbing, and electrical work and I knew how to sand and paint. We were finally settled in our own home and were able to return the travel trailer to our friend, Mr.

Turner. He had been a neighbor and friend of Gene for many years.

Even though we were now living in the house, it had to pass the City Code Inspection. That meant everything had to be working properly before it was considered "livable." "Livable" did not mean we needed to have the curtains on the windows and carpet on the floors, and all the rooms painted. Those thing would take us another six months to one year.

We had been wise enough to have a large 2-car garage built to the rear of our property before we started on the house. That's where we stored our clothes, furniture, tools, etc. while we were working on the house. I suggested we have a bathroom installed in the garage for washing our hands and brushes. It turned out that Sammie and Marie stayed in the Garage after we were allowed to stay in the house. That meant we were all on the property and available for work at all times.

We had to "tape and bed" and paint all the ceilings and walls. The door facings and window facings had to be built and installed. We put the washer and dryer in it's space so that we could do laundry at home and not go to the laundromat.

I was the "Official Painter" and my job was to "tape and bed" all the walls and ceilings, then paint them. I also had to sand and paint all the trim work, doors, and cabinets. I was happy to get that job because I like to paint and no one else did. Gene did all the hard work, such as digging the ditches for the plumbing and sewer lines and laying the pipes.

Since we were doing all the work ourselves, we needed a large "tractor-type" or "backhoe type" to use to dig the ditches. Gene asked his younger brother and some of the other men he knew about finding one. Gene and I drove to a small town south of us because someone told us where to find one. The price on that one was $8,000.00, and was a little out of our budget.

Then his brother told us about one in Louisiana. We headed for Louisiana and found it, but had a hard time making contact with the owner. When we did, he priced it at $1,500.00, which was well within our price range and exactly what we needed. The problem we had now was to get it home.

Since his brother was in the earth moving business, parking lots and building sites, he said he would go and get it for us with his trailer. We paid him $200.00 to transport it to our house. It wasn't a "nice garden tractor" but a John Deer 750

Backhoe and would do all the "digging" we needed to do. After the house was completed and all the lines put in, we sold the Backhoe at a profit.

But until then, Gene used it to dig a hole for the sewer line which crossed the back of our property and then crossed the property to the side and rear of our property to U.S.

Highway 80, which was a very busy highway. Thank God, he did not have to cross that.

He was digging alongside the building, which housed a motorcycle shop, and cut their telephone lines and a "saltwater" line from the oil well nearby. Those all had to be repaired by us. Then he could finish his digging and lay our sewer line. All lines must be inspected by the City Inspector before the ditch can be filled in.

Gene called for the City Inspector, but he was out of town, so they sent the City Inspector from our neighboring town. He inspected the ditch and passed it, and Gene filled it in. A few days later, our City Inspector came out to see how we were doing and saw the ditch filled in. He told Gene that he was the only one who could okay and pass the inspection on the ditch.

He told Gene to dig up the ditch for his inspection. Gene dug up the ditch. The inspector inspected it and passed it. Gene filled in the ditch again. There were several things that did not seem to meet with The Inspector's approval, but I will not elaborate on them. There were many rules and regulations that had to be followed and the Inspector made sure they were.

However, we completed the house according to the plans Sammie and I had worked on while we were living in Mineral Wells. I had designed it, and Sammie drew the plans. Sammie and a couple of his workers had done the heavy work, and Gene and I did the finishing touches.

When Gene sold his house and his Mother's house, he was able to keep the money from his house, but he shared the proceeds from his Mother's house with some members of his family that had help build her house and take care of her.

I was finally living in my "Dream House"-but not for long, just for a couple of years. Then what God had promised me came to pass.

Valura lived for several years after her husband died. As her health and memory grew worse, Gene had his daughter to stay with her some and help with the chores and cooking.

One night his daughter called to let us know Valura was in the hospital. The dementia had gotten much worse and she died that night. For those who don't know what happens to a person with dementia, it also causes their body to shut down because their organs don't know what to do and just quit working.

In her will, she had left everything she had to Gene and I, which included her house. That's when I received the house I did not build and "filled with all goodly things" that God had promised me in His Word.

She had given away many things, but the house was still "full." There was jewelry, not the kind you can buy at Wall-Mart. Two mink coats, one white mink and one brown mink and a short mink jacket. The coats were beautiful, but just a little too late. If a person wore them in public, the people yelling for "animal rights" would throw rocks at you or something just as bad. So they have remained in the closet all these years. When it snows, sometimes I wear the White Mink to church because of the cold weather.

All of her clothes, silverware, china, and crystal was still in the house and the Baby Grand Piano. Everything a person could needed to "set up housekeeping" was there.

Now what do we do? I had given my daughter Theresa and her family, my home in Mineral Wells and Gene had sold his house and his mother's house. And we had finished building my "dream house" only a couple of years ago. We had to decide which house we wanted to sell this time.

The one we built was inside the city limits of White Oak, which meant we had to pay city taxes and obey all of the city rules and regulations. The house we just inherited was outside the city limits of Kilgore on 17 acres of land.

It had that huge garage on the property where Buster and his men had worked on the oil field trucks, etc. There was also a small "Church Building" down on the west corner. The church had been the synagogue for the Jewish residents. They decided to build a larger church and sold their church building "to be moved."

Buster bought the building and had it moved onto his property. He put in a nice paved driveway to the building and a large paved parking. It was a beautiful building that still had the original lights hanging from the ceiling that were put in when it was built in the 1930's. That's where Buster held the Rotary parties.

That may not bother anyone reading this, but it bothered me. That was God's synagogue and was sanctified by Him. Now it was being used for parties where smoking and drinking were being done.

Gene wanted to live in the country, away from all the city rules and regulations, so we sold our home we had built and moved to "the country." The house was made of white brick with a fireplace and den area, a sitting room, a kitchen and another den area. There were two baths, one in the kitchen area and one across the hall from the master bedroom and guest bedroom.

Yes, we sold our home, but while we were waiting for a buyer, we started re-modeling the house in the country. Most women are not satisfied with a new home until they make all the changes they desire. Those changes will make it "Her New Home and will suit her family style." It seemed to be only a short time since we finished building our new house and now we were working on another one.

The important changes for us were the bedrooms and bathrooms. None of the bedrooms were connected to the bathroom. We added onto one bedroom and cut a door into the bathroom. Then we built another bathroom to accommodate the "now guest bedroom." Those were the only major changes we made. Of course, I had to paint all of the inside of the house.

Then I worked on building flower beds around the outside of the house. The original landscape of the house was what I would call "formal." However, all of the shrubs were old and some had died, so we dug up most of them. I put one row of white bricks around the flower beds to keep the grass from growing into them. Then I planted various flowers and roses. Now, this was our home.

This is the one God promised me from His Word that I would not build. Some-times we may think God has forgotten about promises He has made to us or things He will do for us, but God never forgets.

He has a time and a place for every answer and when He does answer our prayers, they will be at the right time and the right place. Just trust Him, He knows how to do it and take care of you in the right way, which is much better than you could ever have imagined. Believe me. I know. Thank you Father for all your many Blessings.

CHAPTER 33

GENE TELLS ME HIS LIFE STORY

Gene had lived his life and had complications just as I did. I told him that his biggest problem was marrying a girl named "Betty," and that he could have at least picked out someone with a different name. He married her about five months after our breakup, in March, while I was still in college.

I found out about it and wrote him a long letter begging him not to do it. It may have been about five years later while I was visiting at home, I went to see his Mother. They were living in a nice brick home in the west side of town.

We were sitting in her living room and she told me about my letter. She said he received it the day of the wedding and sat on the back steps reading it for a long time. I knew Gene was not the type of person who would go back on his word, and his Mother knew that also. He went through with the wedding, and they had a boy and a girl baby later.

Their marriage lasted about six years. She remarried and her husband adopted their son because Gene was "on the road driving truck" all the time and was never at home to take care of him. His Mother and Dad took their daughter to raise and legally adopted her.

Then he married again. Her name was Bertie. That name was also similar to my name, "Betty." She seemed to get along very well with his Mother. They divorced after five years, then re-married and were married for four years. They were divorced when he had the truck wreck. I told him that I may have made some mistakes in my life, but I certainly never re-married my previous husband (spouse).

He remained single for eleven years. His best friend died and his widow showed up at his door wanting a place to live. They were together for seventeen years, then I came back into the picture. I felt I had kept my word to Gene's Mother to leave him alone. I did not try to find out where he was until my Dad died. I asked Shirley, Tommy's wife, if she knew anything about him because they both had gone to the same High School. She said she thought he was killed in a car accident, but did not know for sure.

After we were married, I asked Gene if he had read in the paper about my Dad's death in 1991. He said he did and thought about going to the funeral, but changed his mind. I told him that if he had been there, both of our lives probably would have changed that day.

Buster and his wife were out of town and Gene made a habit of opening up their house every morning, raising the shades, and turned the lights off and then reversing the process every evening.

Gene was working in the large shop behind their house making tabs for door keys by cutting a piece of plexiglass

3 feet long and angled from one foot wide to 16 inches wide and 1/8 inch thick on a table saw. The table saw had a "kick back protector" which he took off because he thought it was in his way. Protectors are put on saws and named "Protectors" for a very special reason.

He was standing directly behind the saw in line with the piece of plexiglass. not watching closely. The saw cut through the angle and the blade caused the plexi-glass to "kick back" which also caused it to pierce his stomach.

He immediately pulled out the piece of plexiglass from his stomach and dropped it on the floor. He wasn't in any pain at that time so he closed the shop down and also the house. He was on his way to his house when his stomach began to hurt because his stomach was filling up with blood. The blood was collecting inside his stomach, not on the outside.

When he arrived home, he asked his wife, Royce, to take him to the hospital. He was admitted, but it took two hours for them to locate the surgeon. When the surgeon arrived, he performed the operation on Gene's stomach and removed seven inches of his small intestines.

Our intestines are not designed to be handled by human hands, and because of the human touch of his intestines, it caused them to grow together about every six years. It also caused a blockage in his intestines which meant he had to have another part of his intestines removed. Over a period of time, he had three of these operations which removed a total of thirty inches of his small intestine.

Not too long after we were living in our new house we had built, he came into the kitchen about ten o'clock at night while I was cleaning up the kitchen. He said, "You better take me to the hospital." He was in pain and had a bowel obstruction caused from his intestines growing together. The same surgeon operated on Gene again and removed seventeen more inches of his small intestine.

I thank God that when the next six years rolled around, he was going to another doctor who knew more about Gene's type of problem. He told Gene that he did not need to have another operation. The problem was resolved in a different way by first swallowing a tiny camera so that the doctor could look into his intestines and see what had happened. With observation and medication, **and prayer,** the problem was resolved.

Gene liked to go to the Kilgore Cafe and have breakfast and drink coffee with his friends. Since I was a late sleeper and did not particularly enjoy breakfast, I was not with him.

He was approaching the intersection at Highway 31 and Highway 1252 and moved to the left turn lane to make his way towards home. Not knowing there was a car following him into the left turn lane, he stopped, then proceeded to make the left turn. The car following him hit him from the rear and caused his truck to go through the intersection out into the oncoming traffic.

When he realized what had happened, he turned into the median which was a ditch about four feet deep. The impact caused the truck to go forward about 200 feet. At the next intersection crossover he drove up onto the pavement and into the southbound lane and then drove back to where the accident happened.

My daughter, Denise, was on her way to work and saw him and stopped to see what had happened. Gene was talking to the woman who was driving the car that hit him, to find out if she was hurt, and she said she wasn't.

A woman and her daughter had been following the lady for several miles and observed some erratic driving. The woman told her daughter to call the police and have her stopped before she hurt someone.

The State Trooper was on the scene within minutes of the occurrence of the accident. Gene told the Trooper he was not hurt and the Trooper told him he could go on home. The Trooper talked with the woman and decided to place her under arrest to get her off the highway.

We lived .6 of a mile from the intersection. Gene drove the truck home and came into the house. I greeted him and did not notice anything wrong until he got into the bright light. That's when I saw that his left eye was black and he had a knot on his head. He told me what had happened, but assured me he was not hurt.

My son-in-law Dave, Denise's husband who lived next door, came in to find out what had happened. He also noticed Gene's black eye and agreed with me that Gene needed to go to the hospital to be checked. We took him to the Emergency Room at the small Kilgore Hospital for examination and X-rays. The accident caused a long irritation of back problems for Gene and a lengthy investigation into the matter, which took several years.

This is only one of the many times God has interceded in our lives. He never turned away from Gene and I and our Family. According to God's Word, He has assigned Angels to each one of us to protect us and help us.

When my children or grandchildren come to visit me and are ready to leave, I always tell them, "Don't drive faster than your angels can fly." I know it's a simple saying, but it lets them know I'm thinking about them and praying for them and want them to have a safe trip home.

God is always there. We need only to call His Name. It took a lawyer several years to reach a settlement about the accident. The Devil was trying to kill Gene, but God had His Angels around him to protect him. Thank You Father for Your Angels. Gene's back still hurts, but he is alive.

CHAPTER 34
GENE'S BIG TRUCK ACCIDENT

Gene told me of an accident he had when he was about 39 years old. He was working for Buster and driving a tractor pulling a flat bed trailer loaded with drilling rig equipment. He was headed north on Interstate 45 out of Conroe, Texas on his way home.

Two trucks passed him as he was running about 55 to 60 mph and waved for him to come on and he passed them going 96 mph. At that instant the left front tire on the tractor blew out. The front of the truck raised up when the tire blew and forced the truck to cross over to the South bound lane of traffic. He was meeting an oncoming car and had to get over which caused him to hit the guard rail on the bridge.

The truck took out about 75 feet of guardrail and then ran off the bridge and hit the concrete retainer wall from the right-of-way down to the creek. Fortunately, the creek was almost dry. The first thing he was aware of was a man holding his head between his legs sitting on the ground. The man told him his neck was broke and for him to lay still.

At that time he could hear the ambulance approaching, then passed out again. The next thing he was aware of was when the attendants in the hospital were removing his boots which was very painful. He asked that the boots be cut off but they would not. The attendants asked him if he knew the phone number of his parents and he told them the number and also his home phone number.

Then he heard the voice of who he thought to be the hospital Administrator talking to his mother on the phone. He advised them to be careful coming to the hospital and that Gene probably wouldn't be alive when they got there. His parents arrived at the hospital that night.

A doctor advised him that his neck was broken, back was broken in three places, and his pelvis was crushed and put him in ICU. While he was in ICU he was kept sedated during that time. One of the attendants said they wanted to transfer him to a larger hospital in Houston, but he said he preferred to remain there. His parents stayed for a week while he was in ICU and then returned home.

He remained in ICU for an additional week, then they moved him to a private room and put him in traction. His parents returned again and stayed with him for about three days.

He was not allowed to have any water or liquid to drink. He asked his mother to get him some cut flowers, so she asked his father to get the flowers for him. His motive for getting the flowers was to get access to the water they were in. And he drank the water from the flowers after he was told not to have any liquids.

His parents came back every weekend for about two months. He remained in traction for about 63 days. At that time he was given a wheelchair and was able to go wherever he desired. He was in the hospital for a total of 93 days then released to go home. He was taken to his home in Kilgore by ambulance where he and his wife Bertie lived.

The hospital referred him to a bone specialist in Longview. He went to see the doctor the first week he was home. His heel was still hurting and he could barely walk or stand on it. The attendants in the hospital did not X-ray his foot, but the doctor in Longview did and found that he had a crushed heel bone. He advised him it would take two years for it to heal and it did.

He was unable to return to work for a year after seeing the bone specialist, because the Doctor would not release him for work. He occupied his time by building some miniature oil derricks and sculptures out of welding rods, etc. Some of these that he made are now on display at the Kilgore Oil Museum.

He told the Specialist he needed to go back to work because he needed some money coming in as the insurance company had discontinued paying him. The Specialist advised him not to go back to work, and that he would take care of any problems with the insurance company. The Doctor phoned them immediately to advise them he was releasing Gene for light duty only. Gene could drive a truck or car but could not perform any manual labor.

The accident happened about 3:00 pm on September 10, 1969 and he was finally released to perform manual labor in January 1971.

While he was in the hospital, the ambulance attendants came back to the hospital to check on him. Gene asked the name of the man that was holding his head in between his legs and trying to keep Gene still until the ambulance came. The ambulance attendants advised Gene that no one was holding his head when they arrived. Gene was lying on his back on the ground and no one was around him.

But, we know that God promised us in His Word in Psalms 91:11 "For He shall give His angels charge over thee, to keep thee in all thy ways. :12 They shall bear thee up in their hands, lest thou dash thy foot against a stone." **KJV**

For years, and almost every day, I have repeated those words in Psalms 91:11 and thanked God for his angels he assigns to each of up to keep us from any harm.

I understand that sometimes we may be hurt, because of the situation we allow ourselves to be in or the stupid things we do, but God will not allow us to be killed. The last verse in Psalms 91 is a promise from God that states, "With long life will I satisfy him, and shew him my salvation."

We now know, that at that time, God was not finished with me or Gene. God had "A Work" for us to do together, not apart, even though we were not aware of it.

When we look back on these things now, we can see how God was at work in our lives. He was just waiting for us to "get our stuff together" and turn to Him for guidance and protection.

CHAPTER 35
COUSIN HARRY GORDON

I made my acquaintance with **Harry Gordon Pettey** shortly after I entered college at Stephen F. Austin State Teacher's College in Nacogdoches, Texas in 1950. That was his name at that time. He changed it later to H. Gordon Pettey or just Gordon Pettey. The name of the college was later changed to Stephen F. Austin University.

I had known his parents, Jessie Elmo Pettey, Sr. and his wife Maud G. Pettey, through my Father, Samuel G. Hooper, Sr. They were my Great Uncle and Great Aunt. Uncle Jessie was my Grandmother's, Mamaw, brother.

My Dad took me to Nacogdoches to register me in College and to set up a bank account for me. I have already related how my Dad asked Uncle Jessie to take us to his bank so he could open a bank account for me.

At that time Aunt Maud had The Modern Dry Cleaning shop on the highway in front of their house. Their house was up on a hill and away from the highway.

They were glad to see me but couldn't believe I had walked all that way.

Harry Gordon was there with his friend Dorothy. I only remember being in the Sitting Room with Harry and his friend and I was sitting on a day bed and Harry was doing most of the talking. He asked me if I always kept my finger nails that long. Well, yes, I had. They were quite long. He proceeded to cut my nails off because he said no one in College had nails like mine that were that long.

He also told me to stop wearing stockings and wedge heel shoes because no one else did. My Step Mom and Dad thought that was the way girls dressed at college. I had seen pictures in the magazines of girls dressed like that. Those must have been some colleges up North, but not in Texas!

Harry Gordon Pettey was born February 14, 1929 and was a Junior at College and was three years older than me. I was only a Freshman and he would not have had anything to do with me if we had not been related.

I was a skinny, 99-pound girl, with long hair and long nails, and wore stockings and wedge heel suede shoes to College. I'm sure I must have been a sight-to-see, fresh from the country and now going to college. Nevertheless, he was very kind to me and never forgot me, and I never forgot him and the kindness he showed me.

It was years later when I saw him again at one of the Pettey Reunions at the Old North Church in Nacogdoches in about 1963. He told me he had been working or managing the famous Johnny Case's Restaurant on Highway 80 in Longview.

That was a well-known restaurant throughout East Texas. I stopped in to see him for a few minutes while in Longview once. He was busy working on the menus for the day and couldn't talk very much with me. At that time, I was married and living in the Dallas Area with three children.

It was about then that Harry Gordon and Vivian Pettey, Uncle Charlie's daughter, discussed producing a book of The Pettey's of East Texas. I understand that they collaborated on the book for some time and then had it printed and offered it for sale at a cost of $15.00. This was a time when money was scarce for us and most of the nation. I couldn't seem to get the $15.00 together for the book.

In about 2010 my oldest daughter asked me again about the person who signed the Declaration of Independence named William Hooper and was he related to us. I didn't know so I decided it was time for me to find out who he was as well as some of our relatives that we weren't sure about.

I joined Ancestry.com and found more information than I knew how to use. It was a treasure of information that traced our relatives back to the time they came to America from Europe. This was when I decided to try and contact Harry Gordon to find out if he could help me with my research.

I found his Email address through another cousin and his brother, Jessie. Some of the information I obtained about Harry Gordon came from his Cousin Lana. She is the same person that was at Uncle Jessie's house when I visited once. Uncle Jessie and Aunt Maud took me and Lana to the Fair one afternoon.

I contacted him by Email and much to my surprise he sent back an answer. His Email read something like this, "I checked my Email and out popped a letter from someone I hadn't heard from for a long time." I was delighted when he answered my letter.

He lived only a few blocks from my son Michael who lived in the Carswell Air Force Base Area in Fort Worth. We made arrangements to meet at his house in a couple of days.

He was the same "Old Cuz" I remembered from long ago, and always called me "Cuz." He gave me some pointers in gathering information and putting it into printable form. I told him I had no desire to publish a book, but I wanted to make a book with a loose leaf notebook for my children and family so they would know about our family history.

In October 2011, my husband and I went on a vacation through Mississippi, Alabama, South Carolina, and North Carolina. Harry told me to go north of Huntsville, Alabama and to Moores Mill where our Great-Great Grandparents, William Eli Pettey (Petty), Sr. and wife Lucretia "Lucy" Wright, are buried next to the road at the edge of a corn field.

William Eli's grave and Lucretia's both have headstones. William's headstone and grave are kept up by the Daughters of the American Revolution because he fought in the Revolutionary War. But Lucretia's grave is so grown over it is barely visible because they are not responsible for her grave.

Their graves are at the edge of the road in a corn field with only a small ditch separating them from the pavement of the two lane country road. The pictures are in my "Book" about the Petteys and the Powers, and the Mays and the Hoopers of East Texas. The Book has not been published because it was never intended to be published. It was written only for my family and for their information. I made 25+ copies of the Book, which contained 620 pages. It took me about six months.

Harry Gordon Pettey told me about his travels around the world and some of the stories he had written. He didn't talk much about his family, but if you asked him about an old church or something about Texas History, he could tell you lots of stories. He loved to tell history stories.

He was my Dearest Friend and I miss our visits and communications. He was always looking for someone to marry, but never found her. I received a rare hand-typed letter from him post marked January 4, 2016 after not hearing from him for a time. That was a week or two before he died.

He never mentioned his family to me, or that he had been married and had two sons. Most of my information about him was gathered from his writings, pictures, and notes that were sent to me by his best friend. He had been a teacher, a radio announcer, traveler, and gatherer of Texas History. I went through the papers and then sent them on to his brother, Jessie.

The Obituary that is printed in Find A Grave Memorial reads, "Obituary for Dr. Gordon Pettey. Dr. Gordon Pettey, 86, passed away on Wednesday, January 27, 2016. Gordon was born on February 14, 1929 in Nacogdoches, Texas. He proudly served in the United States Army during the Korean War, where he survived being run over by a tank.

Gordon was an avid Texas History Buff and wrote many books about Texas History. He was founder, operator and author of Texas Historical Press.org, He received his Doctorate at Stephen F. Austin University. He was a great outdoors man, full of life and loved to spend time at his property in Oregon."

I was given a loose leaf notebook with pages he had written which seem to be his memoirs. His handwriting was almost not legible, but I did give it a try anyhow. He wrote about many things, people and places.

I might mention here that the official spelling of the Pettey name is "Pettey." Some other people, not our family, spell their name "Petty." This is what he wrote.

HARRY GORDON PETTEY, HIS STORY

I'VE LIVED THROUGH:

1. The Great Depression of the 30's.
2. The Polio Epidemic and World War II, Korean War, Vietnam War.
3. A President Assassinated, John F. Kennedy
4. An earthquake in Acapulco.

5. A blizzard in the High Sierras – could not see the highway.

6. Iced wings on my airplane in Salt Lake City. The Cuban missile crisis.

7. The atomic plant melt down in Chernobyl-Bella Russe. It floated right over the house where I lived.

8. Drove through Pamplona, Spain when I was blind.

9. Saw the terrible attack on the Twin Towers of New York and watched them fall. This changed the world.

BIRTH AND EARLY CHILDHOOD
1929-1939

I was born when there weren't any tractors. Horses and mules were the power and used as "bull dossers". Most people still lived on farms and had no electric power or gas. The economy was from cotton and corn. They had no electric motors to do their work. Some people did have an old car.

The average house in the countryside had a cast iron wood burning stove on legs.

The remainder of his manuscript was not legible. I sent all of the papers, his friend had sent to me, on to his brother Jessie so that they would remain in Harry Gordon's Family. He had befriended me during my first year in college. Then when I decided to venture into the story telling era of my life, he was a great help to me.

He was a great friend, my best friend, told many stories, and wrote many stories. I hope his work will live far into the future. He died on the operating table, when the operation went "bad." Rest in peace, dear friend. Your Old Cuz misses you.

CHAPTER 36
GETTING INTO THE ROUTINE

Our home is built. Gene is working for Mr. Tisdale now and I am being the "good housewife" I needed to be. We were very happy and quite active in Tommy's church also.

After our wedding, Gene and I both were attending Tommy's church together. Gene was elected to the office of Trustee, and I was teaching Children's Church. Tommy had asked me to teach Children's Church from the time Gene and I got married, but I had turned him down. I explained that I would like to sit in church with my "new husband" for a while, rather than be separated from him while teaching Children's Church.

The Children's Church was held in another part of the building at the same time the Sunday Morning Worship Service was held. It consisted of children from about four or five years old to ten or twelve years old. There wasn't any prepared material for the lessons, so I decided the best place to start would be at the beginning of the Bible and go forward.

Gene and I had a "wood working shop" in our garage. I made some displays for the lessons. The children seemed to enjoy the displays. When we came to the part where Moses was leading the Children to the Promised Land, I thought it would be nice to make a model of the tabernacle and figures for the houses (tents) around it.

Some tents were made out of paper, but the top of the tabernacle was made with some pieces of fur that I had. Actually, we all had a good time working on it.

Tommy decided to have a Revival and all was going great. After two weeks, he asked if the congregation would like to continue the Revival for an additional two weeks. Everyone liked the Evangelist and voted to continue the Revival. Then we continued for an additional two more weeks, for a total of six weeks.

I'm not sure exactly how long it was after the Revival that we experienced "A Walk Out" in the church. We were told that some of the members contacted "all of the members privately" and discussed the "Walk Out." They said that some of the members were not happy with the way things were being done, and that they liked the Evangelist and wanted to form a church with him in a nearby town.

They also complained that Tommy did not let his Associate Pastor preach as often as they thought he should. However, when this happened, Tommy had just let him preach for two weeks.

We did not find out about their "Secret Plans" until Gene and I returned to church that Sunday night. When we entered the sanctuary, Tommy was draped over the altar crying and praying. There were a few members there, our life-long friends that we called our other family who lived a couple of houses from us when we were growing up.

We were told that these "select members" had contacted every member of the church to discuss their plans and get everyone's approval. I was shocked and amazed that someone would do such a thing. I had never heard of this happening before. Also, those "select members" who said they had contacted **ALL** the members were not exactly telling the truth.

Those "select members" had not contacted me and Gene, nor Sammie and Marie, nor our life-long friends. I am positive they knew that our "group" would never have voted for such a "hideous" thing and would have tried very hard to stop it.

God had delivered Tommy from drinking, drugs, cigarettes and every other vile thing and made a preacher out of him. All of our family believed that if God had not changed him from the way he was living, he would have been dead long ago. I thank God for what He did for my brother.

It had not been God at work to destroy the church and my brother. God would continue to build and enlarge it and make it the Church He wanted. All Churches belong to God, with Jesus at the head, and are not the property of any individual. However, the church that those people started did not last very long. I don't believe it was built on The Rock, Jesus and the Word of God.

What Sandra, Charlie, and I had wanted finally came to pass. We were settled in and living next to each other. Sammie was doing carpenter and construction work for different ones and was living in their neighborhood. He also had a contract to build the "handicap ramps" for people coming out of the hospital with disabilities.

The prayer I prayed in Mineral Wells from Psalm 37:3, "Trust in the LORD, and do good; so shalt thou dwell in the land, and verily thou shalt be fed. :4 Delight thyself also in the LORD; and He shall give thee the desires of thine heart. :5 Commit thy way unto the LORD; trust also in Him; and He shall bring it to pass."

I had kept these verses in my heart all those years, and God had made them come to pass. God is always true to His Word if you will only Believe and Trust Him, He will do the same for you.

There was a small Synagogue, a Jewish church building, on the property that we had inherited. We were still living in the house Gene and I had built, with Sammie's help. Gene came home from being at the Synagogue and asked me if I wanted to open up the Synagogue, make it a church, and be the preacher. I was very, very shocked. I had never thought of such a thing.

We discussed it and decided, with God's help, we would try. Again, there was a lot of remodeling to be done to the inside of the building. It had been used by Buster for his Rotary Club parties and Bar-B-Ques.

The building was in perfect condition, except that it had only one bathroom. Here we go with the bathrooms again. The one bathroom was designed for ladies, but desired improvement. There was an office which could be made into the men's bathroom. All those problems were now solved. The building even had a kitchen.

So we built and remodels bathrooms, and painted the inside of the building. The original lights hanging from the ceiling were still there. This building was built in about the 1930's and functioned as the Synagogue for the congregation for many years. I believe they outgrew it and needed to build a larger building. This one was sold to Buster and he moved it onto his property. I'm not sure how long it had been on his property. It was a beautiful white brick building.

It took us several months to get it ready to hold services. When we told Tommy that we were leaving his church to start a new church in the Synagogue, he was very upset. Naturally, he did not want us to go because we were a vital part of his church. I was the teacher for Children's Church and Gene was a Trustee. The name TRUSTEE was used instead of Deacons or Elders.

We had prayed about our leaving and felt that it was what God wanted us to do. So we started. Some times Gene and I were the only ones there, except for the Lady Bugs and Moths. After several months, Gene came in contact with an old friend of his, Mr. Turner, and told him about the church.

He and his wife became our first members. They were both older than Gene and I, and told me about going to a "Lady's Church in Spring Hill many years ago whose name was Kate." I told them that it was my Aunt Kate's church that Gene and I had attended while we were in High School, fifty years ago. His wife was not in very good health and did not attend church regularly.

One Monday night, about 11:00 pm, Gene came to the kitchen where I was and told me he needed to go to the hospital. He was having problems with his stomach where it had been cut open when the table saw kicked back and cut open his stomach. I knew this probably meant another operation, and it did. I took him to the hospital and he was admitted immediately,

The next night, Tuesday, was our regular service night. I called Mr. Turner and told him we would not be there. He said he would be praying for Gene to have a speedy recovery, and he did.

We saw an advertisement in the paper for church pews for sale. That's the one thing we really needed. We made arrangements to buy them and bring them back to the church. Now the church was complete.

But, the church wasn't growing, so I got the idea of putting an ad in the paper. The ad read, "We have a church building that needs a congregation." I received several phone calls, but then I received the one from a minister who told me they were meeting in a community room at a trailer park and were interested in our building.

Gene and I went to one of their services to "check them out." We were very pleased with what we heard and saw. Then we invited them to come look at our "little church." They said it was ideal for them and we closed the "deal" with a hand shake. There was no money involved because we did not believe that was what God intended. They began their worship services there the next Sunday.

We did not lease or sell the building and property to them. We prayed about it and felt that God wanted us to give it all to them. So we did. The pastor had not had a church in several years. He said some of his friends were telling him that he needed to start preaching again. So he did.

They used the Synagogue building for several years while they were collecting money to build a larger building. By this time, the little building was quite full at every service. They built the new building and were going to use the "little church" for "Youth Services."

Gene came home one afternoon and asked me to go with him to look inside the "little church." He seemed upset. When we walked in, we saw that the church pews had been removed and taken to be used in the new building and that was okay. There were several large "bean bags" around instead of chairs.

I had worked very hard myself painting and fixing those tall walls, that were now painted black. We could not believe how they had changed the inside of the building from what we had spent almost a year to beautify, remodel, and rebuild.

Gene looked at me and said, "Let's go." We could not bear to look at it. He took his keys to the Preacher and told him how disappointed we were and that we would no longer be associated with the church. No one seemed to think they had done anything wrong. Also, they did not seem too concerned about our leaving.

We now think that God wanted us to move on. Maybe He thought our work was finished there. We immediately started looking for another church to attend and visited three of the Assembly of God churches in the area.

On Sunday, after leaving one of the churches we had visited, we drove by and parked outside of the third church. The first person we saw coming out of the church was a man wearing overalls.

After Gene's first operation from the plastic cutting his stomach, he could not bear anything tight around his stomach. Buster had suggested he wear overalls. He has worn overalls for many years working and to church.

We decided we would visit that church the following Sunday. We did and found some of the kindest and sweetest people we have ever known. It reminded me of the church I attended in Mineral Wells. I left a lot of dear friends there.

We were told that the Pastor of the church had a stroke just a few weeks before our visit. He was in a nursing home. They were having guest preachers for the Sunday Morning Services.

Not very long after we started attending regularly, I was asked to substitute teach the Adult Sunday School Class we were attending. I don't know why I am always asked to teach some kind of Sunday School Class wherever I go. I think God has branded my forehead "Teacher" or maybe I just look like a "Teacher." It makes no difference whether I am at church or at work, they always seek me out to "Teach" or to "Train".

The Sunday School Teacher was having some serious health problems and ask me to teach the class "full time." I did, and after several years, she left the church because of personal reasons.

The selection process for a new Pastor took a year. During that time we joined the church. Some of the preachers were just filling in, and some were applicants for the Pulpit. Then the Pastor's wife announced that the Pastor would not be returning and had resigned because of his health. He had been the Pastor of the church for thirty-two years and everyone loved him dearly. He died a year after the new Pastor came.

The selection was made for the new Pastor and we were blessed with a wonderful Pastor and his wife. His wife went through some very difficult and serious health problems. At the end of nine years he resigned from the church and from "full-time" ministry. We were again looking for and trusting God for a new Pastor, a New Shepherd.

We had several applicants over a long period. At that time, I was praying for God to send us our "New Shepherd that He had chosen." I never put any restrictions or any special qualifications for the New Pastor. I left it up to God's choice.

Our New Pastor comes from South Texas, has a beautiful wife who plays the piano and he plays guitar. When God allowed the Israelites to choose their "King" he was not the one God would have picked, and it did not turn out well. But God has chosen Pastor Dale Wommack for us and I am sure that he has been sent by God. Thank You, Father.

CHAPTER 37
UNCLE PAUL, THE PREACHER

This is the same "Uncle Paul" that tried to teach me how to swim, and also the Step Father of "My Cousin Bill." He was one of my favorite relatives whom I loved very much.

I told earlier in my story about how my Dad's Father had died from pneumonia after plowing the field in the rain while he had the measles. Since my Grand-mother, Mamaw, was a young woman with a baby boy to raise and another child on the way, she remarried an older man with about five children, some were already grown. That man was my Uncle Paul's Father, and the father of my Aunt Alpha. These two siblings were my Dad's half brother and sister, but they were as close as any brother or sister I had ever known. In fact, I did not know about this relationship until I was in my teens.

My Uncle, Paul Joseph Paramore, was born July 9, 1910 in Shelby County, which included Center and Paxton, Texas. I was also born in Shelby County Texas. He was about five eight or five nine feet tall with beautiful brown curly-wavy hair and was a very hansom man. Mamaw told me a story about him when he was a very young man. I'm not sure which of these occurrences happened first, I'll just tell them in the order in which she told me.

Mamaw said that Paul came into the house one day asking where his Uncle Ollie was and she told him. She asked him why was he in such a hurry to see Ollie, her brother. His answer was, "I need for him to tell me about Jesus." Then he left.

Between Mamaw and Uncle Paul, they told me how he met his wife. He had met her at a Dance Hall there in Longview and later married her. She had not been married before, but had a small boy. I guess he was "pretty well smitten by her," because he married her. Aunt Connie was a beautiful and sweet person.

Mamaw told me that she was upset because he married "that woman with a child." But Connie was the sweetest and dearest of all of her daughter-in-laws. Come to think of it, she only had two daughter-in-laws, Connie and my Mother. My Mother is the one that left my Dad and us five children to be with another man.

I told you in another story that Uncle Paul and Aunt Connie, and my "Cousin Bill" had lived behind our house on the next street. Our house was on Culver and their house was on the street behind our house. There were no fences, so we could walk from our back yard into their back yard.

It was probably in those same years that Uncle Ollie and his family came to visit us quite often. They could go to see Uncle Paul and his family, and them come around the block and visit us. Uncle Ollie was one of Mamaw's five brothers.

He was my Dad's Uncle and my Great Uncle. I'm not sure when he became a Preacher and where he preached.

I believe Mamaw's daughter, Alpha, was still living at home, her daughter, Kate, was married and living somewhere in the vicinity. Her brother, Will, may also have been living in Longview at that time.

When Uncle Ollie came to visit us, his daughter Doris, son O.N. Jr., and daughter Patsy would go with me to my bedroom where we could play or visit. We always had fun when they came around.

I don't know when Uncle Paul entered the Ministry. The first that I remember was when he came to our house and was the Pastor of a church in Mobile, Alabama. I may have been in my early teens at that time.

I came home from school and my Dad told me that Uncle Paul had been to visit us that day, but left before I came home from school. He told my Dad a story of how some of the congregation had accused him of "curling his hair" because it was very "nice and curly" and they wanted to "put him out of the ministry."

They were very particular about those things in those days. The congregation did not believe in curling your hair. He was also doing some Antique Business as a second income.

He was having problems with his Step Son, Bill. Because of this, Bill was allowed to live with his Grandparents in the next small town from ours. It was only about ten miles from my home. I remember Bill as being a strong willed person with a temper, and quite large for his age.

This was in the 1939 or '40's. Pentecostals were and still are very strict about their beliefs. I'm sure that if the church members had found out that Bill was Aunt Connie's illegitimate child, they would have asked them to leave the church.

Bill spent his teen age years living with his Mother's parents and coming to our house as often as he could. He was only one year older than me, and we always had fun together. We did not break the rules or get into trouble.

If I remember correctly, they lived in Mobile for many years. Then Bill went into the Army, came out and got married and had a son. Bill was driving eighteen wheeler trucks on long runs when I heard from him many years later.

I have already told about what happened to him when he had a stroke and was hanging out of his cab all night in the company parking lot in Houston. Then he was transferred to the hospital in Tyler so he could be near his family and friends.

I'm not sure, but I had the impression that Uncle Paul was the pastor of the same church all those years in Mobile. I calculate it to be between 40 to 50 years. Then they moved from Alabama to Tyler to be near Bill and help him with his rehabilitation. Then several years later Bill died as a result of the stroke.

Since Uncle Paul and Aunt Connie were living only thirty miles from us, they came over at thanksgiving and

Christmas. Our family, Sammie, Charlie, and Sandra were very happy to have them living so near after all those years of living so far from us.

Gene and I went to see Uncle Paul one afternoon and he explained to us that Aunt Connie and he had gone to a church for a type of Business Meeting for that District. Aunt Connie started up the steps and lost her balance and fell back and hit her head and broke her arm. She was taken to the hospital in Tyler where the Doctor told Uncle Paul that Aunt Connie had a concussion and was now incoherent and would never be the same.

Both of them were getting up in years now. Uncle Paul had a man from his church come and help take care of him and clean the house. Uncle Paul's house was filled with antique furniture and old china. He liked to show them to me and explain their use or tell how old the piece was. He showed me a set of what looked to me like saucers, or small plates, and asked me if I knew what they were for. Of course, I did not know. He explained that the small plates were to put on top of your coffee or tea cup to keep it warm while you drank it.

Today we live in a heated house and don't notice the cold so much unless we go outside. But years ago, all of the houses were not heated, only the rooms that had a fireplace. I can understand how your coffee or tea could quickly get cold in a cold room, but the problem was solved with these little saucers.

When Aunt Connie was well enough, she was transferred to a Nursing Home and remained there until her death on September 4, 2007. Before her death, and during one of our visits to see Uncle Paul, he showed us a "Congratulation Letter" he had received from the Mayor of Tyler because he and his wife had been married for seventy years. That's a long time according to anyone's standards.

Before her death, I would call Uncle Paul to inquire if he would be home because we wanted to come visit him. At that time, his answer was always yes. But after her death, he never did answer his phone. His helper, Nick, would answer the phone and give me some excuse that he was taking Uncle Paul to the doctor or some other type of errand.

I'm not sure now if I ever got to see him after Aunt Connie's death. Aunt Connie's sister lived across the street from them. Once Gene and I had gone to see Uncle Paul even though he, or anyone else, did not answer his phone. I went to see Aunt Connie's sister and she said that Nick was keeping everyone away from my Uncle.

It wasn't too long from then that she called me to say that an ambulance had just come and had taken my uncle to the hospital. I went to see him. He was just lying in his bed in a "ball." He knew exactly who I was but did not move around. At that time he was 97 years old and probably was suffering from Arthritis.

It was only days later that he died on June 1, 2008. When I went to the visitation before the funeral, one of the church members said something about him not having any relatives. I was shocked and said that was some kind of lie Nick was telling everyone.

Uncle Paul had a son living in Longview, an ex-wife, and loads of nieces and nephews, and great nieces and great nephews also living in Longview. I found out that Nick had talked Uncle Paul into signing everything he owned over to him by telling him that no one cared about him and never came to see him. That included his Cadillac he had stored in the garage, his house, and all of the antiques in it.

I told the church member there at the visitation that Nick would not let anyone talk to Uncle Paul on the phone or come to see him. Nick would always answer the phone and give some kind of excuse for them to not come to see Uncle Paul because he was going to a doctor's appointment or something else.

Nick turned my Uncle Paul against me and my family, and took everything Uncle Paul owned. I went to the Court House and was given copies of Uncle Paul's will, which showed he had put everything in Nick's name. I did not have the money to fight against him. I put it into God's hands and God will take care of it now or in heaven.

My uncle and I were very close and I know how much he loved me. Throughout the years, I may not have gotten to see him very often, but when we were together, there always seemed to be a very "closeness." I still have his love with me and will forever. I loved him very dearly and still do.

CHAPTER 38

MY JEEP AND THE ACCIDENT

Throughout my married life, my husbands had bought new cars and brought them home. Even when they let me go with them, they always had the final word. The new car was supposed to be mine. I say that, and though it was my car, I was expected to take the kids to school and to all of their school activities, go to the grocery store and the dry cleaners. It may have been "my car" but it was more like a taxi. I drove it to work every day. None of the cars were ever in my name.

After Pat died and I became a widow there in Mineral Wells, I decided to trade my car and get something that I "really liked." I searched the local car dealers and didn't find anything I liked. I went to the nearby town east and found a car that suited me. It was a two door navy blue Mercury Cougar. I did not have any children living at home now. They were all married, so I didn't need that big "station wagon" type to transport my children and the neighbor children around.

The car was in my name because it was "My Car." I was very proud of my car because I had picked it out, paid for it, and drove it until Gene and I were married for five years, then it needed some minor repairs. Gene and I discussed the situation and because it was getting old, we decided to trade it for another car.

We drove to several auto dealers and looked for a "small, red, 4 door car" that I was praying about. We found one car that I thought was exactly what I wanted. The salesman wanted to take us for a ride, but when he looked for the keys, they were not to be found. There had been a break-in the night before into several of the cars, so all the keys were secured in the office. The keys were so secure that no one could find them.

After waiting for thirty minutes, we decided to go somewhere else. We drove on over to Longview and as we passed a Volkswagen Dealership I saw a small red car that looked exactly like the one I had prayed about. It was a red, 2004 Jeep Liberty and had everything on it I wanted.

Gene and I drove it home that night and went back the next day and signed the papers. Gene went back to the Dealership where we found the first car I liked and where they could not find the keys to it. He thought it would be nice if we both had newer cars that were similar, besides his truck was also ten years old.

They had found the keys later the day we were there and let a man who was a school teacher drive it home. On his way home, he stopped at a red light and someone ran the light and hit the car on the side. The car was totaled out because the damage was very bad. However, the driver was not injured. We were all thankful for that.

My sister Sandra came to visit us for the Thanksgiving holidays in 2013. She lived in South Carolina and flew down to see us and to visit all the relatives. We were told that our brother Lynn, who lived in Dallas, was having car trouble and could not come to see us, and my son, Michael who live in Fort Worth, had the same problem.

We discussed the situation for a day and decided we would go to see them the day before Thanksgiving. They lived about 100 miles away, so we set out on our trip.

The weather was beautiful, sun shining and slightly cool. We stopped for gas before we left town and headed west. We were about forty or so miles into our trip, chatting and having a good time. Even though it was the day before a holiday the traffic was very light on the Interstate.

I was driving the speed limit and came up behind a slower moving car. I looked all around and did not see any other vehicles and proceeded to pull into the left lane. At that instant I heard the sound of a horn and caught the glimpse of something "black" beside my car. I immediately turned the steering wheel to pull back into the right lane when I saw a deep ditch on that side of the highway. Then I pulled the steering wheel to go back into the left lane and saw another deep ditch on that side. I turned the steering wheel again back to the right side.

At that instant I could feel the car begin to slowly turn over from side to side. I cried "Jesus" as it turned over and over at least four times. I think we landed in the right hand ditch, but I'm not sure. When the car finally came to rest, I'm not sure if it was lying on the driver's side or upside down. I know that I was leaning slightly on my left side and saw blood dripping from my head onto my hand.

I could not see her but heard my sister yelling, "Somebody get me out of here." I know that I went in and out of consciousness. Then, two men were standing there trying to pull or lift me out of the car onto the grass. Someone said something about calling an ambulance. The next thing I knew, the ambulance was there and I was being lifted into it. The driver asked if I wanted to go the Tyler hospital or the Lindale hospital? I told him we needed to go back east which would be closer to my home.

The next thing I remember was a doctor standing next to me and saying, "Nurse, hand me a razor." That sure got my attention. He had his hands on my head and I knew that he was going to do some shaving in that area. I said, "please don't shave my head." He told me he was only going to shave my head where he was putting in the stitches. The stitches went from my forehead to the crown of my head.

The doctor asked if we were wearing seat belts and I told him "Certainly." I never drove without my seat belt on and didn't allow anyone in my car to ride without a seat belt on. And it seems, that – Jesus and his angels – is what saved our lives. I found out later that my sister's seat belt was wrapped around her neck and that's what broke her neck.

Someone asked me who I wanted to call. I said to call my husband and my Pastor. I had their phone numbers in my cell phone and on an identification card also. Both of them came immediately. My Pastor prayed for me and my sister. Gene came also, but neither stayed very long because I was still going in and out of consciousness and the attendants were preparing us for at least a night's stay. I spent Thanksgiving and the day after in the hospital. The doctor would not allow me out of the bed.

Sandra was in the intensive care ward with a "Halo" on her head and could not get out of bed either. When the doctor told me I could go home after two days, I went to the intensive care unit to see Sandra. She wasn't doing very well and had a "wire brace" on her head and neck. She didn't know I was there because she had been heavily sedated.

Her husband had immediately left their home in South Carolina when they called to tell him what had happened. He was with her in the Intensive Car Unit when I went in to see her. I told him how horrible I felt and that I almost killed my sister. He said he knew it wasn't my fault and not to blame myself. It was an accident.

Her daughter, Shannon and her grandson, Joshua, drove from Tennessee to be with her. All three of them traveled the thirty miles each day from my home to the hospital to see her. She was in intensive care for two months and continued to wear the "Halo" on her head because of her broken neck.

I had a "Case Worker" assigned to me that came to my home several times a week to help me with some exercises and to assist me walking. I had to use a cane at first to keep from falling. I guess my mental anguish was worse than the actual injuries.

I was sitting in my recliner in the den-kitchen rooms and decided I needed a drink of water. Shannon was standing at the sink in the kitchen. When I reached her she looked at me and said, "Aunt Betty, you're walking." I hadn't realized it because we were all talking and laughing, but I had walked to the sink without my cane. I never used it again.

Shannon's husband came after she had been there for about a week or more. He took their son, Joshua, back home with him because he was supposed to be in school. Shannon and her Dad stayed and continued to go to the hospital every day to see Sandra. She remained in the hospital until after January 1st.

Shannon had asked the doctor about taking the "Halo" off of her mother's head. He said it was not time and that he had put it on and no one could take it off except him.

The next day, while Shannon was at the hospital, she was advised that the doctor had gone on a vacation. Shannon immediately made inquiries about moving Sandra from the hospital in Tyler to Longview so that she would be closer to the family and cut out the thirty mile a day drive back and forth.

Sandra was immediately transported from Tyler to the hospital in Longview. When she arrived at the hospital, one of the doctors checked her and took the "Halo" off her head.

I could now go to visit her because she was in our local hospital. She remained in the hospital there for about one month. Then they released her. She had been away from her home for over three months and was ready to go home. She left the next day for South Carolina.

Gene had gone to the salvage yard where my Jeep was stored to see what it looked like. He looked at me, and all he would say was, "You don't want to see it." I knew from his expression and what he said that it must have looked very bad.

Nevertheless, I thank God every day that He and His Angels protected us that day.

Sandra had X-rays done on her body almost every day while she was in the hospital. She was told to go to her doctor when she arrived home for follow-ups. Several months later, the doctor told her that he had found cancer in her lungs and needed to take treatments. She was a smoker.

She did that for months and then the doctor told her she was okay. That was in 2014. But, that devil called "cancer" never wants to give up. It seems, when we run him out of one place, he goes to another.

In 2016 she seemed to get much worse. Finally, she left her husband and her home in South Carolina and went to stay with her daughter Shannon in Tennessee. She was getting very weak and wasn't able to take care of herself.

I believe it was in August that Tommy and his son, Wesley, drove to Tennessee to visit with her because her health was deteriorating very quickly. Tommy said she was beginning to look bad and she wasn't able to carry on a conversation.

The next month, in September, Shannon called me and said that if I wanted to see her, I had better come now. My Daughter, Denise, and I flew to Knoxville as soon as we could get a flight. When we saw her, she was sitting up in the bed watching TV. She had lost all of her hair, did not know who we were, and could not carry on a conversation. We stayed for several days, then flew back home because Denise had to go back to work.

We all kept in close contact with Shannon to check on Sandra. The morning of October 17, 2016, Shannon called to let us know that Sandra had died. She had made her wishes known to us that she wanted to be cremated.

Shannon brought her ashes back to Longview so that we could scatter them at the graves of her Mother and Father, Grandmother and step Granddad, her brother Jackie, and her Uncle Junior. Some other relatives of hers were also buried in that cemetery.

We had a Memorial Service at Tommy's church, then went to the cemetery to take care of her ashes. Her husband, Don, did not come. He had a stroke about twenty years earlier and did not get around very well because he was partially paralyzed on his left side.

Don lived in their house in South Carolina alone for several years. He hired a woman to come and do the housework and laundry.

I don't know who it was, someone found him flat on his back in the bathroom and had been there for three days. As I said, he was partially paralyzed on the left side and could not pull himself up off of the floor. He was wearing an emergency button around his neck, but when he fell, it had been caught underneath him. He was taken to the hospital where the doctors told him he could never live alone again.

Shannon found a Veteran's Home in Tennessee where he could stay and be near her. He was a Veteran and had served in the Army for twenty years. He stayed there for about a year and had another episode. He is now in a rehab where he is not allowed out of the bed. He also has Dementia and is not expected to live much longer. He died in May 2020.

After the stroke, and as he grew older, some say that he became very hateful. I remember him as being very kind and happy all those years he and Sandra were married and I would visit them. They were married over fifty years.

All I can do now, is cling to my memories and the fun we had together.

CHAPTER 39
I WAS ALMOST MOLESTED

My Dad worked for a very rich man as an architect drawing plans for new houses to be built. It seems his boss was going to Dallas on a Business Trip and asked my Dad if I could go with him to keep him company. That drive usually took two plus hours.

I was about twelve years old and still in school. For me to go on this trip with him, I had to miss school. Dad said it might be a good experience for me and he might buy me something nice.

I'm not sure what time of the year it was, but I do remember that I did not wear a coat. I don't even remember taking any luggage, but I'm sure I did.

The man came by our house about 9:00 am, after the other children had gone to school, and picked me up. I don't know how long or how far we had traveled when he asked me to come on over closer to him. I didn't suspect anything at that time and moved over closer to him. He put his hand on my knee and started rubbing his hand up my leg and slightly pulling my dress up.

Those were the days before all the girls wore shorts or slacks. I did not know what to expect from him, but I knew

I did not like what was happening. I knew very little about sex and things of that nature.

He asked me if I had begun my "period." Again, I wasn't sure what he was talking about. He said, "If you have and are having the "cramps" when you do, I have a good cure for them."

I had not started my "period" and had no idea what he was talking about. I only knew I did not like what was happening and did not like the way the conversation was going. He said something about buying me something nice. I was leaning so hard against the passenger door, I thought it would open and drop me out. If it had, I didn't care, I just wanted out of there, but there was NO WAY OUT!

He drove us to one of the large hotels in downtown Dallas and registered us as Father and Daughter. We went up to the room which had twin beds in it. I was sure glad it didn't have only one big bed. He did not make any advances toward me while we were in the bedroom.

He took me to another room in the hotel where there were other people sitting around and talking. There was a woman in the room with her young son who was about my age. She suggested that we go together down to the restaurant and get something to eat.

We had a good meal. I don't know what was done about the check. I guess the boy must have signed it. Then we went back up to the room where his mother was and the other people. Then his mother suggested we go to a movie, and we did. I don't know what theater we went to or what movie we saw. I believe I was too scared and upset to remember.

I knew I was in a very bad situation and wanted out of it. After the movie, we went back to the room where his mother and the others were. She suggested that I and her son go to her room and go to sleep. I was very relieved that I would not have to stay in the bedroom with my Dad's boss all night long.

The next day we returned home. I now think that I have tried to block most of those memories from my mind, but some of them are so vivid they still remain. I don't think he was on a Business Trip. I think he was on a "Party Trip," and there were things that happened that I don't remember and don't care to remember.

I did not know how to tell my Dad what had happened, so he let me go with his boss on a short trip to a small town just north. He stopped at a "Dime Store," We now call those "Dollar Stores." and took we in so I could pick out something I wanted. I was so scared that I picked out a pair of socks. That was the only thing he ever bought for me and it probably cost 25 cents. On the way to Dallas, he had talked to me about a "watch" but I guess he thought a pair of socks was good enough for me. I never saw a watch.

The nest time he wanted me to go with him to look at some land around the new lake that was being built. It was in the afternoon and my younger brother, Charlie was at home. I asked him to go with me and I made him sit in the middle. We drove around the lake for a short time, and he took us back home.

I think my taking Charlie along might have made him angry. The next time he wanted me to go with him was during a school day, thinking he could get me alone. I pretended to be sick when he came to pick me up and stayed home.

When my Dad came home from work he was angry with me because I hadn't gone with his boss to keep him company. He ordered me to go to his bedroom and took his belt off. I started crying and Dad seemed to know something was wrong. He asked me some questions, which I don't remember. I said that I couldn't tell him and he knew for sure something was wrong.

Dad assured me that I could tell him anything. I told him what had happened and he said to me that I would never have to go with his boss again. He said he knew how he was "about women" but thought I would be okay with him.

To this day, I don't know if Dad ever said anything to his boss or not. That was in 1945 and things weren't the same as they are now. If my Dad had confronted his boss, he could have lost his job. And, after all, jobs were hard to find and Dad had a house full of kids to feed and clothe.

I was about twenty-two years old when I had my next experience. My girlfriend and I had rented a two bedroom house from an elderly man in Dallas. It was time to pay the monthly rent, so I went over to the landlord's house.

He invited me in and seemed very polite. Until he asked me to sit in his lap and talk over the situation. I knew immediately I was in the wrong place and I was alone. I gave him the rent money and left the house as fast as I could.

Gene and I had been married for a few years when I needed to have my eyes examined and to check for any eye problems. He suggested I go where he had always gone. I made an appointment.

I went for my appointment. This was not the first time I had my eyes checked. I had them checked many times before. But this time it was different.

I know that the lighting needs to be dim for a proper examination. The doctor was leaning all over me while he was changing the machine that tested my eyes. I had also told him that I did not want to buy any glasses that day. I was having some eye problems and needed my eyes checked for perhaps an infection.

When he finished checking me, he called for his assistant to take me to pick out some frames for my glasses. I know the assistant could see the look on my face and knew what had happened. I politely told him that I did not want to be fitted for glass that day and I had told the doctor that. I excused myself and left.

I went home and told Gene what had happened. He said he had heard "stories about the doctor." My reply to him was, "Then why did you send me to him?"

My Dad had heard "stories" about his boss, but he allowed his boss to take me on a long overnight trip with him. Then Gene advised me to go to the eye doctor whom he had heard "stories" about.

Today the News is filled with stories about young girls being abducted and killed. I can imagine what they went through before they were killed. Their death was probably a relief for them because of the horror they were experiencing.

I thank God that he has been with me all of my life and protected me from such men as these. I believe that the mother of the young boy in Dallas knew what my Dad's boss had in mind for me when he got me alone in that bedroom. I thank God that she was there and diverted the situation by having her son and myself go away from the "Party" activity.

It's so easy to look back and see God at work. He is always there, never leaves us, but helps us out of bad situations. Jesus said, I will never leave you nor forsake you." Thank You Jesus.

CHAPTER 40
BRENDA'S WEDDING, ETC.

I should have written about this nearer to the beginning of the Book, but since I missed it, I will put it in now. I was living in Euless, Texas just outside of Dallas, Texas when I received a call from my niece Brenda. She is Sammie's middle child and was making plans for her wedding.

I have always been close to Sammie and his family, even though they have lived in Decatur, Illinois for a long time. She called to beg me to come to her wedding which would be on February 14th. I promised her I would come. Years later it turned out that this was not to be her first wedding. There would be three more.

I talked to my Step Mom, the gad-about, and she wanted to go with me. She came from Galveston to Dallas on the bus, and I picked her up at the bus station.

The day came for us to leave, so we all piled in my car, my Step Mom, my daughters Theresa and Denise, and my son Michael.

We traveled through north Texas, Oklahoma, and into Missouri. This was to be a long trip, about twelve hours.

As we left Joplin, Missouri traveling east toward St. Louis, Missouri we noticed some "white stuff" out in the plowed fields. We thought it was left-over cotton from the harvest. BUT, much to our surprise – IT WAS SNOW!

When we left our home in Texas, it was a beautiful sunshiny day and we were wearing short sleeves. We had taken jackets because we knew it would be cold in Illinois, but we weren't in Illinois yet!

If that wasn't bad enough, I looked back at Denise who was looking kind of red. I thought at first it was because she was lying in the sun in the back of the station wagon on a quilt. But, much to my surprise, she had red spots all over her. It was the three-day measles.

I asked my Step Mom if we should turn around and go back home, or if we should continue on. We decided to go on to the wedding because it was just as far to go back as it was to continue on. Denise didn't seem to be sickly or running a fever.

When we got to St. Louis, the snow was getting heavier and deeper. Men were out of their cars and pushing cars up the small inclines because the snow was getting deep and slick.

From St. Louis to Springfield, Illinois I could hardly see the hood of my car. I was driving about ten miles an hour when I saw the snow plow on the other side of the four-lane divided highway.

I looked in the rear view mirror and saw a long line of headlights from the traffic behind me and nothing in front of me. I could hardly see where I was going. I told my

Step Mom, "These people must be fools if they think this Texas Girl is going to lead the way through this blizzard for them!!" I turned my flashers on and stopped.

I didn't know if I was in the middle of the road or the side or if I was still on the pavement. I didn't care. I waited for all of those "idiots" to go around me, and then I followed them hoping and thinking that surely they knew the way.

When we came across the city limit sign for Springfield, Illinois, I pulled into a service station that was well lit so I could rest and get my composure back. My hands were glued to the steering wheel. We had left my home in Euless at seven o'clock in the morning on a bright sunny day and was supposed to be in Decatur, Illinois at seven o'clock that night.

We finally arrived at seven o'clock in the morning after driving all day and all night. What was supposed to be a twelve hour trip turned into a twenty-four hour trip.

As we entered Decatur that morning, we passed a bank with a clock on the front of the building that read 7 am and the temperature was 7 degrees. It was Valentine's Day, the day of the wedding. Brenda had begged me to come to her wedding and I promised I would, but I had just been taught a very valuable lesson – THIS TEXAS GIRL WOULD NEVER GO NORTH AGAIN IN THE WINTER!!

I took my children back on vacations in the summer time. Sammie and Alene took us to many of the historical places around Decatur and Springfield, Illinois where

Abraham Lincoln lived. We went through his home in Springfield and saw his grave and the huge granite block that weighs tons, that was placed on top of his grave so no one could steal his body as someone did once before.

As the years went by, we didn't get to see each other as much as we did in the past because we all had children in school and jobs to go to. But, we always kept in touch. Actually, they were living in Monroe, Louisiana years ago when I first asked Sammie to help me design a house the way I would like to have it built. That was in about 1965. We never did get to build that house, but we did build another one in White Oak, Texas after Gene and I were married.

Sammie and his family lived in Decatur, Illinois until after his children graduated from High School, and Linda was married and had a baby, and Brenda was also married.

Sammie and Alene were living in Houston, Texas in 1976 when they divorced after 28 years of marriage. I don't know the reason. He then married Beulah Marie Ryan on December 24, 1976 in Houston, Texas. Alene married Chuck and they lived in Houston. Alene and I remained friends even though we no longer were related, but we had been friends since 1950.

After my husband Pat Malone died in May of 1995, I wanted to sell my house in Mineral Wells and move back to my home town, Longview. But, first I had work that needed to be done on the house in order to sell it. Some things had never been completed, like installing baseboards and door frames.

In March of 1996, I wrote Sammie and told him that I sure needed his help if he was free to help me do some work on my house. I was also planning to have our Hooper Reunion in May. Much to my surprise, Sammie and Marie showed up at my door on May 1st and stayed for a year and a half until we finished the work on my house. I couldn't have done it without them.

During those times, we would sit each morning drinking coffee, and reading and studying the Bible. He had been going to church when he lived in Decatur and had learned quite a lot about the Bible. I was just a Beginner. I had been in church off and on all of my life, but realized I had not actually learned much about the Bible.

Those were special days and times in my life that I will always remember. He had been studying in Decatur with a man named Dale and taught me some things I needed to know. He taught me about **tithing.** Most people don't know why or how much to tithe, but when I learned that principal and followed it, God started Blessing me and has never stopped. The tithe belongs to God, not us.

Sammie also taught me about giving to others. When I learned to listen to God and give when and where He told me to give, those have been some of the happiest moments of my life. Nothing can compare to the joy and happiness you receive when you Bless someone else. Sammie, and his wife

Marie, and I went to church together at the First Assembly of God Church in Mineral Wells.

After we finished working on my house, we did some "House Flipping" and did very well. Sammie was given the contract for building ramps at houses for people how were released from the hospital and were using a wheelchair.

One day he told me he was going back to Decatur. That was the last thing I wanted to hear from him. He and Marie went back to Decatur and I tried to sell my house. That story is told in another part of the Book.

Sammie and Marie returned to Texas and went to Longview where Gene and I, Charlie and Deanna, and Sandra and Don were settling in where we had purchased the property and house that Tommy had told us about.

Sammie helped Sandra make some changes to the house she had chosen. When they were finished, he built Charlie and Deanna's house. By this time, I am living in an apartment with Sammie and Marie. Then through my job at the Longview News Journal, I found out where Gene was and we were married.

Now it's time for Sammie to build the house he and I had planned when he was staying with me in Mineral Wells. The first thing we did was to have the garage delivered. It was a large two-car metal garage with ample room for a workshop and cars. We used the workshop to store our tools and material for the house. Sammie was the contractor and

Gene and I did whatever we could to help. All of the details are told in "Building Our Home."

One Friday evening, Gene and I invited Sammie and Marie to join us for a Catfish Dinner where we had often eaten before. Again, Sammie told me they were moving back to Decatur, Illinois. I told him that was the worst thing he could do. All of his Blessings were here, not there. Nevertheless, they moved back to Decatur. I told Gene I would never see my brother Sammie again.

He became very ill in Decatur and was in the hospital for some time. His children were told that they needed to come to see him because it would probably be the last time. I wasn't able to go at that time. His three children gathered around him.

On April 6, 2006 in the hospital in Decatur, Illinois, he went home to see his Savior with his family gathered around him.

When I think of him now, I remember the "true stories" he would tell. One was about our Great Grandmother, Eliza Jane Pettey, my Dad's grandmother. He said they would walk around in her garden looking a things. Then he would hear her talking. He said he would ask her, "Grandmother, who are you talking to. She would tell him Jesus." She was always talking to Jesus.

She told Sammie that she had prayed and asked God to protect her children. She promised God she would follow

Him all of her life if He would keep her boys from being killed in a war. This was at the time of the Civil War.

Years later, her boys joined the Army during World War I. Not one of her sons or grandsons were ever wounded or killed during any war. Actually, I don't know of any male in our family being killed in any war.

Sammie also told me about his bicycle being stolen when he was a boy. One Sunday morning during church he told our Dad that God had just told him where his bicycle was and he wanted to go and get it. Dad did not want to leave church, but he did and took Sammie where he said his bicycle was and took a policeman with them.

When they saw the bicycle, Dad said it was not Sammie's because it was a different color. Someone scraped on it and they could see that it had been re-painted a different color, but the old paint and color was visible when the new paint was scraped away. Sammie got his bicycle back because God told him where it was. God is always speaking to us, but we are not always listening.

We had always been very close because he was the oldest son and I was the oldest daughter in our family. He may have done some things wrong, or things others did not approve of, but, don't we all make mistakes? I know I certainly do, especially when I'm not listening to God for direction.

I still love my brother Sammie, no matter what. I thank God for him.

CHAPTER 41
DELLA COMES HOME

After seeing Della again after ten years there at Dad's in Galveston, there was no way I could keep her away from the family. She was our sister and Dad's daughter. She was living in Texas City and working at a bar.

Theresa had located her siblings who were adopted out. Patti was one of them.

Patti tells us that a friend of hers said to her, "You should go and see this woman who is working at a bar in Texas City. She looks just like you."

Patti checked it out and much to her surprise, the woman did look like her. Patti did not tell me of their conversation, but they did get together.

Della was living with a man named Charlie in Texas City. She left the bar and went to work driving a taxi. Charlie was driving a commuter van for sailors who were on leave from their ships in Texas City. These were merchant sailors. They seemed to have a good life and relationship together.

Charlie and Deanna and their girls had come to our first Family Reunion in their travel trailer. Charlie had promised his girls he would take them to Galveston after the Reunion was over.

We all loved to go to Galveston and to the beach. We talked it over and off we go. Sandra and I took my granddaughter Emily and my grandson Ryan with us. Della returned to Texas City with Charlie. Texas City is only ten miles from Galveston. Charlie and Deanna took their girls in their travel trailer. We were on our way to Galveston and the beach.

This was just one of the times we would go to the beach at Galveston. From then on, everyone went whenever they got a chance. Sandra and I took the grand kids and Denise and I took them sometimes. One of the things we always had to do while we were there, was to ride the Ferry Boat.

In that area, instead of trying to build long bridges across the ocean water, Ferry Boats were used and they were free. We would park our cars in the designated parking area, board the Ferry, and go for the round trip. We had the ocean breeze in our face and it was delightful.

After this trip, Della and Charlie insisted that we stay with them whenever we came to Galveston. They were very good hosts for us. Charlie had his large van that he drove to transport sailors, and he always took us out at night to eat.

From the very first time, Charlie said to Ryan, "Ryan, you sit up front with me." He was extra fond of Ryan. We would spend part of the day at the beach, then Charlie and Della would take us to a very nice place to have seafood. Those were the days and they went on for years!!!

After my grandson Ryan's death, we didn't go to Galveston very often, but I did keep in touch with Della. It was very hard for me to call Della and Charlie and tell them about Ryan's death. I knew Charlie would take it very badly.

Texas City had an unfortunate disaster. There was a bad chemical spill that polluted the air and Della breathed it in. After that, she had lung problems and breathing problems and was under a doctor's care for years.

One day Della called to tell me that Charlie (her husband) was in the hospital and not expected to live. He died a short time after that. I'm sure Ryan was there to welcome him home.

As I have already told, Della died on October 6, 2017 in the hospital in Texas City. It saddens me to think that she did not have any family or friends around her at that time. No one called me, but, I'm sure Jesus welcomed her home.

My grandchildren that I took to the beach in Galveston are all grown now and have children of their own. Gene has no desire to go to the beach, probably because he did not grow up spending summer vacations at the beach as we did.

However, some of my fondest memories will be when we were children and Dad took us to the Beach at Galveston. Then taking my Grandchildren to the beach so they could enjoy the fun I had when I was little. Thank You Father, for watching over us on all those trips.

CHAPTER 42
OUR VACATIONS

We had not been on a "regular" vacation since we were married in 2000. We have been married now for ten years and it is 2010. Gene and I talked about it and decided it was time to take one. We agreed on going to Yellowstone National Park because neither of us had ever been there.

I got my maps out and started researching. We decided we would not make any reservations. We would just go wherever we wanted to, eat when we were hungry, and sleep when we were tired. That way, if we saw some place or attraction we wanted to see, we could stop and look as long as we desired.

We started out on May 19, 2010 traveling north into Oklahoma. I had traveled that highway many times when I lived in Oklahoma City years earlier. I knew there was a Gene Autry Museum off the Interstate, because I had seen the signs. That was our first stop. It was a small museum, but very interesting, and I am very glad we stopped. The museum constantly played Gene Autry music.

We spent our first night in Oklahoma City. We stopped along the way at every museum and attraction that interested us. One of the places that caught our interest was in Concordia, Kansas where we happened to find The

National Orphan Train Complex. I had seen a movie about the Orphan Train shortly before we left on vacation and wanted to visit the Museum.

The Museum contained many of the original posters from that era as well as the clothes worn and stories of the founders of the Train. Between the Museum and the Visitor Center are metal images (figures) of Orphans playing in the yard. It was a visit I will never forget.

The story is that there were many orphans in the New York City area and around it. They had been orphaned because of their parent's death from different kinds of illnesses and diseases.

A preacher came up with the idea of adopting the children out to people in the west where the population was not so crowded. He thought the people would be more willing to take them and furnish them with a good home. Thus was formed the Orphans Train to transport them to the western United States. The orphans were not sent west unless they had a home to go to and people who wanted them.

We traveled on west to Mount Rushmore to see the carvings of the Presidents, It was fabulous. Then we went to see the mountain carving of Crazy Horse which was not complete. They were both breathtaking.

We stopped at Sturgis, South Dakota because Gene wanted to see the Motorcycle Museum. He had motorcycles when he was younger. He bought one after we were married, but it was too heavy and he could not hold it up. Sturgis is where the Annual Motorcycle Rally is held every year. People come from all over the United States for the Rally.

We went to Old Fort Meade, The Peace Keeper Fort, in South Dakota. It was here that the Star Spangled Banner was first used in military ceremonies, starting its beginning to become our National Anthem. Fort Mead was a "Home Away from Home" for many in the depression years of the 30's when it was used as a base for 16 Civilian Conservation Camps.

We took Interstate 90 to Sundance, Wyoming and saw The Devil's Tower,

America's First National Monument. This is called the Gateway to Wyoming. It is said that this is where The Sundance Kid got his name.

Going on west, we could see some beautiful snow capped mountains in the distance. We had never seen mountains such as these. They stretched from the north to the south as far as we could see. As we neared them, they became larger and taller.

That's when we realized we were heading straight for them and had to go over them. We started up the East Side driving up a narrow winding road at about 15 mph. We were very excited when we finally reached the top, only to realize we had to go down the other side.

There were no towns along the route up or down and we were running low on gas. We had seen only a couple of houses along the highway. We finally reached the bottom and the town of Greybull, Wyoming which had a service station. There was a lady working there who came out, filled our gas tank, and washed our windshield. At least, after traveling so far for gas, we did get excellent service.

We checked our map to find out exactly where we were and much to our surprise, we had just crossed over the Grand Tetons. We also knew why they were named the Grand Tetons. They certainly were grand, wide, and tall and beautiful.

We traveled to Cody, Wyoming and spent the night. The next day we ventured into Yellowstone National Park. Much to our surprise, snow was covering the ground. Naturally, I had to make a snow ball and pretend I was going to throw it at Gene while he sat in the car and watched me.

We saw Old Faithful, but there were also smaller geysers everywhere. It took all day to drive through the Park. There were buffalo everywhere.

Our next stop was Cheyenne, Wyoming where we visited the Cheyenne Depot. The entrance to the Depot has two huge, large statues of cowboy boots painted beautiful colors. Inside were wood carvings displayed and miniature trains. It was all very interesting. Across from the Depot was a small park with a statue of a horse made out of screws and bolts.

As we traveled south towards home, there were antelopes everywhere. When we arrived at the Texas Welcome Center, there was another horse statue with Indian paintings that covered it. As we traveled on south, we saw the famous Cadillac Ranch on the north side of Amarillo, Texas. I think there where about six old Cadillacs standing on end. People were allowed to spray paint the old cars in any manner they desired. Empty paint cans were everywhere.

We were on the Freeway going through Wichita Falls and the water pump went out on our Jeep. That forced us to spend the night there. Our Son-in-law, Dave, owned a trailer that could transport cars. We phoned him, and he was there the next morning to take us the remainder of the way home with our "sick Jeep."

We arrived home on June 2, 2010. Thank God, our car trouble did not occur until we were almost home. It could have been in the Grand Teton Mountains, or Yellowstone National Park with all the buffalo. We know that things can go wrong, but God protected us all the way and we were never stranded in some place where we could not get help.

The trip was wonderful and exciting and we thank God for the opportunity he gave us to see part of our Nation we had never seen before.

Later that year we received a phone call from our friends Mike and Dixie whom we knew through church. Mike had had a very serious motorcycles accident and the doctors though he might lose his foot. They wanted us to come to Estes Park, Colorado to visit them.

We had already been through Colorado, but this was to be a long trip, so we spent the night in a motel in Dumas, Texas. We had stayed there before and knew it was a very nice motel. The next day we drove through to Estes Park to meet with Mike and Dixie. The doctor had told Mike he probably would not lose his foot.

Estes Park is a beautiful place where groups of people and companies come tor a day or a week. The moose roam freely in the town and in the park. You might encounter one coming into a store because they are not afraid of people.

The rooms Dixie had reserved for us were at the edge of a Golf Course. There seemed to be herds of Moose in the area. One was the leader, grandfather, of the herd. Every afternoon he would lay down on the greens at the Golf Course for hours and the golfers could not play golf. He would give a loud bellow and all the others would gather around him.

There were crowds of people standing in the trees along the edge of the Golf Course watching the Moose. Our rooms were just a few feet from the Golf Course fence and we could stand on our balcony and watch them or stand at the fence around the Golf Course and watch them. They were quite fascinating to watch.

After several days, we left Mike and Dixie and went back south, then traveled west to Durango, Cortez, the San Juan Mountains, and Four Corners where the states of Utah, Colorado, Arizona, and New Mexico come together. I stood on the border line of all four states. All of the souvenir stands are run by Indians.

Gene wanted to go to Monument Valley where many of the cowboy and western movies were filmed. We were entering the desert and the scenery was most beautiful. Some of the cone shaped mesas and hills looked like large ice cream sundaes with all the different layers and colors of sand.

We traveled on through Utah where the scenery was breathtaking. This is all part of the Navajo Nation. The entrance gate to Monument Valley was several miles from the Visitor's Center which was built high atop one of the mesas. We could see for miles from the Center.

All of this area belongs to the Hopi Indians. We talked at length with one of the Indians at the Information Desk. We decided to drive through the valley instead of taking the tour. That wasn't exactly the right choice. We hadn't gone very far when we got stuck in the sand, because the road was only a "sand trail." We had to turn around and go back to the Visitor Center.

The rock formations were very beautiful. There was the same breathtaking beauty as we drove through Arizona. We spent the night in Flagstaff and then turned East to start our return home.

We saw the Painted Desert and the Petrified Forest. I had been there when my children were little and we were on our way to visit my brother Charlie in California. The colors were outstanding. Changes had been made since my last visit. Places were fenced off to keep people out. I noticed that everywhere we went. Many areas were no longer open to the public.

We stopped at the Route 66 Automobile Museum in Santa Rosa, New Mexico where we saw some beautiful old cars. Old cars fascinate me. We were getting tired of traveling at that time and made our way home.

In 2011 we waited until October because it is too hot to travel in the South in the Summertime. We started traveling East and our first stop was The Vicksburg National Military Park at Vicksburg, Mississippi. Neither of us had gone through the Cemetery before and found it very interesting and large.

We drove slowly and checked out each of the many statues' memorials in the Park. Each of the Battle Field areas were marked with monuments and statues and descriptions of the battles. We spent most of the day driving through the Park.

My Cousin Harry Gordon Pettey had told me about one of our Great Grandfathers who fought in the Revolutionary War and was buried at Moores Mill, Alabama. I knew I must see his grave while I was in Alabama.

The directions I found on Find-A-Grave did not give the directions correctly. It is listed as a Cemetery, but actually, it consists of two graves at the edge of a ditch at the edge of a cornfield. The two graves are the only ones there. We had some difficulty in finding them.

Rev. William Eli Pettey and his wife, Rev. Lucretia "Lucy" Wright Pettey are both buried side by side. The DAR maintains the grave of William because he fought in the American Revolution, but they are not obligated to maintain his wife's grave. Her grave is very much overgrown and barely visible from the road. But William's grave is well kept and has a bronze plaque marking his grave. I was actually amazed that we even found their graves.

We visited Stone Mountain, Georgia and saw the different state memorials, which were many. On the side of the mountain were carvings of President Lee and his riders.

We arrived at my sister Sandra's home just in time for Gene's Birthday. We visited with them for two days, then traveled on northward, stopping at different points of interest.

One of these was at Greensboro, North Carolina where 1,900 Redcoats under the command of Lord Cornwallis attacked the Rebels. Nathaniel Green deployed 4,400 rebels at the Battle of Guilford Courthouse on March 15, 1781. Cornwallis held the field after an intense fight, but lost a quarter of his army.

We spent another day there and saw the statue of William Hooper who fought there. It was a cool and rainy day, but we got our umbrellas out and forged ahead. There was one section designated to William Hooper and John

Penn because they were delegates from North Carolina and signers of the Declaration of Inde-pendence. Their remains were re-interred here in 1894. I have researched William Hooper trying to find out if there is a connection in our ancestry, but ran into blank spaces between his family and our family.

On October 12th we arrived at Monticello, the home of President Thomas Jefferson and his family. It was raining, so we got out our umbrellas again and traveled on.

The Name "Monticello" means "House on The Hill." We were only allowed to visit the second floor. Jefferson's study displayed his wing-back chair. Each arm of the chair had a candle stand on it for studying at night. There was a stand in front of the chair with three places to hold books because he read three books at one time. He was a very brilliant man.

He was the author of the Declaration of Independence and an architectural genius. His garden had over 400 different kinds of vegetables. He also had a flower garden and an orchard.

We visited the home of Betsy Ross and Christ Church in Philadelphia. The church is very important because of the people who attended there and are buried in its cemetery. Some of those buried there include Benjamin Franklin and his daughter Sarah, Michael Hillegas – first Treasurer of the United States, Benjamin Franklin Bache, grandson of Benjamin Franklin, Elizabeth Graeme Ferguson, poet and writer, Robert Morris, signer of the Declaration of Independence and the Constitution and financier of the American Revolution, James Wilson, signer of the Declaration of Independence and Associate Justice of the Supreme Court, Pierce Butler, signer of the Constitution from South Carolina, General John Forbes, Commander during the French and Indian war, Andrew Hamilton, "The Philadelphia Lawyer," Jacob Brown, signer of the constitution from Delaware, and many, many more.

Next we went and stood in line to see the Liberty Bell which was the purpose of our trip and vacation North. There is never an admission charge to see the Liberty Bell, but many times the lines to see it are quite long.

The second reason for our trip North was to visit Hooper Island, Maryland. We had to cross Hooper Strait to get to Hooper Island. The town is a very small, quiet community and fishing port. The first place we saw was Hooper Island Hardware Store which was closed for the day, this being Sunday. There was also a Hooper Island Volunteer Fire Department. We drove around the town and did not see much activity.

While we were approaching and "touring" Hooper Island, I could not help but think of my Father, Samuel George Hooper, and cry. He had searched and looked hoping to find just one of his relatives, but to no avail. He never had the resources that we have now such as the Internet where you can find any information you desire. If I had known about Hooper Island, I would have brought my Father here to see it and maybe visit with some of the people.

We left Maryland and proceeded to Knoxville, Tennessee where we visited with my Niece Shannon, her husband James, and son Joshua and spent the night with them.

We then went to Nashville, Tennessee and toured the Country Music Hall of Fame and President Andrew Jackson's home, and Elvis Presley's home.

We went from Tennessee to Arkansas where we stopped at Lonoke, Arkansas to visit my half-sister Patricia and her husband. I had not seen her in person for many years, but kept in touch by letters and cards. They welcomed us and housed us and then we were on our way home again.

My niece, Linda Diane Hooper, Sammie's oldest daughter, had asked me to come to Decatur, Illinois to see her roommate join the church they attended. It was in September 2012, and no danger of a snow storm, so off we go again. I love to travel if the weather is nice.

We stopped to visit with Charlie's daughter, Michelle and her family in Paris, Texas. We left there and traveled through Oklahoma to Bartlesville, Oklahoma. The next day we went to Commerce, Oklahoma to see Mickey Mantle's Home. He was raised in a simple little wooden frame home. There was a metal barn beside the house where Mickey was supposed to have practiced pitching baseballs.

We were in Independence, Missouri when Linda called to "remind us of my promise to be there for her roommate, Bonnie's day to join the church. I had been mistaken and thought it was to be the next week. We changed our plans and drove to Saint Louis and spent the night.

The next day, we drove to Decatur, Illinois and spent two nights there in a very nice motel. Linda's house was small and did not have room for us. We did enjoy the ceremony at the church. They served lunch after the ceremony and we met some very friendly people there.

We traveled back to Springfield, Illinois to visit Abraham Lincoln's home and his Memorial Tomb. As I stated before, everything had changed since my visit many years ago. However, it was still quite interesting.

We went next to Hannibal, Missouri, the home of Mark Train, Samuel Longhorn Clemens. We spent two days there looking at the places where he played and worked. We took a boat ride on the Mississippi River so we could see the banks of the river and some of the areas where he had played.

From there we went to St. Joseph, Missouri and visited with Charlie's daughter, Colleen and her children. I had never seen her two youngest children, a boy and a girl. Her daughter, Mikela, was born on my birthday, October 18th and was almost grown. I had always told her that she stole my birthday because it was mine first.

We didn't spend the night there, but continued on to Independence, Missouri to visit President Harry Truman's home and museum. The museum had a replica of the Oval Office that was in the White House. He and his wife are buried on the grounds next to the Museum.

We stopped in Carthage, Missouri to see the "Precious Moments" Museum and displays of beautiful figurines. My Daughter, Denise, had been there and told me to be sure and see it because it was beautiful.

We went to Rogers, Arkansas and saw the B-B Gun Museum. I never thought there would be a B-B Gun Museum. While at Rogers, we went to the War Eagle Mill and Museum and the restaurant. All of these places were very interesting.

After these excursions, we haven't traveled much except for a short trip on weekends. But now, as we are getting older, and all of my brothers and sisters are gone on to be with the LORD, we haven't done that in several years.

With God's help, we were able to see places in America that we had never seen before and will never see again. The only place I did not get to visit was The Valley in South Texas where much of our fruit and vegetables are grown.

We still have plenty of years left, God promised us 120 years, and maybe I can have one of my Grandchildren drive us to South Texas to see The Davis Mountains and any other place that might catch our fancy.

I thank God for all the things I have seen and experienced. Many people never get to leave their back yard. Thank You Father for Blessing me and my Family.

CHAPTER 43
MY GREAT GRANDMOTHER PETTEY

My Great Grandmother Eliza Jane Welch Pettey was my Grandmother Ida, My Mamaw's Mother. After our mother left us, we never had any family connection with her family, the Ellises. I did see her brother, my Uncle Thurman, during a trip to visit him in Houston when I was about twenty-two years old.

My Dad's father, Peter Preston Hooper, died when Dad was about three years old. That severed our relationship with the Hoopers because my Mamaw married a man named Paramore. I never heard anyone speak of the Hooper side of the family except my Dad when he would tell me how much he longed to find or know about his Hooper relationship.

I pray that God will help and guide me through this story about her because I am repeating things I was told. Eliza Jane Welch was born about 1840. She died in 1943 at the age of 103. She was a tall woman. I believe that is why my Dad, Mamaw, and all of her brothers were very tall. My Dad was six foot and two inches tall. Mamaw was six foot tall. Mamaw's brothers were at least six foot six inches tall. Some were nearer to seven feet. When someone would say to me, "Look at that tall man," I would always say "Where."

I lived with tall people and very seldom saw anyone as tall as them.

It may have been because of her height, or because of osteoporosis which made her walk slumped over. She always wore a bonnet, the type that most farm women wore. She had been raised on a farm, as was many people in those days, but she had left the farm many years before.

She also wore sun glasses, something like the "John Lennon" sun glasses. She wore them, inside the house and especially outside. I never saw her without her sunglasses.

I read our Family History about her and found out that the light, any kind of light, hurt her eyes. We know now, through medical science, that this was due to a vitamin deficiency. He problem could have been corrected by taking Vitamin D.

I never did see my Grandmother's eyes to know what color they were.

As I have related before, Sammie told me about her and how she was always talking to Jesus. She told Sammie about the Covenant she had made with God. It takes two to make a Covenant. God's part of the Covenant was to keep her male descendants from being sacrificed on the battle field. She promised she would always serve Him, and she did. She knew her Bible and God's promise in Genesis 17:7 God said, "I will establish my Covenant between me and thee and thy seed after thee in their generations for an everlasting Covenant, to be a God unto thee, and to thy seed after thee."

And in Isaiah 54:10 God reminds us, "The mountains shall depart, and the hills be removed; but my kindness shall not depart from thee, neither shall the Covenant of my peace be removed, saith the LORD that hath mercy on thee."

If you are not familiar with God's Covenant promises, the fact is that His Covenant is from everlasting to everlasting, and to our children and our children's children.

Great Grandmother raised her children according to God's Word. She married my Great Grandfather after the Civil War. I'm not sure if that is why she was so concerned about her sons being killed in battle, but I'm sure she saw a lot of blood-shed in her lifetime.

She had seven children, two girls and five boys. Two of her sons, and several of her grandchildren served in the military, as well as great grandchildren and none were ever killed or wounded in battle. In fact, according to my information, none ever reached the battlefield.

My nephew, Sammie's son, James Terry Hooper, was in the Army during Desert Storm and was sent to Germany and was supposed to go and join the battle at Desert Storm. The night before, their orders were canceled. I will always believe that God was at work. If it was necessary for HIM to cancel a battle to protect my Great-Grandmother's great-great grandson, HE could do it.

Of the seven children she raised, two became Assembly of God pastors, and all of her children served the LORD.

Her son, William Pettey, was pastor of the Assembly of God Church on the corner of Fourth and Marshall that my Dad built. Her son, Oliver Newton Pettey also served as pastor at one time, as well as her son William Pettey.

Her son William was in a Nursing Home in his elder years. My Brother Tommy tells me that when he would go to visit him, the first thing he would say was, "Do you know Jesus Christ as your personal LORD and Savior." Uncle Will was 105 years old when he went to meet his Savior.

Not only did God keep his Covenant with my Great Grandmother, he also gave them long life. In Psalms 91:16 God promises, "With long life will I satisfy him and shew him my salvation." Her son Ollie (Oliver) was 98 when he died. My Mamaw was 98 when she died, but almost 99 years old. Her son, my Uncle Paul, was 98 when he died.

I have already told you about how God spoke to my Dad while he was coming home from town, and told him to build His Church. When my Dad said to God that he did not know how to build a Church. God said to him, "I will teach you." In Psalms 32:8 God says, "I will instruct thee and teach thee in the way which thou shalt go: I will guide Thee with mine eyes."

My Dad's name is Samuel and you can read about how God spoke to a man named Samuel three times in I Samuel 3:3-8 and called him to serve Him. It amazes me that so many of my Great Grandmother's children and Grandchildren became preachers and served God all of their lives. All of those that I knew are now living in Heaven with Jesus.

Mamaw's daughter, Kate, would go to the jail on Sunday morning and preach to the prisoners. She also had a radio program on Sunday morning. I was very young at that time, but I remember "parts" of Sammie and I accompanying her and singing. I would stand on a piano bench in a small room and look through the big plate glass. Aunt Kate was 82 when she died and was living with her Cousin Doris, which was Uncle Ollie's daughter.

You would think that with such a background and upbringing that my brothers and sisters and myself, would have followed the path laid out for us. Not one of us did. All eight of us went out into the world as soon as we were old enough to leave home. But, I also know that the Holy Spirit was tugging at our heartstrings all those years. As for me, I was sixty-three years old when I finally gave in and gave up and gave my heart to Jesus.

I have faced death at least five times in my life, maybe more if I try very hard to remember them all. But God kept his hand over me. I heard a woman say once that God would not let her die because He was not finished with her yet. I believe God is not finished with me yet, just as he was not finished with my Great Grand-mother and Mamaw because He still had work for them to do.

I do not know what else He has in store for me, but I know He still has work for me to do that He only wants me to do. He will reveal what that work is when He is ready to tell and show me. I have now been teaching Sunday School for many years and will continue o do so as long as I am able, or if God gives me another job that He wants done.

Never forget, the Seeds we plant will continue to produce a harvest for many years, some after we are gone. They may be "good Seeds" or "bad Seeds" so be careful what you plant.

The Seeds of Faith that my Great Grandmother planted about 1860 are still growing and producing fruit today. Also, the Seeds that her children planted as Pastors, and her Grandchildren and Great Grandchildren are still bearing fruit.

Never give up on your Seeds, but Believe that your Seeds will produce and they will. The Seeds that my relatives planted for me and in me took forty years to produce. I thank God every day that He never gave up on me and all of my family.

When I think of my Great Grandmother, I remember Psalms 105:8, "He hath remembered His Covenant for ever, the Words which He commanded to a thousand generations."

And to God be all the Praise and Glory.

CHAPTER 44
GENE'S GARDEN

Gene has always planted a garden, but now that we are finished with traveling "the world" he is working harder at it. He usually made his garden plots with a tiller, and lots of hard work. It wasn't unusual for the weeds and grass to overtake it.

I read in a Gardening Book, years ago when I lived in Mineral Wells, that the best way to make a small garden was by building "flower beds." He had never seen that done and didn't want to take my advice for several years. During that time, he was daily fighting weeds and grass in his garden.

This kind of garden is called "A Raised Bed Garden." After several years of fighting weeds in the place where he had chosen to make his garden on the ground, he decided to listen to what I had to say about it.

The beds are made by placing one railroad tie, 16 feet long, on top of another 16 foot tie, and one 4 foot tie on top of another 4 foot tie across the end to form a bed and to form a box. Then black plastic is placed inside the box to cover the ground and any holes that may be in the railroad ties. This will keep the grass and weeds from growing through the plastic and into the bed.

The box is then filled with good gardening soil to within a couple of inches from the top of the box. The soil can then be mixed with some good fertilizer or you can wait until you are ready to plant and put the fertilizer around your plants or seeds.

When working your garden, you can sit on the railroad ties. If there is grass or weeds growing in the bed, it is easy to pull them out by hand or use some small tool. This saves your back and your knees. There is no need to have a plow or a tiller with this garden bed.

It is not necessary to have rows three or four feet apart. All the work done in or to the garden bed is done while sitting on the railroad ties. You can sit on either side or the ends to work the beds. Then you can reach across to the middle to plant or pull weeds. Never make the bed wider than you can reach from the side to the middle of the bed. The width is determined by the length of your arm. You will find that very little weeds or grass grow in your beds, which is WONDERFUL!!

After your Raised Beds are made, the only tools you need are a trowel and a small rake like tool. Everything is done by hand. You will need cages for the tomatoes or cucumbers just as you did for your garden that was planted on the ground.

Watering is also simple and easy, because it can be done while sitting on the ties.

Gene put two poles, one on each end, in the bed and attached some "chicken wire" to each end for the vegetables to grow up on. It depends on what vegetables you want to grow. Peas and beans need something to grow "up" on, as well as cucumbers. The support for the vegetables is the same as needed for a garden grown on the ground.

Gene can harvest as much, if not more, vegetables from his beds as he did with his "ground" garden. He started with one bed and now has three. He grows enough vegetables for us and to give to our neighbors, and also to take to our fellow Christians at Church.

Some people have asked us, "How large is your garden?" They are actually asking, "How many acres of garden do you have?" Everyone is amazed when we tell them that our garden consists of three flower beds.

It's a good thing to pray over your seeds and plants before planting and also after they are planted. I pray and ask God to Bless our garden so that we will have enough to share with our friends and fellow Christians. The first time you try this you will be amazed at how much vegetables you can produce in that small area.

When someone asks Gene about growing things in his garden, he tells them to come and look at his beds. They are amazed when they see them.

People who don't have a big space for a "flower bed garden" like to plant a "container garden." Those work very well also. They can be placed side-by-side with the "raised garden." Gene has about eight containers that he plants tomatoes, bell peppers, and hot peppers in. He puts one plant in each container.

As we get older, we need God's help and advice from others who know how to keep us from all the toil it usually takes to make a garden. It is expensive to build the raised gardens at first, but they are used year after year for many years. They are time savers, work savers, and back and knee savers.

Ask God to Bless you before you start and He will make it even more easy. He does for us. We grow tomatoes, black-eyed peas, cucumbers, bell peppers, hot peppers, corn, squash, turnip greens, onions, as well as several varieties of some of the vegetables.

We are Blessed to have my daughter Denise, and her husband Dave living next door, as well as Gene's son Randal and his wife Nadine living behind us. Our Granddaughter Haleigh grew up next door to us and then left to attend Dallas Baptist University. She graduated on May 14th.

We are now 87 and 88 years young, and there are times when we need a little help with our garden. Our family is always ready and willing to help.

God has truly been good to me and my family and has Blessed us all these many years. I would have been dead long ago if it wasn't for God. He gave us our heart's desire by bringing Gene and I back together after fifty years of being apart.

Thank You Father for watching over us and keeping us safe when Satan tried to kill us. It's all because of You, Your mercy, and Your Grace. Thank You for Blessing us each and every day and every step of the way. He was always there!!

CHAPTER 45
IT'S NOT OVER YET

While trying to finish This Book and making sure I have covered everything, God reminds me of last summer. It was Saturday morning and Gene wasn't feeling well. He had been passing blood in his stool for two days.

On Friday, he said he was feeling better, so I thought he was okay. But, on Saturday he looked terrible and told me he thought he was dying.

I went into the den and sat down in my chair and began to cry and pray for God to help us. I prayed, "Please send the ministering angels to help us, because I don't know what to do or what to pray." God said in Hebrews 1:13 "Are they not all ministering spirits, sent forth to minister for them who shall be heirs of salvation?" I sat there and cried and prayed for about 45 minutes.

Then I heard a knock at our back door and saw through the window that it was my Brother Tommy and his wife. I had not called him or anyone else to tell them about Gene and what he had said. I told Tommy what had happened and said, "Do you have your oil (anointing oil) in your pocket." Of course he did, being a Pastor, he never went anywhere without it.

We prayed and believed God had answered our prayers. Gene said he felt better, so Tommy left to finish his errands. Then Gene said he didn't feel any better and for me to call the ambulance. He stayed overnight at the hospital while they ran tests on him.

Sunday morning, his Doctor that performs the Endoscopy procedures, came to the hospital and gave him one of those "tiny cameras" to swallow so that he could see what was going on in his stomach. GUESS WHAT!! He could find nothing wrong.

Then the Doctor looked at Gene's list of medications and saw that he had been taking a "baby aspirin" every day, plus an Aleve, when he had a pain. He had been hurting for several days. Taking the aspirin and the Aleve is what caused his bleeding. The Doctor strongly advised Gene not to take aspirin and Aleve together ever again. Gene was allowed to go home that day.

He began to feel much better that night at home. We believe God healed Gene when Tommy, his wife Rose, and I prayed for him. Praise God for answering our prayers!!! Just remember, when you know God's Word and pray His Word back to Him, He will always answer you. That's the secret to prayer. Don't pray some "off the wall" prayer you may have made-up yourself. God remembers His Word and always responds. God likes to be reminded of His Promises, and wants to know if you remember them.

The morning of February 26, 2020, I had gone to the Lab to have some "Blood Work and Testing" done which was ordered by my doctor for my next routine checkup. When I returned home, I was surprised that Gene was not home. He had not told me of any reason why he would leave or go to town while I was gone.

I waited for a few minutes, then called him on his cell phone. When he answered his voice was shaky and he said, "You better call the Police because I've been in an accident and I can't seem to get them to answer on my phone."

He said he was on his way home from the grocery store after buying some fruit. He loves fruit. He was on the overpass going over the Interstate headed north when an eighteen wheeler came up the entrance ramp from the Interstate onto Highway 42. The truck collided with Gene's truck on the passenger's side of his pick-up truck. Gene said it lifted up his truck and he thought his truck was going to be pushed into the oncoming traffic lane.

I don't know how long he had been trying to call the Police. When they answered my call there seemed to be some confusion. The Dispatcher said she thought she was receiving notification from two different sources about an accident. One person said they were calling about an accident in Longview and the other person didn't know exactly where the accident was.

I waited on the phone and could hear what they were telling the Dispatcher. Their information didn't seem to agree with any of the information I had. When she was ready I gave her the information Gene had given me about the accident.

I thought my daughter, Denise, was home because her can was in her driveway when I arrived home. I tried to call her but she didn't answer. Then she called me back immediately to say that she left home just after I arrived home. She was on her way to town when she came upon the accident.

There just happened to be a Police Officer following her in the line of traffic when they arrived at the scene of the accident and he took over the investigation.

She saw what she thought was Gene's pick-up truck on the side of the highway. Then much to her amazement she saw Gene standing there. He seemed quite shook up, nervous, and having trouble breathing.

Because of past experiences we have all had with accidents and confusion, she told the Police Officer to call an Ambulance and a wrecker, which he did. By doing that, the pick-up would be towed to where it could be checked for damage, and the Ambulance could take Gene to the hospital and the doctors could determine how badly he was injured.

She called me again to let me know what was happening, and that she was coming to get me and take me to the hospital where Gene would be.

When we arrived at the hospital, Gene was already in the Emergency Section. The doctor and nurses were checking his neck and back because he had complained they were hurting. They took him to X-Ray and them to MRI. They kept him under close observation and continued to run tests on him.

His blood sugar tested high as well as the potassium in his blood. They checked those about every hour. We did not think he would be allowed to go home that night because of some of the medical problems he was having.

The doctor discussed his condition with us and said he would allow him to go home that night if he promised to follow his instructions and have his "blood work" done the next day and see his personal physician.

He also told him to drink a lot of water and to take the medication he had prescribed for him. We agreed and we headed for home about 7:30 pm in Denise's car. It had been a long, tiring day for all of us.

The next day Gene complained about a lot of soreness in his neck and back, which was to be expected after the accident. I tried to make an appointment for him to see his Family Doctor, but the earliest was in four days as it was a weekend.

When our Family Doctor checked Gene, he saw that Gene's blood pressure was quite high and told him to go to the lab and have test made. He also gave him a new "Blood Pressure medication."

It has been several weeks now since the accident and Gene seems to be doing better physically. He was told to go to the Chiropractor weekly for treatments on his back and neck. We don't know how long it will take Gene to completely recover.

We know that the accident could have turned out much worse if God had not "Given His Angels charge over Gene to keep him in all of his ways They shall bear thee up in their hands, lest thou dash thy foot against a stone (or an eighteen wheeler hits you in the side)." Psalm 91.

The Devil tries to kill us daily. That's what God's Word teaches us, but Jesus came that we might have "life and have it more abundantly."

I thank God every day for protecting Gene and I and also Blessing us each day. Without Him, we would be lost and Satan would have killed us long ago. Glory to God for His faithfulness and His Blessings pouring out from the windows of heaven daily.

CHAPTER 46
OUR NEW SHEPHERD

Brother Ron, our Shepherd of seven years, retired from ministry on September 29, 2019. His wife, Sue, had been having some very serious health problems for several years. Once she had to go to Dallas for special treatments that required her to stay in isolation for a week. I thought she was doing better, but no one truly knows what a person is going through while having serious health problems.

God had guided Gene and I to this small, but friendly church nine years ago when the pastor at that time was in a Nursing Home recuperating from a stroke. After a year he had given up the Pulpit, and after another year he died.

We were again looking for some to fill the place left by Pastor Ron. The announcement of a "Vacancy" is handled by those in charge at the Regional level.

Since Gene was still on The Board, he and three others would be required to interview the Candidates and make arrangements for them to come and preach. They prayed and finally agreed on one of the Candidates, but he could not come right away.

Some of the rules have been changed about the interviews and how many times a Candidate may be required to come and preach. The rule now requires them to submit their resume and come to preach only once.

After going through the procedure, we voted. The "For Vote" did not carry by a two-thirds majority. That meant we were still looking for a Shepherd.

During this time, the Regional Directors had sent us an "Interim Pastor" to help us while we were without "A Shepherd" to lead us. They were excellent Ministers and everyone liked them. We had asked the Interim Pastor if he would take over the job of being our "New Shepherd." He explained that he was quite busy in his job of "Interim Pastor" and did not feel he would be able to fill the job. He was also in his seventies, and he and his wife, who was a retired school teacher, did not feel they should take on a full time position at their age.

They remained our Helpers while we waited for more Candidates to apply. The two that had previously applied, had now withdrawn their applications.

We continued on without any new Candidates. Then in March 2020, we received a resume from a new Candidate who lived in South Texas. He stated that he and his wife wanted to move to East Texas. I do not know the reason.

One of the Board Members contacted him by phone and made arrangements for him to come. He stated that he could only be at our church on a Tuesday for an interview with the Board Members, and on Wednesday Night for Service. They decided that would be satisfactory.

This was at the time when the COVID-19 had broken out. We were still having services at our Church at that time. He and his wife came. She is a School Teacher. This was during Spring Break for all the schools, and the School Officials in Texas had thought it best for the children to take another Week of Spring Break and not return to school at the present because of the virus.

I'm sure that's why he and his wife decided to stay until Sunday. After the Morning Service, several of the Board Members took them out to lunch. Our Church loves to eat, and never passes up an opportunity to go out to eat.

The following Sunday was designated as our "Voting Day." However, during the week, the Assembly of God Officials and President Trump decided that everyone should remain at home "voluntary shut-ins" to keep from spreading the virus.

The Board decided we would have a "Drive-by Voting." All of our members were contacted and advised to drive by the church at 10 am on Sunday Morning. Each person would be given a small piece of paper on which they could write "Yes" or "No" for their vote.

Since Gene and I have only one car now, and he is on the Board, that meant we would go to church together, I would vote and remain at the church in prayer while everyone else came and voted.

This plan was working out perfect. I went into the Sanctuary to pray while Gene helped with the Voting. After about fifteen minutes, I thought I heard some "commotion" in the hallway and decided I should go and investigate.

Much to my surprise, they were counting the Votes. It didn't take but a minute to get the results. We now have a New Shepherd to lead this flock. Everyone was in agreement and came to Vote as they had been instructed.

We had been without a "Shepherd" to lead our flock for about six months. I know some of the members must have fretted and were discouraged. One of our Board Members resigned and left the church.

But then, when it seemed to get worse, God put us in touch with a wonderful man and woman whom He had chosen for our New Shepherd. God knew what we needed, and not so much as to "what we wanted."

We are like little children and don't always know what's good for us. That's why we need a "Good Shepherd" who will lead and guide us in the right direction. The direction God wants us to follow.

There is an old "Country and Western Song" from several years ago titled "Thank God for Unanswered Prayers." I thank God now for our "Unanswered Prayers." God knows what we need more than we do. He knows what the future hold for all of us, not just the Church. And He knew who would be the best person to guide us through what may be some very trying days.

President Trump has agreed to open the churches now, and our New Shepherd and his wife, Reverend Dale

Wommack and wife Susan, are here now. I believe they are exactly what we need. Thank God for choosing our New Shepherd and his Wife to come and help us and teach us. I know they will be an asset to our church.

Thank God for His Mercy and Grace, and for all of His Blessings.

CHAPTER 47
THE YEARS OF SORROW

There is the saying, "When it rains, it pours." It is now in the year of 2020 and I have seen or heard or experienced the deaths of so many of my relatives and friends.

It was in December of 2002 that my cousin Doris Pettey Medlin left us for a much better life. In 2003 someone left us each month of that year. I remember our dear neighbor Margarette Grimes left April 28, 2003. We had a funeral to attend every month of 2003.

There were many others who left us that year, but the most important ones were my Grandson Ryan on August 24, 2003 and Gene's Mother in October.

My brother Charlie died at his home he had built in White Oak on February 28, 2003. Sammie died three years later in Decatur, Illinois on April 5, 2006.

The first member of our "Little Church" Mr. Turner died December 13, 2008. Alene, Sammie's first wife and my friend since I was about sixteen years old, died on October 16, 2009. Maxine, Jackie's first wife and the Mother of my nephew Jackie Preston, died May 20, 2011.

Gene's adopted younger brother, "Little Gene" died February 10, 2012. Gene's daughter, Martha Carol, took her life March 25, 2012. Then on October 3, 2012, the man Gene worked for after Buster retired, Mr. Tisdale died.

Martha Carol's son, Joe Lee, took his life on May 4, 2013. My brother Tommy's wife, Shirley died on December 28, 2015 during an operation.

My dear cousin Harry Gordon, the one who helped me and advised me at the beginning of my first year at college, died on January 27, 2016 during an operation. He had been very helpful and instrumental in getting me started on writing the story of my life and my family. I did not find out about his death until about a month later.

In October of 2017, I received a phone call from a young lady whom I did not know. She told me that my sister Della had died in the hospital in Texas City. That was eighteen days after her death and no one had notified me, not the hospital, not the police, and not the morgue.

My daughter, Denise, and I left the next day to investigate the situation. We had been told that her body had finally been released to a funeral home in the area. We met with Della's daughter, Patty, at the funeral home and made the arrangements for the cremation. I paid for everything because it always seemed that no one had any money when emergencies arose. I had promises of repayment, but nothing ever came of those promises.

After Denise and I returned home, I received a phone call from the funeral home that the morgue had requested the return of Della's body for some unknown reason. Finally on November 16, her body was returned to the funeral home for cremation.

My youngest brother Alfred Leonard, Lynn, died on September 5, 2018 in Dallas. There was some delays in my receiving Della's and Lynn's ashes. After our Thanksgiving Dinner in 2019, I took their ashes to the cemetery with my son Michael, nephew Preston, and Preston's daughter Breonna, and laid them to rest with our Dad, Step Mom, Jackie, Sammie, Sandra, Uncle Junior, Big Mama, Daddy Bill, and Mamaw's last husband Daddy Jim.

Gene's only sister, Edna, died on July 27, 2019, leaving him without any siblings. Our family just keeps getting smaller and smaller.

My Stepbrother, Tommy, and I are the only two left of the eight children. Tommy's son, Robert Keith died in December 1958 after a fall from a train. He has one other son living, Wesley.

My Sister's daughter, Shannon, keeps in touch regularly with us, and a few of the others sometimes. Shannon called me to tell me that Don McKay, Sandra's husband has died.

But most of the other family members don't contact us very often. I suppose that all comes with getting older. We have our "old" ways and are not quite "up to" their modern ways.

I think back now and wish I had kept much closer contact with my aunts and uncles. They were all good and loving people, but it seems we just didn't have the time then.

God Forgive us all. Thank You Father, Son, and Holy Spirit, for helping me through my story and giving me the words to put on paper so that all may read about Your great Mercy, and Grace, Your Protection all these years, and all the Blessings You have Bestow on Us.

I love You Father, my Savior Jesus, and The Holy Spirit.

AMEN

UNTIL NEXT TIME, GOD BLESS YOU

I have loved my God for as long as I can remember and I know He has loved me all of my life. It has taken me many, many years to know and understand how God has watched over me and protected me and blessed me even when I did not know He was there, and certainly did not deserve His blessings. But still, He was always there.

Luke 7:45 (Jesus said) Thou gavest me no kiss; but this woman since the time I came in hath not ceased to kiss my feet. :46 My head with oil thou didst not anoint; but this woman hath anointed my feet with ointment. :47 Wherefore I say unto thee, Her sins, which are many, are forgiven; for she loved much; but to whom little is forgiven; the same loveth little.

Printed in the United States
By Bookmasters